G000160517

1995
FLEET HANDBOOK

Keith A. Jenkinson

An Autobus Review Publication

© Autobus Review Publications Ltd. 1994

Published by Autobus Review Publications Ltd.,
42 Coniston Avenue, Queensbury, Bradford BD13 2JD

ISBN 0 907834 33 7

NOTES FOR THE USE OF THIS BOOK

The fleet lists contained in this book are arranged in standard format as follows :

Column 1. Fleet number. ('s' suffix indicates vehicles in store, 'w' suffix
indicates vehicles withdrawn awaiting disposal).

Column 2. Registration number

Column 3. Year first licensed

Column 4. Chassis make and model

Column 5. Body make, type and seating capacity (see notes below)

Column 6. Previous owner and date of acquisition (italics indicate
purchase prior to the company joining the Stagecoach Group)

Body type :

B	Single deck bus
C	Single deck coach
CH	Double deck coach
CO	Convertible open-top double deck
DP	Dual Purpose single deck
DPH	Dual Purpose double deck
FH	Full front double deck bus
H	Double deck bus
O	Permanent open-top double deck

Entrance position.

D	Dual door
F	Front entrance
(FC)	Rear freight compartment
FL	Front entrance & fitted with tail lift
FT	Front entrance & fitted with toilet
R	Rear entrance
RD	Rear entrance with platform doors
RO	Rear entrance with open staircase

Seating capacity : For double deckers the upper deck seating
capacity is shown first, followed by that for the
lower deck.

Contents

Fleet lists correct as at 1 December 1994

Introduction

Born in 1980 as a consequence of the Transport Act of that year, Stagecoach began life as an express coach operator, running a service from Dundee to London on four nights each week. The success of this operation led to the service being extended to Aberdeen and from this humble beginning has grown the now international Stagecoach empire.

The first experience of local bus operations came on 22 December 1980 when the company took over McLennan of Spittalfield's service from Perth to Errol and some five years later, on 7 November 1985, the whole of the A. & C. McLennan business was acquired. Prior to this, Stagecoach had expanded its coaching operations with the purchase of Adamson & Low of Edinburgh, although this business was subsequently resold to one of its original ownwers.

The privatisation of the National Bus Company paved the way for Stagecoach to gain a firm foothold in the operation of local bus service and after failing to capture City of Oxford Motor Services, it achieved its first success on 2 April 1987 when it purchased Hampshire Bus and its associated Pilgrim Coaches. Before the year ended, Cumberland Motor Services and United Counties Omnibus Co. were also added to Stagecoach's growing portfolio whilst in Glasgow, as a result of deregulation, a new company was set up under the title Magicbus in October 1986 to operate a number of services in that city.

Looking further afield, Stagecoach undertook some consultancy work overseas and in 1988 joined with Speedybus Services Ltd. in Hong Kong to form a company under the title of Speedybus Enterprises. Rather than being an operating company, this new venture supplied double deck buses under advertising contract lease agreements to operators in mainland China and it was not until March 1989 that any overseas bus operations of their own were gained when Stagecoach purchased the massive UTI company in Malawi. The company's overseas activities were further expanded in 1990 when Gray Coach Lines of Toronto, Canada was purchased, although this was subsequently sold two years later.

Seeking further expansion on the home front, Stagecoach turned its attention towards several of the privatised former NBC subsidiaries and in April 1989 purchased Ribble and East Midland from their respective management teams, thus strengthening their position south of the border. Having now taken the decision to give full concentration to the running of local bus services, the Perth-based coaching operation was, in August, sold together with a number of vehicles and the company's Walnut Grove headquarters to National Express who rebranded the services concerned Stagecoach-Caledonian Express. As a consequence of this sale, Stagecoach shortly afterwards established a new head office in the centre of Perth where it remains today. Before the year ended, more purchases were made in southern England bringing Southdown, Hastings & District and Portsmouth Citybus into the Stagecoach fold, although the latter was sold to Transit Holdings in January 1991. In Scotland, Inverness Traction was purchased from the receiver in November and was immediately placed under the control of Magicbus.

As was to be expected, interest was shown in the Scottish Bus Group when it was announced that its subsidiaries were to be sold to the private sector and in 1991 Stagecoach successfully bid for Bluebird Northern and Fife Scottish, albeit only acquiring the latter after some protracted negotiations. A further company acquired during that year was Kenya Bus Services, thus giving the Group an even greater presence in East Africa whilst in October 1992 Stagecoach ventured into the southern hemisphere with the purchase of Wellington City Transport in New Zealand. During the year which followed, the Hants & Surrey operations of Alder Valley were purchased and were placed under the control of Stagecoach South as an expansion of its operating territory. On the debit side, the Glasgow-based Magic bus operation was sold in April 1992 to Kelvin Central Buses to enable a bid to be made for Strathclyde's Buses, although in the event this proved to be unsuccessful.

4

Back in the U.K. another milestone was reached when, in April 1993 Stagecoach Holdings successfully applied for listing by the London Stock Exchange. This was followed by further expansion and consolidation with the acquisition of East Kent, Grimsby Cleethorpes Transport and the Western Travel Group together with the operations of Lancaster City Transport. Additionally, having sold its stake in Speedybus Enterprises, Stagecoach began operations in Hong Kong with a small unit providing a residents service, thus continuing its presence in the colony.

The most recent developments, which have taken place during 1994, have brought Western Scottish, Busways, Cleveland Transit and Kingston-upon-Hull City Transport into the ever-expanding Stagecoach Group and with the purchase of Selkent and East London from London Buses has given them their first foothold in the capital. In addition a 20% shareholding has been purchased in Mainline of Sheffield and SB Holdings, parent of Strathclyde Buses, GCT and Kelvin Central Buses, paving the way for a greater shareholding or total takeover in the years ahead.

Over the years, a number of smaller independent operators have also been purchased through various of the Stagecoach companies as was Barrow Borough Transport in order to eliminate competition and further consolidate their position in certain areas, whilst the Group's recent appearance in Darlington led to the almost immediate demise of the local council-owned company. No doubt more acquisitions will be made in the future as and when opportunities arise in order to protect Stagecoach's ever-growing empire.

Thus Stagecoach Holdings at the end of 1994 operate buses in seven different countries spread across four continents and undoubtedly further developments in the years ahead will ensure that the Group maintains its current position as the world's largest independent bus operator.

Our thanks are extended to all the operating companies within the Stagecoach Group for their assistance in the compilation of this book. As it is, however, not an official publication of Stagecoach Holdings plc, any correspondence relating to its content etc. should be addressed to the publishers and not to the company itself whose officials are often too busy to answer enthusiasts questions etc. It should also be pointed out that all the garages of the Stagecoach Group companies are private property and that these should under no circumstances be entered without having first gained permission as trespassing tarnishes the otherwise good image of bus enthusiasts

Busways
Travel Services Ltd.

PART OF THE STAGECOACH GROUP

Busways Travel Services Ltd., Manors, Newcastle-upon-Tyne NE1 2EL
Welcome Passenger Transport Ltd., Manors, Newcastle-upon-Tyne NE1 2EL

Formerly Tyne & Wear PTE which was created on 1 January 1970 by the merging of Newcastle and South Shields Corporations and by the addition of Sunderland Corporation on 1 April 1973. In August 1973 the businesses of Armstrong of Westerhope and Galleys Coaches, Newcastle were purchased as was Economic of Whitburn on 1 January 1975. After being sold to its management/employees in May 1988, further consolidation was achieved in November 1989 with the acquisition of Tyne & Wear Omnibus Co. and in August 1993 with the purchase of Welcome Passenger Services. Both the latter were absorbed into Newcastle Busways on 1 November 1994 whilst seven days later a new operation was started in Darlington under the Stagecoach Darlington name. Currently, Busways is divided into eight operating units, each of which maintains its own livery and fleet name

Livery : ARMSTRONG GALLEY - Light blue, orange red & yellow; BLUE BUS SERVICES - Dark blue & cream; ECONOMIC - Brown & cream; FAVOURITE - Orange, brown & white; NEWCASTLE BUSWAYS - Yellow, white & maroon; SOUTH SHIELDS BUSWAYS - Yellow, white & blue; SUNDERLAND BUSWAYS - Yellow, white & green; STAGECOACH DARLINGTON - Stagecoach corporate livery. *Most of the existing liveries are to be retained for a period of three years.*

Depots : Byker, Newcastle (Newcastle Busways, Armstrong Galley & Blue Bus Services); Darlington (Stagecoach Darlington); North Hetton (Favourite); Slatyford, Newcastle (Newcastle Busways); South Shields (South Shields Busways, Economic); Sunderland (Sunderland Busways).

Armstrong Galley   Fleet list

3	ONL645X	1982	Leyland PSU5D/5R	Plaxton Sup.V C53F	*Jumbulance 1985*
4	KSU454	1985	Leyland TRCTL11/3R	Van Hool Alizee C48FT	
5	KSU455	1985	Leyland TRCTL11/3R	Van Hool Alizee C48FT	
6	KSU456	1985	Leyland TRCTL11/3R	Van Hool Alizee C48FT	
7	KSU457	1988	Leyland TRCTL11/3RZ	Plaxton 3500 C51FT	
8	KSU458	1986	Leyland Royal Tiger	Van Hool Alizee C49FT	
9	KSU459	1986	Leyland TRCTL11/3RH	Van Hool Alizee C48FT	
14	644HKX	1985	Leyland TRCTL113R	Plaxton 3500 C51FT	*Fowler, Holbeach Dv 1987*

4-6 were originally registered B104/5/3DVK. 8/9 were originally registered C110/09PCU. 14 was originally registered B643JAV.

15	1JVK	1988	Leyland TRCTL11/3R	Plaxton 3500 C51FT	
16	2JVK	1989	Leyland TRCL10/3ARZM	Plaxton 3300 C53F	*Shearings, Wigan 2.93*
17	491JVX	1988	Leyland TRCL10/£ARZM	Plaxton 3200 C53F	*Shearings, Wigan 2.93*
18	552UTE	1988	Leyland TRCL10/3ARZM	Plaxton 3200 C53F	*Shearings, Wigan 2.93*
19	813VPU	1992	Volvo B10M-60	Plaxton Excal. C49FT	*Parks, Hamilton 12.93*

15-19 were originally registered F900JRG, F715-7ENE & J423HDS

51	KSU461	1985	MCW Metroliner	MCW CH53/16DT	
55	KSU465	1986	MCW Metroliner	MCW CH53/16DT	
56	KSU466	1986	MCW Metrorider	MCW CH53/16DT	*London Buses 4.87*

51/5/6 were originally registered A751CRG, C155LJR & C103DYE

81	L81YBB	1993	Volvo B10M-60	Plaxton Ex'liner C44FT	
82	L82YBB	1993	Volvo B10M-60	Plaxton Ex'liner C46FT	
83	L83YBB	1993	Volvo B10M-60	Plaxton Ex'liner C46FT	
84	L84YBB	1993	Volvo B10M-60	Plaxton Ex'liner C46FT	
85	KSU462	1992	Volvo B10M-60	Plaxton Excalib. C46FT	*Parks, Hamilton 12.93*
86	KSU463	1992	Volvo B10M-60	Plaxton Excalib. C46FT	*Parks, Hamilton 12.93*
87	KSU464	1992	Volvo B10M-60	Plaxton Excalib. C46FT	*Parks, Hamilton 12.93*

85-7 were originally registered J420/2/4HDS

Blue Bus Services   Fleet list

61	HTY139W	1980	Leyland PSU3E/4R	Duple Dom. C49F	*Grey Green 7.88*
63	HTY138W	1980	Leyland PSU3E/4R	Duple Dom. C49F	*Grey Green 7.88*
65	TBC1X	1981	Leyland PSU3F/4R	Plaxton Sup.V C53F	*Nottingham 5.88*
66	TBC2X	1981	Leyland PSU3F/4R	Plaxton Sup.V C53F	*Nottingham 5.88*

61/3 were previously registered KSU460/3 and were originally FYX819/21W

---

244 - 312   1978 Leyland AN68A/2R   Alexander AL H49/37F

244	SCN244S	268	SCN268S	277	SCN277S	303	VCU303T
261	SCN261S	273	SCN273S	302	VCU302T	312	VCU312T

500	MVK500R	1976	Leyland AN68A/2R	Alexander AL H48/34F
507	MVK507R	1976	Leyland AN68A/2R	Alexander AL H48/33F
509	MVK509R	1976	Leyland AN68A/1R	Alexander AL H48/33F
519	MVK519R	1976	Leyland AN68A/2R	Alexander AL H48/33F
521	MVK521R	1976	Leyland AN68A/2R	Alexander AL H48/33F
532	MVK532R	1976	Leyland AN68A/1R	Alexander AL H48/33F

---

541 - 544   1976 Leyland AN68A/2R   Alexander AL H48/34F

541	MVK541R	542	MVK542R	543	MVK543R	544	MVK544R

---

551 - 565   1977 Leyland AN68A/2R   Alexander AL H48/33F

551	MVK551R	558	MVK558R	563	MVK563R	565	MVK565R

796	LDB796	1960	Leyland PSUC1/1	Willowbrook DP43F	(Preserved)

1401 - 1420   1986 Mercedes Benz 709D   Reeve Burgess B20F

1401	D401TFT	1406	D406TFT	1411	D411TFT	1419	D419TFT
1402	D402TFT	1409	D409TFT	1415	D415TFT	1420	D420TFT
1403	D403TFT	1410	D410TFT				

1422 - 1452   1987 Mercedes Benz 709D   Reeve Burgess B20F

1422	E422AFT	1425	E425AFT	1447	E447AFT	1452	E452AFT
1424	E424AFT						

1604	TPJ55S	1977	Bristol LHS6L	ECW B35F	*South Yorks PTE 12.86*
1605	TPJ60S	1977	Bristol LHS6L	ECW B35F	*South Yorks PTE 12.86*
1606	TPJ62S	1977	Bristol LHS6L	ECW B35F	*South Yorks PTE 12.86*
1607	TPJ64S	1977	Bristol LHS6L	ECW B35F	*South Yorks PTE 12.86*
1610	WEX927S	1977	Bristol LH6L	ECW B43F	*T & W Omnibus 11.89*

1614	AFB594V	1980	Bristol LH6L	ECW	B43F	*T & W Omnibus 11.89*
1615	TTC787T	1978	Bristol LH6L	ECW	B43F	*T & W Omnibus 11.89*
1616	WEX928S	1978	Bristol LH6L	ECW	B43F	*T & W Omnibus 11.89*
1617	WAE187T	1979	Bristol LH6L	ECW	B43F	*T & W Omnibus 11.89*
1619	DTL548T	1979	Bristol LH6L	ECW	B43F	*T & W Omnibus 11.89*
1663	H401DMJ	1990	Renault S75	Reeve Burgess	B29F	*Welcome 8.93*
1666	J226JJR	1991	Renault S75	Reeve Burgess	B28F	*Welcome 8.93*
1672	J232JJR	1991	Renault S75	Reeve Burgess	B28F	*~Welcome 8.93*
1674	K341PJR	1992	Renault S75	Reeve Burgess	B28F	*Welcome 8.93*
1675	K342PJR	1992	Renault S75	Reeve Burgess	B28F	*Welcome 8.93*
1701	J701KCU	1992	Dennis Dart 9.8SDL	Plaxton Pointer	B40F	
1702	J702KCU	1992	Dennis Dart 9.8SDL	Plaxton Pointer	B40F	
1744	L744VNL	1993	Dennis Dart 9.8SDL	Plaxton Pointer	B40F	
1745	L745VNL	1993	Dennis Dart 9.8SDL	Plaxton Pointer	B40F	
1746	L746VNL	1993	Dennis Dart 9.8SDL	Plaxton Pointer	B40F	
1800	RAH681F	1968	Bristol RELL6G	ECW	B53F	*Milton Keynes City 4.94*
1802	TRY118H	1969	Bristol RELL6L	ECW	B48F	*Ipswich 11.87*
1803	LPU452J	1971	Bristol RELL6G	ECW	B53F	*Milton Keynes City 4.94*
1804	EHU383K	1972	Bristol RELL6L	ECW	B50F	*Milton Keynes City 4.94*
1805	EPW516K	1972	Bristol RELL6G	ECW	B53F	*Milton Keynes City 4.94*
1806	PVT221L	1972	Bristol RELL6L	ECW	B53F	*Milton Keynes City 4.94*
1808	HPW522L	1972	Bristol RELL6L	ECW	B53F	*Milton Keynes City 4.94*
1810	YWC16L	1972	Bristol RELL6L	ECW	B53F	*Colchester 8.88*
1811	YWC18L	1972	Bristol RELL6L	ECW	B49F	*Colchester 3.88*
1812	OWC720M	1972	Bristol RELL6L	ECW	B53F	*Colchester 3.88*
1813	OWC722M	1972	Bristol RELL6L	ECW	B49F	*Colchester 8.88*
1814	OWC723M	1972	Bristol RELL6L	ECW	B49F	*Colchester 4.88*
1815	SWC25K	1972	Bristol RELL6L	ECW	B49F	*Colchester 3.88*
1816	SWC26K	1972	Bristol RELL6L	ECW	B49F	*Colchester 3.88*
1817	JMW166P	1975	Bristol RESL6G	ECW	B43F	*Thamesdown 7.87*
1818	JMW167P	1975	Bristol RESL6G	ECW	B43F	*Thamesdown 1.88*
1819	JMW169P	1975	Bristol RESL6G	ECW	B43F	*Thamesdown 7.87*
1820	JMW169P	1975	Bristol RESL6G	ECW	B43F	*Thamesdown 1.88*
1821	JMW170P	1975	Bristol RESL6G	ECW	B43F	*Thamesdown 10.87*
1822	TDL567K	1971	Bristol RELL6G	ECW	B53F	*Hylton Castle 3.93*
1823	NKG246M	1973	Bristol RESL6G	ECW	B44F	*Milton Keynes City 4.94*
1824	OCK363K	1972	Bristol RESL6G	ECW	B47F	*Milton Keynes City 4.94*
1825	OCK369K	1972	Bristol RESL6L	ECW	B47F	*Milton Keynes City 4.94*
1826	KTX242L	1972	Bristol RESL6G	ECW	B47F	*Milton Keynes City 4.94*
1832	LBN201P	1975	Leyland PSU3C/4R	Plaxton Elite	DP51F	*Southend 12.87*
1833	LBN202P	1975	Leyland PSU3C/4R	Plaxton Elite	DP51F	*Southend 2.88*
1847	MTE16R	1976	Leyland PSU3E/4R	Plaxton Derwent	B48F	*GM Buses 6.87*
1868	AHN388T	1978	Leyland PSU3E/4R	Plaxton Sup.V	B53F	*Cleveland Transit 5.90*
1895	OTD824R	1977	Leyland PSU3E/4R	Plaxton Sup.IV	DP51F	*GM Buses 7.87*

509/19, 1604-7/10/5/6/9 & 1803/4/6/22-6 are held in reserve

Economic Bus Services Fleet list

---

115 - 127 1989 Leyland LX112L10 Leyland B49F

115	F115HVK		118	F118HVK	125	F125HVK	127	F127HVK
117	F117HVK						

271	SCN271S	1978	Leyland AN68A/2R	Alexander AL	H49/37F
274	SCN274S	1978	Leyland AN68A/2R	Alexander AL	H49/37F
279	SCN279S	1978	Leyland AN68A/2R	Alexander AL	H49/37F

641 - 649

1985 Leyland ONLXB/1R — Alexander RL H45/31F

641	C641LFT	644	C644LFT	646	C646LFT	648	C648LFT
642	C642LFT	645	C645LFT	647	C647LFT	649	C649LFT
643	C643LFT						

675	H675BNL	1990	Leyland ON2R50C13Z4	Northern Counties	H47/30F
676	H676BNL	1990	Leyland ON2R50C13Z4	Northern Counties	H47/30F
1227	SVK627G	1969	Leyland PDR1A/1	Alexander	O44/30F
1749	L749VNL	1993	Dennis Dart 9.8SDL	Plaxton Pointer	B40F
1750	L750VNL	1993	Dennis Dart 9.8SDL	Plaxton Pointer	B40F

Favourite Services Fleet list

62	HTY137W	1980	Leyland PSU3E/4R	Duple Dom. C49F	*Grey Green 7.88*	
71	CMJ447T	1978	Leyland PSU3E/4R	Plaxton Sup.IV C53F	*Southend 2.88*	

62 was previously registered KSU464 and was originally FYX820W

262 - 297

1978 Leyland AN68A/2R — Alexander AL H49/37F

262	SCN262S	286	SCN286S	288	UVK288T	297	UVK297T

540	MVK540R	1976	Leyland AN68A/2R	Alexander AL	H48/34F
561	MVK561R	1976	Leyland AN68A/2R	Alexander AL	H48/33F
564	MVK564R	1976	Leyland AN68A/2R	Alexander AL	H48/33F
1437	E437AFT	1987	Mercedes Benz 709D	Reeve Burgess	B20F
1444	E444AFT	1987	Mercedes Benz 709D	Reeve Burgess	B20F

1634 - 1640

1987 Renault S56 — Alexander AM B25F

1634	E634BVK	1636	E636BVK	1638	E638BVK	1640	E640BVK
1635	E635BVK	1637	E637BVK	1639	E639BVK		

1748	L748VNL	1993	Dennis Dart 9.8SDL	Plaxton Pointer	B40F	
1770	M770DRG	1994	Dennis Dart 9.8SDL	Plaxton Pointer	B40F	
1771	M771DRG	1994	Dennis Dart 9.8SDL	Plaxton Pointer	B40F	
1863	ESU263	1984	Leyland TRCTL11/3R	Plaxton 3500	C49FT	*11.92*
1869	AHN389T	1978	Leyland PSU3E/4R	Plaxton Sup.V	B53F	*Cleveland Transit 5.90*
1870	AHN390T	1978	Leyland PSU3E/4R	Plaxton Sup.V	B53F	*Cleveland Transit 5.90*
1876	CBB476V	1980	Leyland PSU3F/4R	Duple Dom.	C53F	
1877	CBB477V	1980	Leyland PSU3F/4R	Duple Dom.	DP47F	
1896	OTD825R	1977	Leyland PSU3E/4R	Plaxton Sup.IV	DP51F	*GM Buses 7.87*

1863 was originally registered A899PPP.

Newcastle Busways Fleet list

247 - 300

1978 Leyland AN68A/2R — Alexander AL H49/37F

247	SCN247S	253	SCN253S	259	SCN259S	298	UVK298T
248	SCN248S	254	SCN254S	260	SCN260S	301	VCU301T
249	SCN249S	255	SCN255S	263	SCN263S	304	VCU304T
250	SCN250S	256	SCN256S	281	SCN281S	309	VCU309T
251	SCN251S	257	SCN257S	294	UVK294T	310	VCU310T
252	SCN252S	258	SCN258S				

314 - 363   1980   Leyland AN68A/2R   Alexander AL H49/37F

314	AVK134V	327	AVK147V	340	AVK160V	352	AVK172V
315	AVK135V	328	AVK148V	341	AVK161V	353	AVK173V
316	AVK136V	329	AVK149V	342	AVK162V	354	AVK174V
317	AVK137V	330	AVK150V	343	AVK163V	355	AVK175V
318	AVK138V	331	AVK151V	344	AVK164V	356	AVK176V
319	AVK139V	332	AVK152V	345	AVK165V	357	AVK177V
320	AVK140V	333	AVK153V	346	AVK166V	358	AVK178V
321	AVK141V	334	AVK154V	347	AVK167V	359	AVK179V
322	AVK142V	335	AVK155V	348	AVK168V	360	AVK180V
323	AVK143V	336	AVK156V	349	AVK169V	361	AVK181V
324	AVK144V	337	AVK157V	350	AVK170V	362	AVK182V
325	AVK145V	338	AVK158V	351	AVK171V	363	AVK183V
326	AVK146V	339	AVK159V				

413	JFT413X	1982	Scania BR112	Alexander RH H47/31F	
414	JFT414X	1982	Scania BR112	Alexander RH H47/31F	

421 - 430   1991   Scania N113DRB   Alexander H47/31F

421	H421BNL	424	H424BNL	427	H427BNL	429	H429BNL
422	H422BNL	425	H425BNL	428	H428BNL	430	H430BNL
423	H423BNL	426	H426BNL				

554	MVK554R	1976	Leyland AN68A/2R	Alexander AL H48/33F	
555	MVK555R	1976	Leyland AN68A/2R	Alexander AL H48/33F	
556	MVK556R	1976	Leyland AN68A/2R	Alexander AL H48/33F	

601 - 640   1985   Leyland ONLXB/1R   Alexander RL H45/31F

601	C601LFT	612	C612LFT	622	C622LFT	632	C632LFT
602	C602LFT	613	C613LFT	623	C623LFT	633	C633LFT
603	C603LFT	614	C614LFT	624	C624LFT	634	C634LFT
604	C604LFT	615	C615LFT	625	C625LFT	635	C635LFT
605	C605LFT	616	C616LFT	626	C626LFT	636	C636LFT
606	C606LFT	617	C617LFT	627	C627LFT	637	C637LFT
608	C608LFT	618	C618LFT	628	C628LFT	638	C638LFT
609	C609LFT	619	C619LFT	629	C629LFT	639	C639LFT
610	C610LFT	620	C620LFT	630	C630LFT	640	C640LFT
611	C611LFT	621	C621LFT	631	C631LFT		

684 - 697   1987   Leyland ONLXB/1RH   Northern Counties H43/30F
(ex.London Buses 1991)

684	E911KYR	688	E917KYR	692	E921KYR	695	E925KYR
685	E912KYR	689	E918KYR	693	E922KYR	696	E925KYR
686	E914KYR	690	E919KYR	694	E923KYR	697	E927KYR
687	E915KYR	691	E920KYR				

901 - 920   1989   Scania N113CRB   Alexander PS B51F

901	F901JRG	906	F906JRG	911	F911JRG	916	F916JRG
902	F902JRG	907	F907JRG	912	F912JRG	917	F917JRG
903	F903JRG	908	F908JRG	913	F913JRG	918	F918JRG
904	F904JRG	909	F909JRG	914	F914JRG	919	F919JRG
905	F905JRG	910	F910JRG	915	F915JRG	920	F920JRG

921 - 926

1990 Scania N113CRB   Alexander PS B51F

921	G921TCU	923	G923TCU	925	C925TCU	926	C926TCU
922	G922TCU	924	G924TCU				

---

927 G113SKX 1989 Scania N113CRB   Alexander PS B51F   *Demonstrator 3.91*

---

928 - 937

1991 Scania N113CRB   Alexander PS B51F

928	H928EFT	931	H931EFT	934	H934EFT	936	H936EFT
929	H929EFT	932	H932EFT	935	H935EFT	937	H937EFT
930	H930EFT	933	H933EFT				

938	G108CEH	1990	Scania N113CRB	Alexander PS B49F	*Stevenson, Spath 5.93*
952	M952DRG	1994	Scania L113CRL	Northern Counties DP49F	
953	M953DRG	1994	Scania L113CRL	Alexander AF B51F	
1201	M201DRG	1994	Dennis Lance 11SDA	Plaxton Verde B49F	
1204	M204DRG	1994	Dennis Lance 11SDA	Optare Sigma B47F	

1404 - 1418

1986 Mercedes Benz 709D   Reeve Burgess B20F

1404	D404TFT	1412	D412TFT	1414	D414TFT	1417	D417TFT
1408	D408TFT	1413	D413TFT	1416	D416TFT	1418	D418TFT

1421 - 1455

1987 Mercedes Benz 709D   Reeve Burgess B20F

1421	E421AFT	1429	E429AFT	1435	E435AFT	1441	E441AFT
1423	E423AFT	1430	E430AFT	1436	E436AFT	1442	E442AFT
1426	E426AFT	1432	E432AFT	1438	E438AFT	1443	E443AFT
1427	E427AFT	1433	E433AFT	1439	E439AFT	1455	E455AFT
1428	E428AFT	1434	E424AFT	1440	E440AFT		

1651	F651KNL	1988	Iveco 49.10	Carlyle B23F
1654	F654KNL	1988	Iveco 49.10	Carlyle B23F

1679 - 1688

1991 Optare Metrorider   Optare B29F
(ex.Welcome 8.93)

1679	J371BNW	1682	J374BNW	1685	J377BNW	1687	J379BNW
1680	J372BNW	1683	J375BNW	1686	J378BNW	1688	J380BNW
1681	J373BNW	1684	J376BNW				

1689 - 1693

1992 Optare Metrorider   Optare B29F
(ex.Welcome 8.93)

1689	K162FYG	1691	K164FYG	1692	K165FYG	1693	K166FYG
1690	K163FYG						

1703 - 1721

1992 Dennis Dart 9.8SDL   Alexander AM Dash B40F

1703	K703PCN	1708	K708PCN	1713	K713PCN	1718	K718PCN
1704	K704PCN	1709	K709PCN	1714	K714PCN	1719	K719PCN
1705	K705PCN	1710	K710PCN	1715	K715PCN	1720	K720PCN
1706	K706PCN	1711	K711PCN	1716	K716PCN	1721	K721PCN
1707	K707PCN	1712	K712PCN	1717	K717PCN		

1739 - 1743

1993 Dennis Dart 9.8SDL   Alexander AM Dash B40F

1739	L739VNL	1741	L741VNL	1742	L742VNL	1743	L743VNL
1740	L740VNL						

1902	M902DRG	1994	Volvo B10B	Alexander AF B51F	

221, 332/5/45/55, 414/4, 554-6 & 1651/4 are held in reserve

South Shields Busways Fleet list

116 - 124

1989 Leyland LX112L10   Leyland B49F

116	F116HVK	120	F120HVK	122	F122HVK	124	F124HVK
119	F119HVK	121	F121HVK	123	F123HVK		

126	H126HCU	1990	Leyland LX112L10ZR1S	Leyland DP47F		
140	LCU112	1964	Daimler CCG6	Roe H35/28R	(Preserved)	

264 - 300

1978 Leyland AN68A/2R   Alexander AL H49/37F

264	SCN264S	275	SCN275S	284	SCN284S	291	UVK291T
265	SCN265S	276	SCN276S	285	SCN285S	292	UVK292T
266	SCN266S	278	SCN278S	287	UVK287T	295	UVK295T
267	SCN267S	280	SCN280S	289	UVK289T	299	UVK299T
269	SCK269S	282	SCN282S	290	UVK290T	300	UVK300T
270	SCN270S	283	SCN283S				

951	M951DRG	1994	Scania C113CRL	Northern Counties Paladin B49F	
1202	M202DRG	1994	Dennis Lance 11SDA	Plaxton Verde B49F	
1405	D405TFT	1986	Mercedes Benz 709D	Reeve Burgess B20F	
1407	D407TFT	1986	Mercedes Benz 709D	Reeve Burgess B20F	
1431	E431AFT	1987	Mercedes Benz 709D	Reeve Burgess B23F	
1445	E445AFT	1987	Mercedes Benz 709D	Reeve Burgess B20F	
1446	E446AFT	1987	Mercedes Benz 709D	Reeve Burgess B20F	
1448	E448AFT	1987	Mercedes Benz 709D	Reeve Burgess B20F	
1449	E449AFT	1987	Mercedes Benz 709D	Reeve Burgess B23F	
1450	E450AFT	1987	Mercedes Benz 709D	Reeve Burgess B20F	
1451	E451AFT	1987	Mercedes Benz 709D	Reeve Burgess B23F	
1453	E453AFT	1987	Mercedes Benz 709D	Reeve Burgess B23F	

1454 - 1460

1987 Mercedes Benz 709D   Reeve Burgess B20F

1454	E454AFT	1457	A457AFT	1459	E459AFT	1460	E460AFT
1456	E456AFT	1458	E458AFT				

1664 - 1669

1991 Renault S75   Reeve Burgess Beaver B28F
(ex.Welcome 8.93)

1664	J553NGS	1665	J225JJR	1667	J227JJR	1669	J229JJR

1751 - 1759

1993 Dennis Dart 9.8SDL   Alexander AM Dash B40F

1751	L751VNL	1754	L754VNL	1756	L756VNL	1758	L758VNL
1752	L752VNL	1755	L755VNL	1757	L757VNL	1759	L759VNL
1753	L753VNL						

1766 - 1769

1994 Dennis Dart 9.8SDL   Plaxton Pointer B40F

| 1766 | M766DRG | 1767 | M767DRG | 1768 | M768DRG | 1769 | M769DRG |

| 1801 | ECU201E | 1968 | Bristol RESL6L | ECW B45D | (Preserved) |
| 1872 | CMJ450T | 1978 | Leyland PSU3E/4R | Plaxton Sup.IV C53F | *Southend 2.88* |

269/84/99 are held in reserve

Sunderland Busways   Fleet list

101 - 107

1988 Leyland LX112L10   Leyland B49F

| 101 | F101HVK | 103 | F103HVK | 105 | F105HVK | 107 | F107HVK |
| 102 | F102HVK | 104 | F104HVK | 106 | F106HVK | | |

108 - 114

1989 Leyland LX112L10   Leyland B49F

| 108 | F108HVK | 110 | F110HVK | 112 | F112HVK | 114 | F114HVK |
| 109 | F109HVK | 111 | F111HVK | 113 | F113HVK | | |

204 - 223

1980 Leyland AN68A/2R   Alexander AL H49/37F

204	EJR104W	209	EJR109W	214	EJR114W	219	EJR119W
205	EJR105W	210	EJR110W	215	EJR115W	221	EJR121W
206	EJR106W	211	EJR111W	217	EJR117W	222	EJR122W
207	EJR107W	212	EJR112W	218	EJR118W	223	EJR123W
208	EJR108W	213	EJR113W				

650 - 665

1985 Leyland ONLXB/1R   Alexander RL H45/31F

650	C650LFT	654	C654LFT	658	C658LFT	662	C662LFT
651	C651LFT	655	C655LFT	659	C659LFT	663	C663LFT
652	C652LFT	656	C656LFT	660	C660LFT	664	C664LFT
653	C653LFT	657	C657LFT	661	C661LFT	665	C665LFT

667 - 674

1990 Leyland ON2R50C13Z4   Northern Counties H47/30F

| 667 | H667BNL | 669 | H669BNL | 671 | H671BNL | 673 | H673BNL |
| 668 | H668BNL | 670 | H670BNL | 672 | H672BNL | 674 | H674BNL |

677 - 683

1987 Leyland ONLXB/1RH   Northern Counties H43/30F
(ex.*London Buses 1991*)

| 677 | E901KYR | 679 | E906KYR | 681 | E908KYR | 683 | E910KYR |
| 678 | E905KYR | 680 | E907KYR | 682 | E909KYR | | |

800 - 839 1977 Daimler FE30AGR Alexander AL H44/30F

800	OCU800R	821	OCU821R	827	RCU827S	834	RCU834S
806	OCU806R	822	OCU822R	828	RCU828S	835	RCU835S
813	OCU813R	823	OCU823R	829	RCU829S	836	RCU836S
816	OCU816R	824	OCU824R	830	RCU830S	837	RCU837S
818	OCU818R	825	OCU825R	832	RCU832S	838	RCU838S
819	OCU819R	826	OCU826R	833	RCU833S	839	RCU839S
820	OCU820R						

954	M954DRG	1994	Scania L113CRL	Alexander AF	B51F
1203	M203DRG	1994	Dennis Lance 11SDA	Plaxton Verde	B49F
1218	KBB118D	1966	Leyland PDR1/1	MCCW	O44/34F

1621 - 1633 1987 Renault S56 Alexander AM B25F

1621	E621BVK	1625	E625BVK	1628	E628BVK	1631	E631BVK
1622	E622BVK	1626	E626BVK	1629	E629BVK	1632	E632BVK
1623	E623BVK	1627	E627BVK	1630	E630BVK	1633	E633BVK
1624	E624BVK						

1694 - 1700 1992 Iveco 59.12 (ex.Welcome 8.93) Dormobile B27F

1694	K330RCN	1696	K332RCN	1698	K335RCN	1700	K337RCN
1695	K331RCN	1697	K334RCN	1699	K336RCN		

1722	K722PCN	1992	Dennis Dart 9.8SDL	Alexander AM Dash B40F

1723 - 1738 1993 Dennis Dart 9.8SDL Alexander AM Dash B40F

1723	K723PNL	1727	K727PNL	1731	L731VNL	1735	L735VNL
1724	K724PNL	1728	K728PNL	1732	L732VNL	1736	L736VNL
1725	K725PNL	1729	L729VNL	1733	L733VNL	1737	L737VNL
1726	K726PNL	1730	L730VNL	1734	L734VNL	1738	L738VNL

1760 - 1765 1994 Dennis Dart 9.8SDL Plaxton Pointer B40F

1760	L760ARG	1762	L762ARG	1764	L764ARG	1765	L765ARG
1761	L761ARG	1763	L763ARG				

1864	FYX824W	1980	Leyland PSU3E/4R	Duple Dom. DP49F	*Grey Green 7.88*	
1901	M901DRG	1994	Volvo B10B	Alexander AF B51F		

221, 800/6/11/3/23/36/39 & 1218 are held in reserve

Fleet list

801 - 831

1977 Daimler FE30AGR   Alexander AL H44/30F
(ex.Sunderland Busways 11.94)

801	OCU801R	804	OCU804R	814	OCU814R	817	OCU817R
802	OCU802R	807	OCU807R	815	OCU815R	831	RCU831S
803	OCU803R	808	OCU808R				

1653 - 1661

1988 Iveco 49.10   Carlyle Daily B23F
(ex.Blue Bus Services 11.94)

| 1653 | F653KNL | 1658 | F658KNL | 1659 | F659KNL | 1661 | F661KNL |

1668 - 1673

1991 Renault S75   Reeve Burgess Beaver B28F
(ex.Welcome Services 11.94)

| 1668 | J228JJR | 1670 | J230JJR | 1671 | J231JJR | 1673 | J233JJR |

1676	K343PJR	1992	Renault S75	Reeve Burgess B28F	Welcome 8.93
1677	K344PJR	1992	Renault S75	Reeve Burgess B28F	Welcome 8.93
1678	K345PJR	1992	Renault S75	Reeve Burgess B28F	Welcome 8.93
2006	F496NTR	1988	Iveco 49.10	Robin Hood B25F	United Counties 11.94
2007	F494NTR	1988	Iveco 49.10	Robin Hood B25F	United Counties 11.94
2008	F495NTR	1988	Iveco 49.10	Robin Hood B25F	United Counties 11.94
2009	D606MKH	1987	Iveco 49.10	Robin Hood B25F	KHCT 11.94
2010	D604MKH	1987	Iveco 49.10	Robin Hood B25F	KHCT 11.94
2011	D607MKH	1987	Iveco 49.10	Robin Hood B25F	KHCT 11.94
	G22CSG	1989	Renault S56	Reeve Burgess B25F	Fife Scottish 12.94
	G23CSG	1989	Renault S56	Reeve Burgess B25F	Fife Scottish 12.94
2101	PES188Y	1983	Leyland TRCTL11/3R	Duple Gold.IV C51F	Fife Scottish 11.94
2102	PSE189Y	1983	Leyland TRCTL11/3R	Duple Gold.IV C51F	Fife Scottish 11.94
2103	PES190Y	1983	Leyland TRCTL11/3R	Duple Gold.IV C55F	Fife Scottish 11.94
2104	A940XGG	1984	Leyland TRCTL11/3R	Duple Laser C46F	Fife Scottish 11.94
2105	A941XGG	1984	Leyland TRCTL11/3R	Duple Laser C51F	Fife Scottish 11.94
2106	A942XGG	1984	Leyland TRCTL11/3R	Duple Laser C46F	Fife Scottish 11.94
2107	PSO179W	1981	Leyland TRCTL11/3R	Duple Gold.IV C51F	Bluebird Buses 11.94
2108	CSO388Y	1982	Leyland TRCTL11/3R	Duple Gold IV C51F	Bluebird Buses 11.94
2109	CSO389Y	1983	Leyland TRCTL11/3R	Duple Gold.IV C51F	Bluebird Buses 11.94
2110	VSS3X	1982	Leyland TRCTL11/3R	Duple Gold.IV C51F	Bluebird Buses 11.94
2111	CSO387Y	1983	Leyland TRCTL11/3R	Duple Gold.IV C51F	Bluebird Buses 11.94
2112	RRS226X	1982	Leyland TRCTL11/3R	Duple Gold.IV C51F	Bluebird Buses 11.94

*2101 were previously registered MSU463/45 & GSU341/4/2/3 and were originally SFS583/2Y,
VTY130Y & A507/5/6PST. 2107-9 were previously registered CSU922 & TSV777/8 and were originally
BSG545W & ASA 7/8Y. 2111/2 were previously registered TSV781 & 1412NE and were originally
ASA11Y & KSL41X.*

2121	TRN805V	1979	Leyland LN10351B/1R	Leyland B44F	Ribble 11.94
2122	NEO833R	1977	Leyland LN11351A/1R	Leyland B49F	Ribble 11.94
2123	SNS822W	1980	Leyland NL116AL11/1R	Leyland B52F	Ribble 11.94
2124	AHH201T	1978	Leyland LN10351B/1R	Leyland B44F	Ribble 11.94
2125	MAO368P	1976	Leyland LN11351/1R	Leyland B52F	Ribble 11.94
2126	WAO397Y	1982	Leyland NL116HLXB/1R	Leyland B52F	Ribble 11.94

2127	OLS806T	1978	Leyland LN10351B/1R	Leyland B44F	Ribble 11.94
2128	SNS828W	1980	Leyland NL116L11/1R	Leyland B52F	Ribble 11.94
2129	UHG739R	1976	Leyland LN11351A/1R	Leyland B49F	Ribble 11.94

2141 - 2146

1986 Mercedes Benz L608D (ex.Ribble 11.94)   Reeve Burgess B20F

2141	D33UAO	2143	D538RCK	2145	D535RCK	2146	D543RCK
2142	D523RCK	2144	D526RCK				

1994 Volvo B10M-55   Alexander PS DP48F

M784PRS	M787PRS	M790PRS	M792PRS
M785PRS	M788PRS	M791PRS	M793PRS
M786PRS	M789PRS		

Included amongst the Stagecoach Darlington fleet at its inception was a number of former Busways Alexander-bodied Fleetlines, one of which - 815 - is seen in corporate livery showing Stagecoach in its destination apperture operating town service 54 to Firth Moor in November 1994. (K.A.Jenkinson)

PART OF THE STAGECOACH GROUP

Cleveland Transit Ltd., Church Road, Stockton-on-Tees TS18 2HW
Cleveland Transit Coaches Ltd., Church Road, Stockton-on-Tees TS18 2HW
KHCT Ltd., Lombard Street, Hull HU2 8QN

Cleveland Transit was created on 1 APril 1974 to take over Teesside Municipal Transport which itself had been formed on 1 April 1968 by the merging of Middlesbrough and Stockton Corporations and the Teesside Railless Traction Board. Operations were expanded on 1 August 1974 with the purchase of Saltburn Motor Services and on 13 December 1993 when a 51% share of Kingston-upon-Hull City Transport was acqyuired.

Livery : TRANSIT - Green, yellow & white; CLEVELAND COACHES - Yellow & orange; KHCT - Blue, white & yellow; TEES VALLEY - Maroon, white & yellow. *Existing liveries are to be retained for a period of three years.*

Depots : Liverpool Street, Hull (KHCT); Lombard Street, Hull (KHCT); Stockton-on-Tees (Transit, Cleveland Coaches & Tees Valley).

Transit   Fleet list

1 - 10
1989 Leyland LX112L10ZR1R   Leyland B49F

1	F601UVN	4	F604UVN	7	F607UVN	9	F609UVN
2	F602UVN	5	F605UVN	8	F608UVN	10	F610UVN
3	F603UVN	6	F606UVN				

11 - 20
1989 Leyland LX2R11C15Z4R   Leyland B49F

11	G611CEF	14	G614CEF	17	G617CEF	19	G619CEF
12	G612CEF	15	G615CEF	18	G618CEF	20	G620CEF
13	G613CEF	16	G616CEF				

| 21 | J901UKV | 1992 | Leyland LX2R11C15Z4R | Leyland B49F | *Demonstrator 10.92* |

22 - 30
1992 Leyland LX2R11C15Z4R   Leyland B49F

22	K622YVN	25	K625YVN	27	K627YVN	29	K629YVN
23	K623YVN	26	K626YVN	28	K628YVN	30	K630YVN
24	K624YVN						

31 - 42
1994 Volvo B10B   Plaxton Verde B52F

31	L31HHN	34	L34HHN	37	L37HHN	40	M40PVN
32	L32HHN	35	L35HHN	38	M38PVN	41	M41PVN
33	L33HHN	36	L36HHN	39	M39PVN	42	M42PVN

101 - 108

1994 Volvo B6   Plaxton Pointer B41F

101	L101GHN	103	L103GHN	105	M105PVN	107	M107PVN
102	L102GHN	104	M104PVN	106	M106PVN	108	M108PVN

---

121 YVN521T 1979 Leyland FE30AGR   NCME H43/31F

---

125 - 141

1980 Leyland FE30AGR   NCME H43/31F

125	GAJ125V	130	GAJ130V	134	GAJ134V	138	JAJ138W
126	GAJ126V	131	GAJ131V	135	GAJ135V	139	JAJ139W
127	GAJ127V	132	GAJ132V	136	GAJ136V	140	JAJ140W
128	GAJ128V	133	GAJ133V	137	JAJ137W	141	JAJ141W
129	GAJ129V						

---

142 - 149

1981 Leyland FE30AGR   NCME H43/31F

142	JAJ142W	144	JAJ144W	146	JAJ146W	148	PEF148X
143	JAJ143W	145	JAJ145W	147	PEF147X	149	PEF149X

---

150 - 155

1982 Leyland FE30AGR   NCME H43/31F

150	VEF150Y	152	VEF152Y	154	YAJ154Y	155	YAJ155Y
151	VEF151Y	153	VEF153Y				

156	YAJ156Y	1983	Leyland FE30AGR	NCME H43/31F
157	YAJ157Y	1983	Leyland FE30AGR	NCME H43/31F

---

204 - 207

1983 Dennis Dominator DD149A   NCME H43/31F

204	A204EHN	205	A205EHN	206	A206EHN	207	A207EHN

208	A208EHN	1984	Dennis Dominator DD149A	NCME H43/31F
209	A209EHN	1983	Dennis Dominator DD149A	NCME H43/31F
211	A211EHN	1983	Dennis Dominator DD149A	NCME H43/31F
212	A212FVN	1984	Dennis Dominator DD149A	NCME H43/31F
213	A213FVN	1984	Dennis Dominator DD149A	NCME H43/31F

---

214 - 218

1985 Dennis Dominator DD149A   NCME H43/31F

214	B214OAJ	216	B216OAJ	217	B217OAJ	218	B218OAJ
215	B215OAJ						

---

219 - 222

1986 Dennis Dominator DDA1009   NCME H43/31F

219	C219WAJ	220	C220WAJ	221	C221WAJ	222	C222WAJ

---

336 - 345

1989 Renault S56   NCME B23F

336	F336VEF	339	F339VEF	342	F342VEF	344	F344VEF
337	F337VEF	340	F340VEF	343	F343VEF	345	F345VEF
338	F338VEF	341	F341VEF				

500	PRX189B	1964	Leyland PD3/4	NCME FCO39/30F	*Southdown 6.88*

Cleveland Coaches   Fleet list

900	CVN400T	1979	Bedford YLQ/S	Duple Dom.II C35F	
901	H201XKH	1990	Leyland Swift	Reeve Burgess C34F	*KHCT 9.94*
902	BPY402T	1979	Leyland PSU3E/4R	Plaxton Sup.IV C53F	
903	BPY403T	1979	Leyland PSU3E/4R	Plaxton Sup.IV C53F	
905	CPY705T	1979	Leyland PSU3E/4R	Plaxton Sup.IV DP55F	*KHCT 9.94*
912	HPY422V	1980	Leyland PSU3F/4R	Plaxton Sup.IV DP53F	*KHCT 9.94*
914	HPY424V	1980	Leyland PSU3F/4R	Plaxton Sup.IV DP53F	*KHCT 9.94*
916	HPY416V	1980	Leyland PSU3F/4R	Plaxton Sup.IV DP53F	
925	HPY425V	1980	Leyland PSU3F/4R	Plaxton Sup.IV C53F	
926	HPY426V	1980	Leyland PSU3F/4R	Plaxton Sup.IV C53F	
927	OHN427X	1981	Leyland PSU3F/4R	Plaxton Sup.IV C53F	
928	OHN428X	1981	Leyland PSU3F/4R	Plaxton Sup.IV C53F	
929	OHN429X	1981	Leyland PSU3F/4R	Plaxton Sup.IV C53F	
933	E333LHN	1988	Dodge S56	NCME DP21F	
935	F335SPY	1988	Renault S56	NCME DP21F	
951	OIB3516	1983	Leyland TRCTL/2R	Plaxton 3200 C49F	
952	OIB3515	1983	Leyland TRCTL/2R	Plaxton 3200 C49F	
953	OIB3514	1984	Leyland TRCTL11/2RP	Plaxton 3200 C49F	
954	OIB3413	1984	Leyland TRCTL11/2RP	Plaxton 3200 C49F	
955	OIB3512	1987	Leyland B50	Roe Doyen C53F	
983	PJI4983	1985	Leyland ONLXB/2R	ECW DPH45/28F	*Clyde Coast 11.92*
986	PJI4986	1988	Volvo B10M-60	Van Hool Alizee C49F	*Excelsior, Bournmth 5.93*

951-5 were originally registered YHN451/2Y, A453/4HPY & D455GHN. 983 was originally registered B577LPE. 986 was previously registered E847SEL, XEL24, E402SEL & XEL606 and was originally registered E304OPR.

Tees Valley   Fleet list

920	YVN520T	1979	Leyland FE30AGR	NCME H43/31F
922	YVN522T	1979	Leyland FE30AGR	NCME H43/31F
923	HPY423V	1980	Leyland PSU3F/4R	Plaxton Sup.IV DP53F
924	E324JVN	1987	Dodge S56	NCME B19F
997	AHN397T	1979	Leyland PSU3E/4R	Plaxton Sup.IV DP55F

ANCILLARY VEHICLES

301	D530HNW	1988	Ford Transit 150	Carlyle .B16F	*West Yorkshire 1988*
303	C301CRH	1985	Ford Transit 150	Carlyle B16F	*East Yorkshire 1993*
323	D323HDC	1987	Dodge S56	NCME B19F	
501	XMS253R	1977	Leyland PSU3/3R	Alexander AY C49F	*Thamesdown 1994*
G16	Q923DAJ	1975	Leyland Clydesdale	Recovery Wagon	
	WAJ299Y	1982	Leyland Terrier	Lorry	
	K634CEF	1993	Vauxhall Astramax	Van	

501 is a driver training vehicle.

KHCT   Fleet list

42	BUT24Y	1983	Dennis Dorchester	Plaxton 3200 C49F	*Leicester 1986*
43	BUT25Y	1983	Dennis Dorchester	Plaxton 3200 C49F	*Leicester 1985*
50	IIL1319	1986	Volvo B10M-61	Plaxton 3200 C50FT	
51	IIL1321	1987	Volvo B10M-61	Plaxton 3200 C44FT	
52	E52WAG	1988	Volvo B10M-61	Plaxton 3200 C50FT	
53	F53EAT	1989	Dennis Javelin	Plaxton 3500 C48FT	
55	F55EAT	1989	Dennis Javelin	Plaxton 3500 C48FT	
56	G56SAG	1990	Volvo B10M-61	Plaxton 3500 C49FT	
60	B60WKH	1984	Leyland NL116HLXCT/1R	Leyland B24DL	
61	YAY21Y	1982	Dennis Lancet SD506	Duple Dom. B25DL	*Leicester 1987*
71	H71XKH	1990	Leyland Swift	Reeve Burgess C34FT	

50/1 were originally registered C50FRH & D51ORH.

106 - 109   1984   Dennis Dominator DDA903   Alexander RL H43/32F

106	B106UAT		107	B107UAT		108	B108UAT		109	B109UAT

110	B110UAT	1984	Dennis Dominator DDA903	Alexander RL CH43/32F
111	C111CAT	1986	Dennis Dominator DDA1007	East Lancs H43/28F
112	C112CAT	1986	Dennis Dominator DDA1007	East Lancs H43/28F
113	C113CAT	1986	Dennis Dominator DDA1007	East Lancs H43/28F
122	C122CAT	1986	Dennis Dominator DDA1006	East Lancs H45/30F

123 - 131   1985   Dennis Dominator DDA1006 East Lancs H45/30F

123	C123CAT		125	C125CAT		129	C129CAT		131	C131CAT
124	C124CAT		128	C128CAT					

132	E132SAT	1987	Dennis Dominator DDA1014	East Lancs H45/21D

133 - 141   1987   Dennis Dominator DDA1014   East Lancs H45/32F

133	E133SAT		136	E136SAT		138	E138SAT		140	E140SAT
134	E134SAT		137	E137SAT		139	E139SAT		141	E141SAT
135	E135SAT								

142 - 151   1988   Dennis Dominator DDA1016   East Lancs H45/31F

142	F142BKH		145	F145BKH		148	F148BKH		150	F150BKH
143	F143BKH		146	F146BKH		149	F149BKH		151	F151BKH
144	F144BKH		147	F147BKH					

152 - 157   1989   Dennis Dominator DDA1027   East Lancs H45/33F

152	F152HAT		154	F154HAT		156	F156HAT		157	F157HAT
153	F153HAT		155	F155HAT					

| 204 | J204JKH | 1992 | Volvo B10M-60 | | Plaxton 3500 C51FT | | |
| 205 | J205JKH | 1992 | Volvo B10M-60 | | Plaxton 3500 C51FT | | |

505 - 515

1980   MCW Metrobus DR102   MCW H43/30F

505	LAT505V	509	LAT509V	512	LAT512V	514	LAT514V
506	LAT506V	510	LAT510V	513	LAT513V	515	LAT515V
507	LAT507V	511	LAT511V				

516 - 530

1981   MCW Metrobus DR102   MCW H43/30F

516	SAG516W	520	SAG520W	524	SAG524W	528	SAG528W
517	SAG517W	521	SAG521W	525	SAG525W	529	SAG529W
518	SAG518W	522	SAG522W	526	SAG526W	530	SAG530W
519	SAG519W	523	SAG523W	527	SAG527W		

601 - 615

1987   Iveco 49.10   Robin Hood B25F

601	D601MKH	605	D605MKH	611	D611MKH	614	D614MKH
602	D602MKH	608	D608MKH	612	D612MKH	615	D615MKH
603	D603MKH	609	D609MKH	613	D613MKH		

701 - 706

1988   Scania N112CRB   East Lancs DP49F

| 701 | F701BAT | 703 | F703BAT | 705 | F705BAT | 706 | F706CAG |
| 702 | F702BAT | 704 | F704BAT | | | | |

801 - 808

1989   Scania N113DRB   East Lancs H51.37F

| 801 | G801JRH | 803 | G803JRH | 805 | G805JRH | 807 | G807LAG |
| 802 | G802JRH | 804 | G804JRH | 806 | G806JRK | 808 | G808LAG |

809 - 816

1990   Scania N113DRB   East Lancs H51/33F

| 809 | H809WKH | 811 | H811WKH | 813 | H813WKH | 815 | H815WKH |
| 810 | H810WKH | 812 | H812WKH | 814 | H814WKH | 816 | H816WKH |

ANCILLARY VEHICLES

WRH484J	1970	Leyland PDR1A/1	Roe H--D	Exhibition Unit
89HBC	1980	Leyland PSU5D/4R	Plaxton Sup. C49F	Driver Trainer
FYB451Y	1985	ERF	Recovery Wagon	
WMJ267K	1971	Ford	Recovery Wagon	
A834ORH	1983	Dodge	Stores Lorry	
G265KJX	1989	Ford Escort	Van	
A23SAG	1983	Freight Rover Sherpa	Van	
G155VBB	1898	Ford Transit	Van	
LWY185P	1976	Bedford-Spencer	Platform	
FAG906Y	1983	Dodge	Van	

89HBC was originally registered CTC133V

Fife ⚡ Scottish

PART OF THE STAGECOACH GROUP

Fife Scottish Omnibuses Ltd., Esplanade, Kirkcaldy, KY1 1SP

Formed as a result of the division of the massive W.Alexander & Sons Ltd. empire on 15 May 1961 to become W.Alexander & Sons (Fife) ltd, the company was given its current title in 1985.

Depots : Aberhill; Cowdenbeath; Dunfermline; Glenrothes; Kirkcaldy; St.Andrews

Fife Scottish   Fleet list

1	D891DSF	1987	Dodge S56	Alexander AM B25F
9	E809JSX	1987	Renault S56	Alexander AM B25F
50	MSU463	1988	MCW MF150/98	MCW DP25F

50 was originally registered F70RFS

51 - 66   1988 MCW MF150/98   MCW B25F

51	F51RFS	55	F55RFS	59	F59RFS	63	F63RFS
52	F52RFS	56	F56RFS	60	F60RFS	64	F64RFS
53	F53RFS	57	F57RFS	61	F61RFS	65	F65RFS
54	F54RFS	58	F58RFS	62	F62RFS	66	F66RFS

67 - 69   1988 MCW MF150/102   MCW DP25F

| 67 | F67RFS | 68 | F68RFS | 69 | F69RFS |

70 - 76   1994 Mercedes Benz 709D   Alexander AM B25F

| 70 | M770TFS | 72 | M772TFS | 74 | M774TFS | 76 | M776TFS |
| 71 | M771TFS | 73 | M773TFS | 75 | M775TFS | | |

77	VLT77	1989	Mercedes Benz 811D	Reeve Burgess B33F	Selkent 11.94
78	M778TFS	1994	Mercedes Benz 709D	Alexander AM B25F	
79	M779TFS	1994	Mercedes Benz 709D	Alexander AM B25F	
80	G280TSL	1990	Mercedes Benz 709D	Alexander AM B23F	Bluebird Northern 9.92
81	G281TSL	1990	Mercedes Benz 709D	Alexander AM B23F	Bluebird Northern 9.92
82	M780TFS	1994	Mercedes Benz 709D	Alexander AM B25F	

77 was originally registered F396DHL.

85 - 94   1993 Mercedes Benz 709D   Alexander (Belfast) B25F

85	K485FFS	88	K488FFS	91	K491FFS	93	K493FFS
86	K486FFS	89	K489FFS	92	K492FFS	94	K494FFS
87	K487FFS	90	K490FFS				

104	TMX404X	1982	Leyland PSU3G/4R	Alexander AYS B53F	Ribble 3.92
122	XMS422Y	1982	Leyland PSU3G/4R	Alexander AYS B53F	Ribble 3.92
123	XMS423Y	1982	Leyland PSU3G/4R	Alexander AYS B53F	Ribble 3.92

138 - 150   1980   Leyland PSU3F/4R   Alexander AYS   B53F

138	WFS138W	141	WFS141W	147	WFS147W	149	WFS149W
139	WFS139W	142	WFS142W	148	WFS148W	150	WFS150W
140	WFS140W						

158	CSF158W	1981	Leyland PSU3F/4R	Alexander AYS	B53F
159	CSF159W	1981	Leyland PSU3G/4R	Alexander AYS	B53F
160	CSF160W	1981	Leyland PSU3G/4R	Alexander AYS	B53F

180 - 189   1982   Leyland PSU3G/4R   Alexander AYS   B53F

180	PSX180Y	183	PSX183Y	186	PSX186Y	188	PSX188Y
181	PSX181Y	184	PSX184Y	187	PSX187Y	189	PSX189Y
182	PSX182Y	185	PSX185Y				

200 - 207   1982   Leyland PSU3G/4R   Alexander AYS   C49F
(ex.Ribble 3.92)

200	XMS420Y	205	TMS405X	206	TMS406X	207	TMS407X

261	CSF161W	1981	Leyland PSU3G/4R	Alexander AYS	B53F
262	CSF162W	1981	Leyland PSU3G/4R	Alexander AYS	B53F

263 - 269   1981   Leyland PSU3F/4R   Alexander AYS   DP49F

263	CSF163W	265	CSF165W	267	CSF167W	269	CSF169W
264	CSF164W	266	CSF166W	268	CSF168W		

270 - 279   1982   Leyland PSU3G/4R   Alexander AT   C49F

270	NFS170Y	273	NFS173Y	276	NFS176Y	278	NFS178Y
271	NFS171Y	274	NFS174Y	277	NFS177Y	279	NFS179Y
272	NFS272Y	275	NFS175Y				

282	GSO82V	1980	Leyland PSU3E/4R	Alexander AYS DP53F	Stagecoach Buses 7.94
283	GSO83V	1980	Leyland PSU3E/4R	Alexander AYS DP49F	Stagecoach Buses 7.94
284	GSO84V	1980	Leyland PSU3E/4R	Alexander AYS DP53F	Stagecoach Buses 7.94

290 - 294   1982   Leyland PSU3G/4R   Alexander AT   C49F

290	RSC190Y	292	RSC192Y	293	RSC193Y	294	RSC194Y
291	RSC191Y						

301 - 310   1994   Volvo B10M--60   Alexander PS   B49F

301	L301PSC	304	L304PSC	307	L307PSC	309	L309PSC
302	L302PSC	305	L305PSC	308	L308PSC	310	L310PSC
303	L303PSC	306	L306PSC				

316 - 323   1980   Leyland NL116L11/1R   Leyland   B52F

316	RSG816V	320	RSG820V	322	RSG822V	323	RSG823V

328	YSX928W	1980	Leyland NL106L11/1R	Leyland	B44F
329	YSX929W	1980	Leyland NL106L11/1R	Leyland	B44F
330	YSX930W	1980	Leyland NL106L11/1R	Leyland	B44F

380 - 388

1980 Leyland NL116l11/1R Leyland B52F
(ex. Northern Scottish 1989)

380	DMS20V	382	DMS22V	386	NLS986W	388	NLS988W
381	DMS21V	385	MSO15W	387	NLS987W		

412	D512CSF	1986	Leyland TRCTL11/3RH	Alexander P	B61F

413 - 419

1987 Leyland TRCTL11/3RH Alexander P B61F

413	D713CSC	415	D615ASG	417	D517DSX	419	D519DSX
414	D614ASG	416	D516DSX	418	D518DSX		

420 - 424

1987 Leyland TRCTL11/2RH Alexander P B57F

420	D520DSX	422	D522DSX	423	D523DSX	424	D524DSX
421	D521DSX						

441 - 445

1985 Leyland TRCTL11/2RH Alexander TC C47F

441	GSU341	443	GSU343	444	GSU344	445	GSU345
442	GSU342						

441-5 were originally registered B207-11FFS.

466 - 470

1983 Leyland TRBTL11/2R Alexander TE C49F (*C47F)
(ex. Kelvin Scottish 1989)

466	MNS6Y	468	MNS8Y	469	MNS9Y	470*	MNS10Y
467	MNS7Y						

477 - 479

1987 Leyland TRCTL11/3RH Alexander TE C53F
(ex. Highland Scottish 1987)

477	D277FAS	478	D278FAS	479	D279FAS

499	MSU499	1987	Leyland TRTL11/3R	Duple 340	C48FT

499 was originally registered D319SGB.

504	IIL3504	1988	Volvo B10M-61	Van Hool Alizee	C49FT	East Midland	6.93
506	IIL3506	1988	Volvo B10M-61	Van Hool Alizee	C49FT	East Midland	6.93

504/6 were previously registered E937/1XSB after being registeed GIL2967 & MIB658 and were originally E626/4UNE.

542 - 554

1994 Volvo BI0M-60 Plaxton Premiere 320 C51F

542	M942TSX	546	M946TSX	549	M949TSX	552	M952TSX
543	M943TSX	547	M947TSX	550	M950TSX	553	M953TSX
544	M944TSX	548	M948TSX	551	M951TSX	553	M953TSX
545	M945TSX						

571 - 577

1993 Volvo B10M-60 — Plaxton Premiere 320 C53F

571	K571DFS	573	K573DFS	575	K575DFS	577	K577DFS
572	K572DFS	574	K574DFS	576	K576DFS		

578 - 590

1993 Volvo B10M-60 — Plaxton Premiere 320 C51F

578	L578HSG	582	L582HSG	585	L585HSG	588	L588HSG
579	L579HSG	583	L583HSG	586	L586HSG	589	L589HSG
580	L580HSG	584	L584HSG	587	L587HSG	590	L590HSG
581	L581HSG						

601 - 605

1992 Dennis Dart 9.8SDL3017 — Alexander AM Dash B40F

601	K601ESH	603	K603ESH	604	K604ESH	605	K605ESH
602	K602ESH						

623 - 628

1993 Volvo B6 (ex.Ribble 3.94) — Alexander AM Dash B40F

623	L423MVV	625	L425MVV	627	L427MVV	628	L428MVV
624	L424MVV	626	L426MVV				

651 - 658

1993 Volvo B6 — Alexander AM Dash B40F

651	L651HKS	653	L653HKS	655	L655HKS	657	L657HKS
652	L652HKS	654	L654HKS	656	L656HKS	658	L685HKS

659	L659HKS	1994	Volvo B6	Alexander Dash B40F	
667	L267CCK	1993	Volvo B6	Alexander Dash B40F	Ribble 3.94
668	L268CCK	1993	Volvo B6	Alexander Dash B40F	Ribble 3.94
669	L269CCK	1993	Volvo B6	Alexander Dash B40F	Ribble 3.94

670 - 673

9914 Volvo B6 — Alexander AM Dash B40F

670	M670SSX	671	M671SSX	672	M672SSX	673	M673SSX

701 - 725

1992 Leyland ON2R50G13Z4 — Alexander RL H47/32F

701	J701WFS	705	J708WFS	719	K719ASC	723	K723ASC
702	J702WFS	706	J706WFS	720	K720ASC	724	K724ASC
703	J703WFS	707	J707WFS	721	K721ASC	725	K725ASC
704	J704WFS	718	K718ASC	722	K722ASC		

737	G337KKW	1989	Leyland ONLXB/1R	Alexander RL DPH51/31F	East Midland 7.92
738	G338KKW	1989	Leyland ONLXB/1R	Alexander RL DPH51/31F	East Midland 7.92
801	KSF1N	1975	Ailsa B55-10	Alexander AV H44/35F	*Highland Scottish 1991*
806	KSF6N	1975	Ailsa B55-10	Alexander AV H44/35F	*Highland Scottish 1991*

810 - 838

1975 Ailsa B55-10 — Alexander AV H44/35F

810	LSX10P	817	LSX17P	832	LSX32P	838	LSX38P
816	LSX16P						

847 - 866   1979   Ailsa B55-10 Mk.II   Alexander AV   H44/35F

847	OSC47V	852	OSC52V	857	OSC57V	862	OSC62V
848	OSC48V	853	OSC53V	858	OSC58V	863	OSC63V
849	OSC49V	854	OSC54V	859	OSC59V	864	OSC64V
850	OSC50V	855	OSC55V	860	OSC60V	865	OSC65V
851	OSC51V	856	OSC56V	861	OSC61V	866	OSC66V

867 - 874   1984   Ailsa B55-10 Mk.III   Alexander RV   H44/37F

867	A967YSX	869	A969YSX	871	A971YSX	873	A973YSX
868	A968YSX	870	A970YSX	872	A972YSX	874	A974YSX

875 - 879   1977   Ailsa B55-10   Alexander AV   H44/35F

875	UFS875R	877	UFS877R	878	UFS878R	879	UFS879R
876	UFS876R						

901 - 907   1986   Volvo B10MD   Alexander RV   CH47/33F

901	C801USG	905	C805USG	906	C806USG	907	C807USG

908	B108CCS	1985	Volvo B10MD	Alexander RV CH47/33F *Volvo demonstrator 1986*
909	E909KSG	1987	Volvo D10M-50	Alexander RV CH45/35F
910	E910KSG	1987	Volvo D10M-50	Alexander RV CH45/35F

914 - 920   1986   Volvo B10MD   Alexander RV   CH47/33F

914	C794USG	918	C798USG	919	C799USG	920	C800USG
915	C795USG						

940 - 942   1989   Volvo D10MD   (ex. Southdown .91)   NCME   CH43/33F

940	F310MYJ	941	F311MYJ	942	F312MYJ

972 - 974   1986   Volvo B10MD   Alexander RV   H47/37F

972	C802USG	973	C803USG	974	C804USG

977 - 986   1985   Volvo B10MD   Alexander RV   H47/37F

977	B177FFS	980	B180FFS	983	B183FFS	985	B185FFS
978	B178FFS	981	B181FFS	984	B184FFS	986	B186FFS
979	B179FFS	982	B182FFS				

987 - 997   1986   Volvo B10MD   Alexander RV   H47/37F

987	C787USG	990	C790USG	993	C793USG	996	C796USG
988	C788USG	991	C791USG	994	C794USG	997	C797USG
989	C789USG	992	C792USG	995	C795USG		

1102	ABV669A	1961	Leyland PDR1/1	MCCW O44/31F	Ribble 5.92
1107	UWV617S	1978	Bristol VRT/SL3/6LXB	ECW CO43/31F	Coastline 5.93
1110	OVV850R	1976	Bristol VRT/SL3/6LXB	ECW H43/31F	Stagecoach Buses 7.94
1111	VTV167S	1978	Bristol VRT/SL3/6LXB	ECW H43/31F	Stagecoach Buses 7.94
1112	RJT153R	1977	Bristol VRT/SL3/6LXB	ECW H43/31F	Stagecoach Buses 7.94

1113	RJT157R	1977	Bristol VRT/SL3/6LXB	ECW H43/31F	Stagecoach Buses 7.94
1114	XAP642S	1978	Bristol VRT/SL3/6LXB	ECW H43/31F	Stagecoach Buses 7.94
1115	EWE204V	1980	Bristol VRT/SL3/6LXB	ECW H43/31F	East Midland 5.94
1116	HWG208W	1980	Bristol VRT/SL3/6LXB	ECW H43/31F	East Midland 5.94
1117	RTH924S	1977	Bristol VRT/SL3/6LX	ECW H43/31F	East Midland 5.94
1118	KWA217W	1981	Bristol VRT/SL3/6LXC	ECW H43/31F	East Midland 5.94
1119	KKY220W	1981	Bristol VRT/SL3/6LXB	ECW H43/31F	East Midland 5.94
1120	DWF198V	1980	Bristol VRT/SL3/501	ECW H44/31F	East Midland 5.94
1121	DWF199V	1980	Bristol VRT/SL3/501	ECW H43/31F	East Midland 5.94
1122	DWF200V	1980	Bristol VRT/SL3/501	ECW H43/31F	East Midland 5.94
1123	RVB973S	1978	Bristol VRT/SL3/6LXB	Willowbrook H43/31F	East Kent 7.94
1124	RVB974S	1978	Bristol VRT/SL3/6LXB	Willowbrook H43/31F	East Kent 7.94
1125	RVB978S	1978	Bristol VRT/SL3/6LXB	Willowbrook H43/31F	East Kent 7.94
1126	TFN990T	1978	Bristol VRT/SL3/6LXB	Willowbrook H43/31F	East Kent 7.94
1127	PRU917R	1977	Bristol VRT/SL3/6LXB	ECW H43/31F	Bluebird Buses 9.94
1128	RPR716R	1977	Bristol VRT/SL3/6LXB	ECW H43/31F	Bluebird Buses 9.94
1129	WHH415S	1978	Bristol VRT/SL3/501	ECW H43/31F	Bluebird Buses 9.94

1102 was originally registered 927GTA

	HDV639E	1967	Bristol MW6G	ECW C39F	Stagecoach Buses 8.94
	HGM335E	1967	Bristol FLF6G (LX)	ECW H44/34F	Stagecoach Buses 8.94
	DSG625	1950	Leyland PS1/1	McLennan C39F	Stagecoach Buses 8.94

HDV639E, HGM335E & DGS625 are preserved by Stagecoach
50-4/63-5 are in the rental fleet

ANCILLARY VEHICLES

1002	K809JSN	1992	Ford Fiesta	Van	
1003	K819JSN	1992	Ford Fiesta	Van	
1004	F153MSR	1988	Ford Fiesta	Van	
1005	G963SSN	1989	Ford Fiesta	Van	
1007	M187VES	1994	Ford Fiesta	Van	
1019	F819LSN	1988	Talbot Express	Van	
1022	NMT722E	1967	Leyland Octopus	Fuel Tanker	Ribble 7.94
1030	Q600NST		AEC Matador	Recovery wagon	
1034	Q204XSC		AEC Matador	Recovery wagon	
1040	C640NHH	1985	Freight Rover	Van	
1049	WXA949M	1973	Leyland PSU3/3R	Breakdown wagon	
1051	XXA851M	1974	Leyland PSU3/3R	Breakdown wagon	
1054	XXA854M	1974	Leyland PSU3/3R	Breakdown wagon	
1055	GST855N	1975	Ford	Breakdown wagon	
1059	XXA859M	1974	Leyland PSU3/3R	Breakdown wagon	
1499	GSU839T	1979	Leyland PSU3E/4R	Alexander B--F	Driver Trainer

The Plaxton Premiere Interurban-bodied Volvo B10Ms used by Fife Scottish on their express services carry Stagecoach Express fleet names as illustrated by 573

YOUR BUS — Hartlepool Transport

Hartlepool Transport Ltd., 1 Church Street, Hartlepool TS18 2HW

Formed on 1 April 1967 by the merging of the 4-vehicle undertaking of Hartlepool Corporation and the 71 bus fleet of West Hartlepool Corporation, Hartlepool Transport left municipal ownership on 29 June 1993 when it was purchased by its employees.

Fleet name : Your Bus, Hartlepool Transport

Livery : Cream & maroon

Depot : Hartlepool

Hartlepool Transport Fleet list

1	SHN401R	1977	Leyland LN11351A/2R	Leyland	B50F	
2	SHN402R	1977	Leyland LN11351A/2R	Leyland	B49F	
3	SHN403R	1977	Leyland LN11351A/2R	Leyland	B52F	
4	SHN404R	1977	Leyland LN11351A/2R	Leyland	B52F	
5	SHN405R	1977	Leyland LN11351A/2R	Leyland	B50F	
6	SHN406R	1977	Leyland LN11351A/2R	Leyland	B52F	
7	SHN407R	1977	Leyland LN11351A/2R	Leyland	B50F	
14	KAJ214W	1980	Leyland NL116L11/2R	Leyland	B46D	
15	KAJ215W	1980	Leyland NL116L11/2R	Leyland	DP48F	
16	KAJ216W	1980	Leyland NL116L11/2R	Leyland	DP48F	
17	KAJ216W	1980	Leyland NL116L11/2R	Leyland	B46D	
18	KAJ218W	1980	Leyland NL116L11/2R	Leyland	B46D	
19	KAJ219W	1980	Leyland NL116L11/2R	Leyland	B50F	
20	KAJ220W	1980	Leyland NL116L11/2R	Leyland	B46D	

21 - 26 — 1983 Dennis Falcon — Wadham Stringer B46D

21	YDC21Y	23	YDC23Y	25	YDC25Y	26	YDC26Y
22	YDC22Y	24	YDC24Y				

27 - 32 — 1985 Dennis Falcon — NCME B47D

27	B27PAJ	29	B29PAJ	30	B30PAJ	31	B31PAJ
28	B28PAJ	30	B30PAJ				

38	RUF38R	1977	Leyland LN11351A/2R	Leyland	B46F	*Brighton & Hove 1990*
40	RUF40R	1977	Leyland LN11351A/2R	Leyland	B44D	*Brighton & Hove 1990*
49	UFG49S	1978	Leyland LN11351A/2R	Leyland	B44D	*Brighton & Hove 1990*
52	UFG52S	1978	Leyland LN11351A/2R	Leyland	B44D	*Brighton & Hove 1990*

59 - 65 — 1970 Bristol RELL6L — ECW B46D

59	LEF59H	60	LEF60H	61	LEF61H	65	LEF65H

67 - 72

1971 Bristol RELL6L   ECW B46D

| 67 | MEF67J | 70 | MEF70J | 71 | MEF71J | 72 | MEF72J |
| 69 | MEF69J | | | | | | |

73 - 79

1972 Bristol RELL6L   ECW B46D

| 73 | OEF73K | 75 | OEF75K | 77 | OEF77K | 79 | OEF79K |
| 74 | OEF74K | 76 | OEF76K | 78 | OEF78K | | |

80 - 84

1973 Bristol RELL6L   ECW B46D

| 80 | SEF80L | 82 | SEF82L | 83 | SEF83L | 84 | SEF84L |
| 81 | SEF81L | | | | | | |

85   GEF185N   1974   Bristol RELL6L   ECW B46D

86 - 90

1975 Bristol RELL6L   ECW B46D

| 86 | GEF186N | 88 | GEF188N | 89 | GEF189N | 90 | GEF190N |
| 87 | GEF187N | | | | | | |

91   GEF191N   1975   Bristol RELL6L   ECW DP47F

92 - 96

1975 Bristol RELL6L   ECW B46D

| 92 | JAJ292N | 94 | JAJ294N | 95 | JAJ295N | 96 | JAJ296N |
| 93 | JAJ293N | | | | | | |

101	XCC94V	1980	Leyland PSU3E/4R	Plaxton Sup IV C53F	*Roberts, Cefn Mawr 1986*
102	BTU33W	1981	Leyland PSU3E/4R	Plaxton Sup IV C53F	*Roberts, Cefn Mawr 1986*
103	FSL61W	1982	Leyland PSU3E/4R	Plaxton Sup IV C53F	*Tayside 1987*
104	FSL62W	1982	Leyland PSU3E/4R	Plaxton Sup IV C53F	*Tayside 1987*
105	HDZ8683	1984	Volvo B10M	Plaxton 3500 C53F	*Allander, Milngavie 1990*

101 - 4 were previously registered XAM829, 93FYB, 666TPJ & 6689DP and were originally UMA953V, WLG380W & GSL307/6W. 105 was previously registered A491WYS & 2367AT and was originally A845UGB.

This rare photograph of Alexander-bodied Volvo B10M M769PRS shows the short-lived Stagecoach Glasgow fleet name. Two days after entering service in that city, this bus was sold together with its sisters to Strathclyde's Buses.   (B.Newsome)

Bluebird Buses 234 is a Reeve Burgess-bodied Mercedes Benz L609D acquired secondhand from Carr & Robbins of Tomintoul in 1990.   (T.W.W.Knowles)

KENYA BUS

Kenya Bus Services Ltd., General Warning Street, 1st Avenue, Eastleigh, Nairobi.

Incorporated in 1934, Kenya Bus Services was purchased together with Kenya Bus Services (Mombassa) Ltd. (whivch began operations in 1936) by United Transport Overseas Ltd. in the 1950s and later passed to the British Electric Traction Group.

Depots : Mombassa; Nairobi.

Kenya Bus   Fleet list

---

321 - 324

1986   ERF Trailblazer 6LXB   Singh B49D

321	KXQ484	322	KXR065	323	KXR282	324	KXR388

| 325 | KYD116 | 1987 | ERF Trailblazer 6LXB | Singh B49D |
| 326 | KYD117 | 1987 | ERF Trailblazer 6LXB | Singh B49D |

---

327 - 331

1988   ERF Trailblazer 6LXB   Singh B49D (+B43D)

327	KYW205	329	KYV457	330+	KYY078	331	KYW206
328	KYV458						

---

341 - 374

1993   ERF Trailblazer 6LXB   Singh B45D (*B49D)

341*	KAC649X	350	KAD527A	359	KAD127C	367	KAD779D
342	KAC929X	351	KAD521A	360	KAD158C	368	KAD826D
343	KAC023Y	352	KAD528A	361	KAD225C	369	KAD899D
344	KAC022Y	353	KAD526A	362	KAD368C	370	KAD994D
345	KAC021Y	354	KAD619A	363	KAD447C	371	KAD021E
346	KAC287Y	355	KAD841A	364	KAD553C	372	KAD261E
347	KAC290Y	356	KAD902A	365	KAD743D	373	KAD360E
348	KAC289Y	357	KAD535A	366	KAD773D	374	KAD407E
349	KAC288Y	358	KAD126C				

---

601 - 604

1990   DAF TB2100DHT   Singh B47D

601	KAA128N	602	KAA351N	603	KAA330N	604	KAA313Q

605 - 616   1992   DAF TB2100DHT   Singh B43D

605	KAC145H	608	KAC253H	611	KAC592J	614	KAC887J
606	KAC146H	609	KAC447H	612	KAC672J	615	KAC519L
607	KAC252H	610	KAC485J	613	KAC865J	616	KAC243K

701 - 718   1979   Leyland Victory Mk.II 6LX   Singh B49D (+B47D; *B48D)
                                                                         (#B56D)

701	KVR629	706	KVR952	711#	KVS328	715	KVT909
702	KVR652	707	KVR995	712	KVT664	716	KVT973
703	KVR787	708	KVS025	713*	KVT703	717	KVU018
704	KVR818	709	KVS307	714	KVT857	718	KVU079
705	KVR866	710+	KVS284				

719	KVU211	1980	Leyland Victory Mk.II 6LX	Singh	B49D
720	KVU156	1979	Leyland Victory Mk.II 6LX	Singh	B49D

721 - 748   1980   Leyland Victory Mk.II 6LX   Singh B49D (#B41D; *B42D)
                                                                        (+B44D; "B48D)

721	KVU237	726	KVX651	731#	KVY237	736	KSJ265
722+	KVU369	727	KVX664	732	KVZ671	746	KSP338
723	KVV809	728	KVY046	733	KVZ703	747"	KSP339
724	KVV957	729	KVY074	734	KVZ919	748	KSP337
725	KVW013	730*	KVY316	735	KSJ158		

749 - 775   1981   Leyland Victory Mk.II 6LX   Singh B49D (*B47D; +B59D)

749	KSW894	756	KTF527	763	KTK846	770	KTQ249
750	KSW877	757	KTF834	764	KTM915	771	KTQ287
751	KSW876	758	KTF809	765	KTM946	772	KTQ398
752	KSW875	759	KTG230	766	KTN216	773	KTR405
753	KSW895	760	KTG376	767*	KTP917	774	KTR553
754	KSW879	761	KTJ159	768	KTQ004	775	KTR630
755+	KTF528	762	KTJ235	769	KTQ164		

776 - 814   1982   Leyland Victory Mk.II 6LX   Singh B49D ("B42D; %B44D)
                            (803 fitted with Leyland TL11 engine)   (+B46D; *B47D; #B48D)

776	KTR678	799	KTY110	805	KUG585	810	KUG978
777	KTT617	800	KUF144	806	KUJ641	811	KUH141
778+	KTT881	801	KUG599	807	KUG850	812	KUH254
779	KTV814	802"	KUG474	808	KUG860	813	KUH275
797#	KTW268	803	KUG560	809	KUG938	814	KUJ561
798*	KTW190	804%	KUH104				

815	KUJ874	1983	Leyland Victory Mk.II 6LX	Singh	B49D
816	KUJ638	1982	Leyland Victory Mk.II 6LX	Singh	B49D

817 - 831   1983   Leyland Victory Mk.II 6LX   Singh B49D (*B37D; #B46D)
                                                                          (+B47D)

817*	KUJ998	820	KUJ890	822+	KUM870	824	KUK271
818	KUJ889	821#	KUM688	823	KUM534	831	KUY105
819+	KUK083						

Wearing Newcastle Busways livery, Alexander-bodied Leyland Atlantean 359 is seen with headlights ablaze in Gallowgate, Newcastle in November 1994.   (Travelscene)

Busways Blue Bus Services fleet has long been famed for its elderly Bristol RE and LH buses, two of which - RESL 1818 and LHS 1607 - are seen here in March 1994.

Illustrating Busways Armstrong Galley coaching fleet is Plaxton Paramount-bodied Leyland Tiger 17 seen in central Newcastle in November 1994.   (Travelscene)

832 - 850

1984 Leyland Victory Mk.II 6LX

Singh B46D (*B38D; #B45D)
("B47D; +B49D)

832+	KWA562	837	KWB994	842	KWE971	847+	KWM059
833	KWA575	838	KWB286	843#	KWK134	848+	KWM145
834	KWA576	839*	KWB295	844	KWK144	849+	KWM189
835	KWA577	840	KWC826	845"	KWL823	850+	KWN536
836	KWA574	841	KWE920	846+	KWL923		

851 - 867

1985 Leyland Victory Mk.II 6LX
(866/7 have 6LXB engines)

Singh B49D

851	KWP262	856	KWR077	861	KWS725	865	KWT146
852	KWQ584	857	KWR105	862	KWS971	866	KWT169
853	KWQ808	858	KWR140	863	KWS985	867	KWT337
854	KWQ914	859	KWS524	864	KWT030		
855	KWQ946	860	KWS690				

868 - 872

1985 Leyland Victory Mk.II 6LXB

Suleman B49D (+B45D)

868	KWV976	870+	KWX892	871	KWX948	872	KWY155
869	KWX587					

873	KWY371	1985 Leyland Victory Mk.II L10	Singh B49D
874	KXA037	1985 Leyland Victory Mk.II L10	Singh B49D

876 - 880

1986 Leyland Victory Mk.III 6LXB

Singh B47D (*B43D)

876#	KXD797	878	KXK503	879	KXD761	880	KXD781
877*	KXK017					

881	KXG262	1985 Leyland Victory Mk.II 6LXB	Singh B49D
882	KXG278	1985 Leyland Victory Mk.II 6LXB	Singh B49D

883 - 900

1986 Leyland Victory Mk.III 6LXB

Singh B49D (+B45D;*B46D)

883	KXH320	888	KXH896	893	KXJ474	897	KXN955
884	KXH321	889	KXH993	894	KXK610	898	KXN982
885	KXH623	890	KXJ010	895	KXK708	899	KXP038
886	KXH624	891+	KXJ173	896*	KXM065	900	KXP187
887	KXH875	892	KXJ369				

906 - 920

1974 Leyland Victory Mk.I 6LX

Singh B48D (*B46D)

906	KPW130	914*	KQB935	915	KQB978	920	KQC946
909	KPW571					

921 - 924

1975 Leyland Victory Mk.I 6LX

Singh B47D (*B48D)

921	KQD110	922*	KQD302	924	KQF075

928 - 937

1976 Leyland Victory Mk.I 6LX   Singh B47D (*B40F, +B41F #B50F)

928	KQV140	932	KQW687	934	KQW802	936#	KQW994
930	KQV261	933	KQW743	935+	KQW958	937*	KQX875
931	KQV346						

938 - 941

1977 Leyland Victory Mk.I 6LX   Singh B47D (*B46D)

| 938 | KRP893 | 939 | KRP967 | 940* | KRP995 | 941 | KRQ083 |

| 942 | KRQ125 | 1978 | Leyland Victory Mk.I 6LX | Singh | B47D |
| 944 | KRS033 | 1978 | Leyland Victory Mk.I 6LX | Singh | B47D |

946 - 959

1979 Leyland Victory Mk.I 6LX   Singh B49D (*B48D)

946	KVK649	950	KVK941	953	KVL232	957	KVN055
947	KVK708	951	KVK993	954	KVL266	958	KVM957
948	KVK751	952	KVL108	956*	KVM733	959	KVN137
949	KVK823						

961	KUF067	1982	Isuzu DQR 6LX	Singh	B49D
962	KUG695	1982	Isuzu DQR 6LX	Singh	B45D
963	KUT967	1983	Leyland Victory Mk.II 6LX	Singh	B49D

964	KNY401	1985	Leyland Victory Mk.II 6LX	Singh	B47D
966	KZF894	1988	Leyland Victory Mk.II 6LXB	Singh	B49D
967	KQB925	1974	Leyland Victory Mk.II 6LX	Singh	B48D
968	KQD250	1975	Leyland Victory Mk.II 6LX	Singh	B48D
969	KPW753	1974	Leyland Victory Mk.II 6LX	Singh	B48D
970	KPW294	1974	Leyland Victory Mk.II 6LX	Singh	B45D

961-3/7-70 are re-manufactured by Kenya Bus Service

991 - 997

1988 Leyland Victory Mk.III 6LXB   Singh B49D (+B43D)

| 991+ | KZC129 | 993 | KZA013 | 995 | KYZ546 | 997 | KZB481 |
| 992 | KZC481 | 994 | KZF416 | 996 | KYD894 | | |

ANCILLARY VEHICLES

011	KNZ965	1972	Leyland Victory Mk.I			Breakdown wagon
012	KPB846	1972	Leyland Victory Mk.I			Breakdown wagon
013	KPC467	1972	Leyland Victory Mk.I			Breakdown wagon
015	KNZ223	1972	Leyland Victory Mk.I	Singh	B59D	Driver trainer
016	KNZ354	1972	Leyland Victory Mk.I	Singh	B59D	Driver trainer
017	KPA095	1972	Leyland Victory Mk.I	Singh	B59D	Driver trainer
019	KSN623	1980				Fork lift
901	KNY921	1972	Leyland Victory Mk.I	Singh	B49D	

Amongst the most recent additions to the Cleveland Transit fleet are a number of Plaxton Pointer-bodied Volvo B6s, one of which - 107 - passes through Stockton Market Place on a dismal November afternoon in 1994.   (K.A.Jenkinson)

Amongst the vehicles transferred to Stagecoach Darlington for the start of its operations were a number of Leyland Tiger coaches including 2110 which was previously in the Bluebird Buses fleet.   (K.A.Jenkinson)

Cleveland Coaches solitary Leyland Royal Tiger Doyen 955 which began life in 1987 registered D455GHN is pictured here at Albert Dock, Liverpool in April 1994 whilst working a private hire duty.   (K.A.Jenkinson)

Following Cleveland Transit's gaining of a 51% stake in KHCT, a Transit-style yellow band has been added to the Hull company's blue & white livery as illustrated by Scania 801. Despite its appearance, the body on this bus is by East Lancashire Coach Builders.   (K.A.Jenkinson)

Kenya Bus (Mombasa) Fleet list

301 - 307

1983 ERF Trailblazer 6LX   Suleman B53D+47 (+B40D+47)
(*B44D+46; #B45D+47; %B46D=47; "B54D+46)

| 301* | KUW565 | 303# | KUY279 | 305 | KUY829 | 307" | KUZ834 |
| 302% | KUW634 | 304+ | KUY289 | 306 | KUZ807 | | |

308 - 312

1984 ERF Trailblazer 6LX   Suleman B44D+45 (+B53D+47)
(*B50D+47; #B40D+46)

| 308 | KWC094 | 310+ | KWE764 | 311* | KWC808 | 312# | KWH535 |
| 309 | KWE546 | | | | | | |

313 - 320

1984 ERF Trailblazer 6LX   Suleman B53D+47 (+B40D+46)
(*B40D+47; #B50D+47)

| 313 | KWP182 | 315* | KWP640 | 317* | KWQ651 | 319 | KWQ732 |
| 314 | KWP609 | 316+ | KWQ159 | 318+ | KWQ673 | 320# | KWT363 |

332 - 338

1987 ERF Trailblazer 6LX   Suleman B53D+47 (+B53D+46)

| 332 | KYG173 | 334 | KYH176 | 336 | KYM857 | 338+ | KYS305 |
| 333 | KYE597 | 335 | KYH535 | 337 | KYN019 | | |

339 - 340

1986 ERF Trailblazer 6LX   Suleman B53D+47 (+B35D+47)

| 339 | KYU264 | 340+ | KYU693 |

737 - 738

1979 Leyland Victory Mk.II 6LX   Suleman B36D+46

| 737 | KVU147 | 738 | KTE926 |

739 - 745

1980 Leyland Victory Mk.II 6LX   Suleman B54D+46 (*B35D+46)
("B36D+46; +B37D+46; #B40D+47; %B44D+46)

| 739+ | KTE936 | 741 | KTE554 | 743# | KSH120 | 745* | KSP840 |
| 740% | KTE447 | 742" | KSH004 | 744 | KSH443 | | |

780 - 787

1981 Leyland Victory Mk.II 6LX   Suleman B53+47D (*B44D+46)
(+B44D+46; #B51D+49)

| 780# | KSW663 | 782* | KSY974 | 784 | KTN321 | 786+ | KTR094 |
| 781+ | KSZ136 | 783+ | KTN313 | 785 | KTN339 | 787 | KTR124 |

788 - 830

1982 Leyland Victory Mk.II 6LX   Suleman B53D+47 (#B40D+34)
(*B37D+46; "B47D+44; %B48D+44; +B47D+46)

788	KTU010	792+	KUD378	796"	KUF366	828	KUK427
789%	KTU064	793"	KUE121	825+	KUF947	829	KUK494
790#	KTW693	794	KUE168	826	KUK401	830	KUK979
791+	KTY066	795	KUF305	827*	KUK402		

875   KXD749   1985 Leyland Victory Mk.II 6LX   Suleman B48D

---

971 - 975   1983 Leyland Victory Mk.II 6LX   Suleman B56F+44 (+B35F+47)
                                                           (*B50F+44; #B53F+47)

971   KUR801   973* KUS386   974+ KUT208   975# KUT615
972   KUR811

---

981 - 984   1985 ERF Trailblazer 6LX   Suleman B55F+31 (*B56F+36)
                                                                  (+B56F+40)
981+ KWY053   982   KWY095   983* KWY472   984   KXA410

ANCILLARY VEHICLE

X8   KVU216   1979 Leyland Victory Mk.II 6LX   Suleman B36D   Driver trainer

---

National Transport Tokens

National Transport Tokens Ltd., Frenchwood Avenue, Preston PR1 4LU

Although not incorporated until 13 October 1972, National Travel Token Limited's history dates back to the late 'sixties when several municipal bus operators in the Manchester area entered into a co-operative agreement to accept each other's travel tokens issued to such groups as postmen and gas and electricity meter readers to enable them to reach the start of their rounds and to schoolchildren for journeys to and from their places of education. As more general travel concessions were introduced, several other operators in the north-west joined the scheme which eventually spread to other parts of the country and as a result, Transport Tokens grew to become a national organisation. Despite its headquaters remaining in Manchester, National Transport Tokens had over 2,000 operator users including bus and taxi companies, British Rail and the Mersey Ferries. Gaining a share in the company through its acquisition of Ribble, Stagecoach purchased Greater Manchester PTE's 50% stake in National Transport Tokens in March 1992 to give it a controlling interest.

National Transport Tokens   Fleet list

B379CHE   1984   Ford Cargo   Box Van   Stagecoach, Perth 2.93

Leaving Glenrothes bus station in the spring of 1994 is Fife Scottish 861, one of a large fleet of Alexander-bodied Ailsa double deckers operated by the company since the late 'seventies. (K.A.Jenkinson)

A large number of Alexander PS-bodied Volvo B10M-55s have been purchased by the Stagecoach Group including this example delivered to Fife Scottish in 1994. (C.Morrison)

Freshly repainted in Stagecoach Group corporate livery is Kenya Bus dual-door DAF 605. (Stagecoach International)

East London still operates a number of Routemasters - the last of the capital's 'real' buses - as illustrated by RML2709 seen here at Victoria bus station sporting promotional lettering above its lower deck windows for route 8.   (K.A.Jenkinson)

Stagecoach EAST LONDON

East London Bus & Coach Co. Ltd., 16-20 Clements Road, Ilford IG1 1BA

East London was formed on 5 December 1988 as a consequence of the restructuring of London Buses Ltd. into eleven semi-autonomous operating companies. Soon after its sale to Stagecoach Holdings on 6 September 1994, the company's small coaching activities were enhamced by those transferred from Selkent Travel. Under the conditions of sale it was required that East London maintains a red livery.

Livery : Red (unrelieved)

Depots : Barking (BK); Bow (BW); Leyton (T); Romford (NS); Stratford (SD); Upton Park (U).

East London Fleet list

DA10 G684KNW 1989 DAF SB220LC550 Optare Delta B36D *Optare Demonstrator 1991*

DA11 - DA29 — 1992 DAF SB220LC550 — Optare Delta B40D

11	J711CYG	16	J716CYG	21	J721CYG	26	J726CYG
12	J712CYG	17	J717CYG	22	J722CYG	27	J727CYG
13	J713CYG	18	J718CYG	23	J723CYG	28	J728CYG
14	J714CYG	19	J719CYG	24	J724CYG	29	J729CYG
15	J715CYG	20	J720CYG	25	J725CYG		

DA30 - DA35 — 1993 DAF SB220LC550 — Optare Delta B40D

30	K630HWX	32	K632HWX	34	K634HWX	35	K635HXW
31	K631HWX	33	K633HWX				

DRL109 - DRL138 — 1993 Dennis Dart — Plaxton Pointer B34F

109	K109SRH	117	K117SRH	125	K125SRH	132	K132SRH
110	K110SRH	118	K118SRH	126	K126SRH	133	K133SRH
111	K211SRH	119	K119SRH	127	K127SRH	134	K134SRH
112	K112SRH	120	K120SRH	128	K128SRH	135	K135SRH
113	K113SRH	121	K121SRH	129	K129SRH	136	L136VRH
114	K114SRH	122	K122SRH	130	K130SRH	137	L137VRH
115	K115SRH	123	K123SRH	130	K130SRH	138	L138VRH
116	K116SRH	124	K124SRH				

DW133 - DW159 — 1993 Dennis Dart — Wright B29F

133	NDZ3133	140	NDZ3140	147	NDZ3147	154	NDZ3154
134	NDZ3134	141	NDZ3141	148	NDZ3148	155	NDZ3155
135	NDZ3155	142	NDZ3142	149	NDZ3149	156	NDZ3156
136	NDZ3136	143	NDZ3143	150	NDZ3150	157	NDZ3157
137	NDZ3137	144	NDZ3144	151	NDZ3151	158	NDZ3158
138	NDZ3138	145	NDZ3145	152	NDZ3152	159	NDZ3159
139	NDZ3139	146	NDZ3146	153	NDZ3153		

DWL15 - DWL26   1993 Dennis Dart   Wright B36F

15	NDZ3015	18	NDZ3018	21	NDZ3021	24	NDZ3024
16	NDZ3016	19	NDZ3019	22	NDZ3022	25	NDZ3025
17	NDZ3017	20	NDZ3020	23	NDZ3023	26	NDZ3026

LS121	THX121S	1977	Leyland LN10351A/2R	Leyland B21DL
LS308	AYR308T	1979	Leyland LN10351A/2R	Leyland B21DL
LS403	BYW403V	1979	Leyland LN190351A/2R	Leyland B36D
MR16	D476PON	1987	MCW Metrorider MF150	MCW B23F

MRL65 - MRL73   1988 MCW Metrorider MF158 ·   MCW B30F

65	E641KYW	68	E644KYW	70	E646KYW	72	E648KYW
66	E642KYW	69	E645KYW	71	E647KYW	73	E649KYW
67	E643KYW						

MRL74	E650KYW	1988	MCW Metrorider MF158	MCW DP33F
MRL75	E705LYU	1988	MCW Metrorider MF158	MCW DP33F
MRL76	E706LYU	1988	MCW Metrorider MF158	MCW DP33F

MRL77 - MRL131   1992 MCW Metrorider MF158   MCW B28F

77	F197YDA	112	F112YVP	119	F119YVP	126	F126YVP
106	F106YVP	113	F113YVP	120	F120YVP	128	F128YVP
109	F109YVP	114	F114YVP	121	F121YVP	130	F130YVP
110	F110YVP	118	F118YVP	125	F125YVP	131	F131YVP
111	F111YVP						

MRL132	F132YVP	1988	MCW Metrorider MF158	MCW DP28F
RB10	G880WML	1989	Renault S75	Reeve Burgess B29F
RB27	H127AML	1990	Renault S75	Reeve Burgess B29F
RB28	H128AML	1990	Renault S56	Reeve Burgess B29F
RM613	WLT613	1960	AEC Routemaster	Park Royal H36/28R
RM1527	527CLT	1963	AEC Routemaster	Park Royal H36/28R
RMA5	NMY635E	1967	AEC Routemaster	Park Royal H32/24F
RMA8	NMY640E	1967	AEC Routemaster	Park Royal H32/24F
RMC1456	LFF875	1962	AEC Routemaster	Park Royal H32/25RD
RMC1461	461CLT	1962	AEC Routemaster	Park Royal H32/25RD
RMC1485	485CLT	19632	AEC Routemaster	Park Royal H32/25RD

RMC1456 was originally registered 456CLT.

RML886	WLT886	1961	AEC Routemaster	Park Royal H40/32R
RML890	WLT890	1961	AEC Routemaster	Park Royal H40/32R
RML898	WLT898	1961	AEC Routemaster	Park Royal H40/32R

RML886/90 are fitted with Cummins engines, RML898 is fitted with an Iveco engine.

RML2272 - RML2303   1965 AEC Routemaster   Park Royal H40/32R
(Iveco engine *Cummins engine)

2272*	CUV272C	2386*	CUV386C	2300	CUV300C	2303	CUV303C

RML2311	CUV311C	1965	AEC Routemaster	Park Royal H40/32R	*London Country 1978*
RML2392	JJD392D	1965	AEC Routemaster	Park Royal H40/32R	
RML2399	JJD399D	1966	AEC Routemaster	Park Royal H40/32R	
RML2402	JJD402D	1966	AEC Routemaster	Park Royal H40/32R	

RML2311 is fitted with a Cummins engine. RML2392/9/402 are fitted with Iveco engines.

Cleethorpes Pier is the location of this view of Grimsby Cleethorpes East Lancs-bodied Dennis Lance no.5 and Alexander-bodied Dennis Dominator 75. (K.A.Jenkinson)

East Midland Leyland Leopard 414 began life in 1980 as a Willowbrook 003-bodied coach, gaining its new Alexander P-type body in 1985. (K.A.Jenkinson)

The coaching operation of Stagecoach Grimsby Cleethorpes continues to operate under the Peter Sheffield fleet name. Now carrying a cherished registration number, Duple Laser-bodied Leyland Tiger 189 was acquired from Lincoln City Transport in 1991 as PYE843Y. (K.A.Jenkinson)

867, a Stagecoach Malawi ERF Trailblazer is pictured being attached to one of its owner's corporate-liveried freight trailers.   (Stagecoach International)

RML2415 - RML2456   1966   AEC Routemaster   Park Royal H40/32R
(Iveco engine - *Cummins engene)
(ex.London Country 1978-80)

2415	JJD415D	2437	JJD437D	2445	JJD445D	2451	JJD451D
2429	JJD429D	2444	JJD444D	2450	JJD450D	2456	JJD456D
2435	JJD435D						

RML2462 - RML2592   1966   AEC Routemaster   Park Royal H40/32F
(Iveco engine - *Cummins engine)

2462	JJD462D	2493	JJD493D	2497*	JJD497D	2565*	JJD565D
2470	JJD470D	2495*	JJD495D	2541*	JJD541D	2581*	JJD581D
2481	JJD481D	2496*	JJD496D	2550*	JJD550D	2592	JJD592D
2488	JJD488D						

RML2607 - RML2749   1967   AEC Routemaster   Park Royal H40/32F
(Iveco engne - *Cummins engine)

2607	NML607E	2641*	NML641E	2670*	SMK670F	2723*	SMK723F
2610*	NML610E	2642*	NML652E	2671*	SMK671F	2738	SMK738F
2616*	NML616E	2657	NML657E	2696	SMK696F	2743	SMK743F
2624	NML624E	2661*	SMK661F	2705*	SMK705F	2748*	SMK748F
2639*	NML639E	2665	SMK665F	2709	SMK709F	2749	SMK749F

RML2760   SMK760F   1968   AEC Routemaster   Park Royal H40/32R
RML2760 is fitted with an AEC engine.

S22 - S29   1991   Scania N113DRB   Alexander H47/31F

22	J822HMC	24	J824HMC	26	J826HMC	28	J828HMC
23	J823HMC	25	J825HMC	27	J827HMC	29	J829HMC

S30	J230XKY	1991	Scania N113DRB	Northern Counties H41/25D
S31	J231XKY	1991	Scania N113DRB	Northern Counties H41/25D

S32 - S71   1992   Scania N113DRB   Northern Counties H41/25D

32	J132HMT	40	J140HMT	57	K857LMK	65	K865LMK
33	J133HMT	41	J141HMT	58	K858LMK	66	K866LMK
34	J134HMT	42	J142HMT	59	K859LMK	67	K867LMK
35	J135HMT	43	J143HMT	60	K860LMK	68	K868LMK
36	J136HMT	44	J144HMT	61	K861LMK	69	K869LMK
37	J137HMT	45	J145HMT	62	K862LMK	70	K870LMK
38	J138HMT	46	K846LMK	63	K863LMK	71	K871LMK
39	J139HMT	47	K847LMK	64	K864LMK		

SP2   K302FYG   1992   DAF DB250WB505   Optare Spectra H44/23D

SLW15 - SLW30   1994   Dennis SLF   Wright B37D

15	RDZ6115	19	RDZ6119	23	RDZ6123	27	RDZ6127
16	RDZ6116	20	RDZ6120	24	RDZ6124	28	RDZ6128
17	RDZ6117	21	RDZ6121	25	RDZ6125	29	RDZ6129
18	RDZ6118	22	RDZ6122	26	RDZ6126	30	RDZ6130

SR1 - SR13   1988   Mercedes Benz 811D   Optare B26F

1	E155CGJ	3	E713LYU	12	F912YWY	13	F913YWY
2	E712LYU	4	E714LYU				

SR1 was previously registered WLT461 and was originally E711LYU.

SR32 - SR119   1989   Mercedes Benz 811D   Optare B26F

32	F32CWY	69	F169FWY	75	F175FWY	86	G86KUB
50	F50CWY	70	F170FWY	76	F176FWY	91	G91KUB
56	F156FWY	71	F171FWY	77	F177FWY	105	G105KUB
60	F160FWY	72	F172FWY	78	F178FWY	106	G106KUB
65	F165FWY	73	F173FWY	79	F179FWY	107	G107KUB
66	F166FWY	74	F174FWY	80	F180FWY	119	G119KUB

T1	THX401S	1978	Leyland TNLXB	Park Royal H44/22D
T2	THX402S	1978	Leyland TNLXB	Park Royal H44/26D

T3 - T6   1978   Leyland TNLXB/2RR   Park Royal H44/22D

3	WYV3T	4	WYV4T	5	WYV5T	6	WYV6T

T7	WYV7T	1979	Leyland TNLXB	Park Royal H44/22D
T8	WYV8T	1978	Leyland TNLXB	Park Royal H44/22D

T9 - T12   1979   Leyland TNLXB/2RR   Park Royal H44/26D

9	WYV9T	10	WYV10T	11	WYV11T	12	WYV12T

T13 - T18   1979   Leyland TNLXB/2RR   Park Royal H44/22D

13	WYV13T	15	WYV15T	17	WYV17T	18	WYV18T
14	WYV14T	16	WYV16T	18	WYVI8T		

T19	WVY19T	1979	Leyland TNLXB/2RR	Park Royal H44/26D
T20	WYV20T	1979	Leyland TNLXB/2RR	Park Royal H44/26D
T21	WYV21T	1979	Leyland TNLXB/2RR	Park Royal H44/22D
T22	WYV22T	1979	Leyland TNLXB/2RR	Park Royal H44/26D
T23	WYV23T	1979	Leyland TNLXB/2RR	Park Royal H44/22D
T24	WYV24T	1979	Leyland TNLXB/2RR	Park Royal H44/22D
T25	WYV25T	1979	Leyland TNLXB/2RR	Park Royal H44/26D
T26	WYV26T	1979	Leyland TNLXB/2RR	Park Royal H44/26D
T27	WYV27T	1979	Leyland TNLXB/2RR	Park Royal H44/22D
T28	WYV28T	1979	Leyland TNLXB/2RR	Park Royal H44/22D
T29	WYV29T	1979	Leyland TNLXB/2RR	Park Royal H44/22D
T30	WYV30T	1979	Leyland TNLXB/2RR	Park Royal H44/26D
T31	WYV31T	1979	Leyland TNLXB/2RR	Park Royal H44/22D
T32	WYV32T	1979	Leyland TNLXB/2RR	Park Royal H44/22D
T33	WYV33T	1979	Leyland TNLXB/2RR	Park Royal H44/26D
T34	WYV34T	1979	Leyland TNLXB/2RR	Park Royal H44/22D
T35	WYV35T	1979	Leyland TNLXB/2RR	Park Royal H44/22D
T36	WYV36T	1979	Leyland TNLXB/2RR	Park Royal H44/26D
T37	WYV37T	1979	Leyland TNLXB/2RR	Park Royal H44/22D
T38	WYV38T	1979	Leyland TNLXB/2RR	Park Royal H44/22D
T39	WYV39T	1979	Leyland TNLXB/2RR	Park Royal H44/26D
T40	WYV40T	1979	Leyland TNLXB/2RR	Park Royal H44/26D
T63	WVY63T	1979	Leyland TNLXB/2RR	Park Royal H44/26D
T64	WYV64T	1979	Leyland TNXLB/2RR	Park Royal H44/22D
T66	WYV66T	1979	Leyland TNLXB/2RR	Park Royal H44/26D
T80	WYV80T	1979	Leyland TNLXB/2RR	Park Royal H44/26D

Not all Stagecoach's vehicles are painted in corporate livery as illustrated by Cumberland's open-top MCCW-bodied Leyland Atlantean 1928 which wears its owner's green & cream Lakeland Experience colours for use on the tourist service from Bowness to Grasmere. (K.A.Jenkinson)

Several Stagecoach North-West Alexander-bodied Leyland Olympians were given promotional lettering for the services upon which they were employed. Leaving Lancaster bus station on the 555 Lakeslink service to Kendal is Cumberland 1022, a coach-seated example which is informing prospective passengers that the 555 Lakeslink is a Network 2000 service. (K.A.Jenkinson)

T140 CUL140V 1979 Leyland TNLXB/2RR   Park Royal H44/26D

T175 - T223
1980 Leyland TNLXB/2RR   Park Royal H44/26D

| 175 | CUL175V | 197 | CUL197V | 222 | CUL222V | 223 | CUL223V |
| 193 | CUL193V | 214 | CUL214V | | | | |

T230	EYE230V	1980	Leyland TNLXB /2RR	Park Royal H44/24D
T246	EYE246V	1980	Leyland TNLXB /2RR	Park Royal H44/26D
T248	EYE248V	1980	Leyland TNLXB /2RR	Park Royal H44/26D

T252 - T263
1981 Leyland TNLXB/2RR   Leyland H44/26D

| 252 | GYE252W | 260 | GYE260W | 262 | GYE262W | 263 | GYE263W |
| 254 | GYE254W | 261 | GYE261W | | | | |

| T264 | GYE264W | 1981 | Leyland TNLXB /2RR | Leyland H44/24D |
| T266 | GYE266W | 1981 | Leyland TNLXB /2RR | Leyland H44/26D |

T268 - T281
1981 Leyland TNLXB/2RR   Leyland H44/24D

| 268 | GYE268W | 272 | GYE272W | 273 | GYE273W | 281 | GYE281W |
| 270 | GYE270W | | | | | | |

T285	KYN285X	1981	Leyland TNLXB /2RR	Leyland H44/26D
T286	KYN286X	1981	Leyland TNLXB /2RR	Leyland H44/24D
T298	KYN298X	1981	Leyland TNLXB /2RR	Leyland H44/24D
T306	KYN306X	1981	Leyland TNLXB /2RR	Leyland H44/24D
T311	KYV311X	1981	Leyland TNLXB /2RR	Leyland H44/26D
T318	KYV318X	1981	Leyland TNLXB /2RR	Leyland H44/24D
T320	KYV320X	1981	Leyland TNLXB /2RR	Leyland H44/26D
T326	KYV326X	1981	Leyland TNLXB /2RR	Leyland H44/26D
T331	KYV331X	1981	Leyland TNLXC /2RR	Leyland H44/26D

T334 - T395
1981 Leyland TNLXB/2RR   Leyland H44/24D

334	KYN334X	366	KYN366X	380	KYV380X	394	KYV394X
340	KYN340X	378	KYV378X	386	KYV386X	395	KYV395X
360	KYN360X	379	KYV379X	387	KYV387X		

T403 KYV403X 1982 Leyland TNLXB /2RR   Leyland H44/23D

T404 - T508
1982 Leyland TNLXB/2RR   Leyland H44/24D

404	KYV404X	453	KYV453X	470	KYV470X	497	KYV497X
406	KYV406X	454	KYV454X	471	KYV471X	498	KYV498X
428	KYV428X	456	KYV456X	473	KYV473X	500	KYV500X
434	KYV434X	458	KYV458X	476	KYV476X	501	KYV501X
437	KYV437X	460	KYV460X	480	KYV480X	502	KYV502X
439	KYV439X	461	KYV461X	486	KYV486X	503	KYV503X
441	KYV441X	462	KYV462X	488	KYV488X	504	KYV504X
444	KYV444X	465	KYV465X	490	KYV490X	505	KYV505X
445	KYV445X	466	KYV466X	492	KYV492X	506	KYV506X
446	KYV446X	467	KYV467X	495	KYV495X	508	KYV508X
448	KYV448X	469	KYV469X	496	KYV496X		

T512 KYV512X 1982 Leyland TNLXB Leyland O44/24D

T513 - T527   1982 Leyland TNLXB/2RR   Leyland H44/24D

513	KYV513X	517	KYV517X	522	KYV522X	526	KYV526X
514	KYV514X	521	KYV521X	525	KYV525X	527	KYV527X
515	KYV515X						

T529 KYV529X 1982 Leyland TNXLB/2RR Leyland H44/23D

T531 - T558   1982 Leyland TNLXB/2RR   Leyland H44/24D

531	KYV531X	540	KYV540X	546	KYV546X	553	NUW553Y
532	KYV532X	541	KYV541X	548	KYV548X	554	NUW554Y
535	KYV535X	542	KYV542X	549	KYV549X	555	NUW555Y
536	KYV536X	543	KYV543X	550	NUW550Y	556	NUW556Y
537	KYV537X	544	KYV544X	551	NUW551Y	557	NUW557Y
539	KYV539X	545	KYV545X	552	NUW552Y	558	NUW558Y
533	KYV533X						

T559 NUW559Y 1982 Leyland TNLXB /2RR Leyland H44/23D

T560 - T564   1982 Leyland TNLXB/2RR   Leyland H44/24D

560	NUW560Y	562	NUW562Y	563	NUW563Y	564	NUW564Y

T565	NUW565Y	1982	Leyland TNLXB/2RR	Leyland H44/23D
T566	NUW566Y	1982	Leyland TNLXB/2RR	Leyland H44/24D
T568	NUW568Y	1982	Leyland TNLXB/2RR	Leyland H44/24D
T569	NUW569Y	1982	Leyland TNLXB/2RR	Leyland H44/24D
T571	NUW571Y	1982	Leyland TNLXB/2RR	Leyland H44/23D

T572 - T631   1982 Leyland TNLXB/2RR   Leyland H44/24D

572	NUW572Y	585	NUW585Y	601	NUW601Y	617	NUW617Y
573	NUW573Y	586	NUW586Y	602	NUW602Y	619	NUW619Y
574	NUW574Y	587	NUW5897Y	603	NUW603Y	621	NUW621Y
575	NUW575Y	588	NUW588Y	604	NUW604Y	622	NUW622Y
576	NUW576Y	589	NUW589Y	605	NUW605Y	623	NUW623Y
577	NUW577Y	590	NUW590Y	606	NUW606Y	624	NUW624Y
578	NUW578Y	591	NUW591Y	608	NUW608Y	625	NUW625Y
579	NUW579Y	592	NUW592Y	609	NUW609Y	626	NUW626Y
580	NUW580Y	593	NUW593Y	610	NUW610Y	627	NUW627Y
581	NUW581Y	595	NUW595Y	613	NUW613Y	629	NUW629Y
582	NUW582Y	597	NUW597Y	614	NUW614Y	630	NUW630Y
583	NUW583Y	598	NUW598Y	615	NUW615Y	631	NUW631Y
584	NUW584Y	600	NUW600Y				

T632 NUW632Y 1982 Leyland TNLXB/2RR Leyland H44/23D

T633 - T646   1982 Leyland TNLXB/2RR   Leyland H44/24D

633	NUW633Y	637	NUW637Y	641	NUW641Y	644	NUW644Y
634	NUW634Y	639	NUW639Y	642	NUW642Y	645	NUW645Y
636	NUW636Y	640	NUW640Y	643	NUW643Y	646	NUW646Y

T647 NUW647Y 1982 Leyland TNLXB/2RR   Leyland H44/23D

T648 - T675   1982 Leyland TNLXB/2RR   Leyland H44/24D

648	NUW648Y	654	NUW654Y	663	NUW663Y	670	NUW670Y
649	NUW649Y	657	NUW657Y	664	NUW664Y	671	NUW671Y
650	NUW650Y	658	NUW658Y	665	NUW665Y	672	NUW672Y
651	NUW651Y	659	NUW659Y	666	NUW666Y	673	NUW673Y
652	NUW652Y	660	NUW660Y	668	NUW668Y	675	NUW675Y
653	NUW653Y	662	NUW662Y	669	NUW669Y		

T684 OHV684Y 1983 Leyland TNLXB/2RR   Leyland H44/23D

T686 - T789   1983 Leyland TNLXB/2RR   Leyland H44/24D

686	OHV686Y	702	OHV702Y	738	OHV738Y	759	OHV759Y
688	OHV688Y	719	OHV719Y	743	OHV743Y	761	OHV761Y
691	OHV691Y	724	OHV724Y	744	OHV744Y	769	OHV769Y
697	OHV697Y	729	OHV729Y	749	OHV749Y	784	OHV784Y
699	OHV699Y	731	OHV731Y	751	OHV751Y	789	OHV789Y

T802 - T922   1983 Leyland TNLXB/2RR   Leyland H44/26D

802	OHV802Y	832	A832SUL	849	A849SUL	902	A902SYE
819	RYK891Y	833	A833SUL	867	A867SUL	905	A905SYE
826	A826SUL	840	A840SUL	873	A873SUL	921	A921SYE
827	A827SUL	846	A846SUL	876	A876SUL	922	A922SYE

T935 - T1050   1984 Leyland TNLXB/2RR   Leyland H44/26D

935	A935SYE	949	A949SYE	965	A965SYE	1026	A626THV
944	A944SYE	953	A953SYE	971	A971SYE	1050	A650THV
945	A945SYE	960	A960SYE	1022	A622THV		

T1128 486CLT   1978 Leyland TNLXB   Park Royal CH43/29F   *West Midlands PTE 1984*
T1128 was originally registered WDA3T.

TPL5 G601XMD 1990 LeylandTRCTL10/3ARZA   Plaxton C53F
TPL7 H642GRO 1991 Leyland TRCTL10/£ARZA Plaxton C53F

VP2   F24HGG   1988 Volvo B10M-61   Plaxton C53F   *Park,s, Hamilton 4.94*

East Midland Motor Services Ltd., New Street, Chesterfield S40 2LQ

Since its acquisition by the Stagecoach Group, East Midland has undergone several changes and has disposed of its subsidiaries Frontrunner South East, Frontrunner North West and Midland Travel. Its operations under the Maun Buses and Mansfield & District names have now been fully absorbed and the company has taken over all the administrative responsibility for Grimsby Cleethorpes Transport which was purchased by Stagecoach Holdings on 18 November 1993.

Depots : Chesterfield; Mansfield; Worksop.

East Midland   Fleet list

31	SKY31Y	1983	Leyland TRCTL11/3R	ECW C51F
32	SKY32Y	1983	Leyland TRCTL11/3R	ECW C51F
37	PJI4316	1983	Leyland TRCTL11/2R	Duple Dom. IV C47F
38	PJI4317	1983	Leyland TRCTL11/2R	Duple Dom. IV C47F

37/8 were originally registered UHE37/8Y.

39 - 44   1983 Leyland TRCTL11/2RH   Alexander T C45F (*C49F)

39	A39XHE	42*	A42XHE	43*	A43XHE	44	A44XHE
41	A41XHE						

49	B49DWE	1984	Leyland TRCTL11/2RH	Alexander TE C49F
52	B52DWE	1984	Leyland TRCTL11/2RH	Alexander TE C49F
53	B53DWJ	1985	Leyland TRCTL11/2RH	Alexander TE C49F
54	B54DWJ	1985	Leyland TRCTL11/2RH	Alexander TE C49F

101 - 109   1993 Volvo Olympian S3-80   Northern Counties H47/29F

101	K101JWJ	104	K104JWJ	106	K106JWJ	108	L108LHL
102	K102JWJ	105	K105JWJ	107	K107JWJ	109	L109LHL
103	K103JWJ						

202 - 211   1980 Bristol VRT/SL3/6LXB   ECW H43/31F

202	EWE202V	205	EWE205V	207	HWG207W	211	JAK211W
203	EWE203V	206	EWE206V	209	JAK209W		

213	KWA213W	1981	Bristol VRT/SL3/6LXB	ECW H43/31F
214	KWA214W	1981	Bristol VRT/SL3/6LXB	ECW H43/31F

215 - 219   1981 Bristol VRT/SL3/6LXC   ECW H43/31F

215	KWA215W	216	KWA216W	218	KWA218W	219	KWA219W

221 - 224

1981 Bristol VRT/SL3/6LXB   ECW H43/31F

221	KKY221W	222	KKY222W	223	KKY223W	224	KKY224W

301 - 305

1981 Leyland ONLXB/1R   ECW H45/32F

301	NHL301X	303	NHL303X	304	NHL304X	305	NHL305X
302	NHL302X						

306 - 311

1982 Leyland ONLXB/1R   ECW H45/32F

306	SHE306Y	308	SHE308Y	310	SHE310Y	311	SHE311Y
307	SHE307Y	309	SHE309Y				

312	UDT312Y	1983	Leyland ONLXB/1R	ECW H45/32F
313	UDT313Y	1983	Leyland ONLXB/1R	ECW H45/32F

314 - 325

1984 Leyland ONLXB/1R   ECW H45/32F

314	A314XWG	317	A317XWG	320	A320YWJ	323	A323AKU
315	A315XWG	318	A318XWG	321	A321YWJ	324	A324AKU
316	A316XWG	319	A319YWJ	322	A322AKU	325	A325AKU

326 - 330

1985 Leyland ONLXB/1R   ECW DPH40/32F

326	C326HWJ	328	C328HWJ	329	C329HWJ	330	C330HWJ
327	C327HWJ						

331 - 336

1986 Leyland ONLXB/1R   ECW H45/32F

331	C331HWJ	333	C333HWJ	335	C335HWJ	336	C336HWJ
332	C332HWJ	334	C334HWJ				

339 - 343

1989 Leyland ONLXB/2RH   Alexander RL DPH51/31F

339	G339KKW	341	G341KKW	342	G342KKW	343	G343KKW
340	G340KKW						

344 - 348

1990 Leyland ON2R56G13Z4   Alexander RL DPH51/31F

344	H344SWA	346	H346SWA	347	H347SWA	348	H348SWA
345	H345SWA						

349 - 353

1991 Leyland ON2R56G13Z4   Alexander RL DPH47/27F

349	J349XET	351	J351XET	352	J352XET	353	J353XET
350	J350XET						

354 - 358

1992 Leyland ON2R50G13Z4   NCME H47/29F

354	K354DWJ	356	K356DWJ	357	K357DWJ	358	K358DWJ
355	K355DWJ						

359 - 363

1992 Leyland ON2550G13Z4   Alexander H43/27F

| 359 | K359DWJ | 361 | K361DWJ | 362 | K362DWJ | 363 | K363DWJ |
| 360 | K360DWJ | | | | | | |

412	DWF22V	1979	Leyland PSU3E/4R	Duple Dominant B55F
413	DWF23V	1979	Leyland PSU3E/4R	Duple Dominant B51F
414	DWF24V	1979	Leyland PSU3E/4R	Alexander P B52F
415	DWF25V	1980	Leyland PSU3E/4R	Duple Dominant B51F
416	DWF26V	1980	Leyland PSU3E/4R	Duple Dominant B55F

412-6 were originally fitted with Willowbrook 003 bodies and were rebodied in 1985.

---

425 - 433

1985 Leyland TRCTL11/2RH   Alexander P B52F

425	B625DWF	428	B628DWF	430	B630DWF	432	B632DWF
426	B626DWF	429	B629DWF	431	B631DWF	433	B633DWF
427	B627DWF						

435 - 453

1993 Volvo B6   Alexander Dash B40F

435	L435LWA	440	L440LWA	446	L446LWA	450	L450LWA
436	L436LWA	441	L441LWA	447	L447LWA	451	L451LWA
437	L437LWA	442	L442LWA	448	L448LWA	452	L452LWA
438	L438LWA	443	L443LWA	449	L449LWA	453	L453LWA
439	L439LWA	445	L445LWA				

614 - 616

1980 Leyland NL106L11/1R   Leyland B44F

| 614 | EKW614V | 615 | EKW615V | 616 | EKW616V |

617 - 621

1980 Leyland NL116L11/1R   Leyland B49F

| 617 | GWE617V | 619 | GWE619V | 620 | HWJ620W | 621 | HWJ621W |
| 618 | GWE618V | | | | | | |

622 - 624

1981 Leyland NL116L11/1R   Leyland B49F

| 622 | MWG622X | 623 | MWG623X | 624 | MWG624X |

625	LAG188V	1980	Leyland NL116L11/1R	Leyland B49F	*East Yorkshire 1988*
626	LAG189V	1980	Leyland NL116L11/1R	Leyland B49F	*East Yorkshire 1988*
627	NRP580V	1980	Leyland NL116L11/1R	Leyland B49F	United Counties .92
628	SVV586W	1981	Leyland NL116L11/1R	Leyland B49F	United Counties .92

---

634 - 636

1983 Leyland NL116HLXB/1R   Leyland DP47F

| 634 | VWA34Y | 635 | VWA35Y | 636 | VWA36Y |

---

637 - 643

1993 Volvo B10M-60   Plaxton Premiere 320 DP51F

| 637 | L637LDT | 639 | L639LDT | 641 | L641LDT | 643 | L643LDT |
| 638 | L638LDT | 640 | L640LDT | 642 | L642LDT | | |

720 - 727

1989   Mercedes Benz 811D   Reeve Burgess B31F

720	G820KWF	722	G822KWF	724	G824KWF	726	G826KWF
721	G821KWF	723	G823KWF	725	G825KWF	727	G827KWF

728 - 730

1988   Mercedes Benz 811D   Optare StarRider B33F
(ex. Maun, Mansfield 2.90)

728	E721BVO	729	E880DRA	730	E481DAU

731 - 751

1993   Mercedes Benz 709D   Alexander (Belfast) B25F

731	L731LWA	736	L736LWA	741	L741LWA	746	L746LWA
732	L732LWA	737	L737LWA	742	L742LWA	748	L748LWA
733	L733LWA	738	L738LWA	743	L743LWA	749	L749LWA
734	L734LWA	739	L739LWA	744	L744LWA	750	L750LWA
735	L735LWA	740	L404LWA	745	L745LWA	751	L751LHL

915	G915KWF	1989	Iveco 49.10	Reeve Burgess	B25F
916	G916KWF	1989	Iveco 49.10	Reeve Burgess	B25F

Grimsby Cleethorpes Transport Ltd., Victoria Street, Grimsby DN31 1NS

Formed on 1 January 1957 by the merging of Grimsby and Cleethorpes Corporations, the undertaking was expanded in 1988 by the acquisition of the Cleethorpes coach operator, Peter Sheffield whose fleet name has been retained.

Livery : Grimsby Cleethorpes Transport - Stagecoach corporate livery replacing orange, white & black. Peter Sheffield - White & purple.

Depot : Grimsby (Grimsby & Cleethorpes Transport & Peter Sheffield)

Grimsby Cleethorpes   Fleet list

1 - 9

1993   Dennis Lance SDA3106   East Lancs B45F

1	K701NDO	4	K704NDO	6	L706HFU	8	L708HFU
2	K702NDO	5	L705HFU	7	L707HFU	9	L709HFU
3	K703NDO						

27 - 30

1988   Leyland TRBLXCT/2RH   Alexander P DP51F

27	E927PBE	28	E928PBE	29	E929PBE	30	E930PBE

31	EJV31Y	1983	Dennis Falcon H	Wadham Stringer Vanguard B45F	
32	EJV32Y	1983	Dennis Falcon H	Wadham Stringer Vanguard B45F	
33	EJV33Y	1983	Dennis Falcon H	Wadham Stringer Vanguard B42F	
34	EJV34Y	1983	Dennis Falcon H	Wadham Stringer Vanguard B42F	

45 - 51
1988   MCW Metrorider MF150   MCW B23F

45	E45HFE	47	E47HFE	49	E49HFE	51	E51HFE
46	E46HFE	48	E48HFE	50	E50HFE		

56 - 58
1988   MCW Metrorider MF150   MCW DP23F

56	E56HFE	57	E57HFE	58	E58HFE

59 - 64
1979   Leyland FE30AGR   Roe H45/29D

59	TFU59T	61	TFU61T	63	TFU63T	64	TFU64T
60	TFU60T	62	TFU62T				

65 - 70
1980   Leyland FE30AGR   Roe H45/29D

65	WFU465V	67	WFU467V	69	WFU469V	70	WFU470V
66	WFU466V	68	WFU68V				

71	A71GEE	1984	Leyland ONTL11/1R	ECW H45/31F	
72	A72GEE	1984	Leyland ONTL11/1R	ECW H45/31F	
73	A73GEE	1984	Leyland ONTL11/1R	ECW H47/28D	
74	A74GEE	1984	Leyland ONTL11/1R	ECW H47/28D	

75 - 78
1989   Dennis Dominator DDA1021   Alexander RH H45/33

75	F75TFU	76	F76TFU	77	F77TFU	78	F78TFU

79 - 81
1990   Dennis Dominator DDA1025   Alexander RH H45/33F

79	G79VFW	80	G80VFW	81	G81VFW

82 - 85
1991   Dennis Dominator DDA1034   East Lancs H45/33F

82	H482BEE	83	H483BEE	84	H484BEE	85	H485BEE

91 - 94
1992   Dennis Dominator DDA1034   East Lancs H45/33F

91	J91DJV	92	J92DJV	93	J93DJV	94	J94DJV

103	BJV103G	1973	Daimler CRG6LX	Roe O45/29D	
113	MBE613R	1976	Leyland FE30AGR	Roe O45/29D	

120 - 124
1978   Leyland FE30AGR   Roe H45/29D

120	OJV120S	122	OJV122S	123	OJV123S	124	OJV124S
121	OJV121S						

125 - 130
1980   Leyland FE30AGR   Roe H45/29D

125	XFU125V	127	XFU127V	129	XFU129V	130	XFU130V
126	XFU126V	128	XFU128V				

Peter Sheffield Fleet list

159	BFW136W	1981	Ford R1114	Plaxton Sup.IV C53F	*Sheffield 1988*
172	XGS736S	1978	Leyland PSU3E/4R	Plaxton Sup.III C53F	*Sheffield 1988*
173	BHO441V	1980	Leyland PSU5C/4R	Duple Dom.II C55F	*Sheffield 1988*
174	MRJ270W	1980	Leyland PSU5C/4R	Plaxton Sup.IV C25DL	*Sheffield 1988*
175	EFU935Y	1983	Leyland PSU5C/4R	Duple Dom.I C53F	*Sheffield 1988*
176	OJL823Y	1983	Leyland PSU5C/4R	Duple Dom.II C53F	*Sheffield 1988*
177	OJL822Y	1983	Leyland PS5C/4R	Duple Dom.III C49F	*Sheffield 1988*
178	PSU787	1986	Leyland TRCTL11/3RZ	Duple Carib. C49FT	*Sheffield 1988*
183	PJI4314	1983	Leyland TRCTL11/2R	Plaxton 3200 C47F	East Midland 1994
184	PSU788	1985	Leyland TRCTL11/3RZ	Duple Carib. C48FT	*Crosville Wales 1990*
185	PSU775	1985	Leyland TRCTL11/3RZ	Duple Carb. C48FT	*Crosville Wales 1990*

176/7 were previously registered PS2743 & PS2945 and were originally EJV419Y & SSG321Y.
178/83-5 were originally registered C495LJV, UWJ33Y & B146/8ACK.

187	PYE841Y	1983	Leyland TRCTL11/3R	Duple Laser C53F	*Lincoln 1991*
188	PYE842Y	1983	Leyland TRCTL11/3R	Duple Laser C53F	*Lincoln 1991*
189	PSU764	1983	Leyland TRCTL11/3R	Duple Laser C53F	*Lincoln 1991*
190	PSU443	1983	Leyland TRCTL11/3R	Duple Laser C53F	*Lincoln 1991*
191	PS2045	1984	Leyland TRCTL11/3R	Duple Laser C57F	*Midland Rec North 1991*
192	PS2743	1984	Leyland TRCTL11/3R	Duple Laser C57F	*Midland Red North 1991*
193	PS3696	1984	Leyland TRCTL11/3R	Duple Laser C57F	*Midland Red North 1991*

189-93 were originally registered PYE843Y, A844SYR & A601-3HVT.

Stagecoach Hong Kong Ltd., Suite 1606, 16/F, Sha Tin Galleria Building, Fo Tan, NT, Hong Kong

After severing its links with Speedybus Enterprises who leased buses to mainland China, Stagecoach International (Hong Kong) Ltd. was set up in 1992 to investigate the possibility of operating services in the New Territories. The first, and to date only, operation, anresidents service service commenced on 24 January 1994 and at the end of 1994 the company was renamed Stagecoach Hong Kong Ltd.

Depot : Fo Tan.

Hong Kong Fleet list

1	FW6766	1993	Volvo B10M-55	Alexander PS B50F
2	FW6555	1993	Volvo B10M-55	Alexander PS B50F
3L	FW6832	1993	Volvo B10M-55	Alexander PS B50F
4L	FW8231	1993	Volvo B10M-55	Alexander PS B50F
5L	FW7894	1993	Volvo B10M-55	Alexander PS B50F

On order for delivery Spring 1995 - 6 Volvo Olympian MkII (tri-axle)-Alexander RH H110D

Stagecoach Malawi Ltd., P.O.Box 176, Blantyre, Malawi

Established by the Overseas Transport Company In 1947 as Nyasaland Transport Company, ownership passed to BET subsidiary United Transport Overseas Ltd. in 1951 and in 1964 the company was renamed United Transport Malawi Ltd. following the country's gaining of independence.

Fleet names : Cityline; Coachline; Intercity; Expressline

Depots : Chichiri; Makata; Lilongwe; Mzuzu. *Outstations : Karonga; Mzimba.*

Stagecoach Malawi   Fleet list

1	BH9601	1988	Volvo B10M-61	Plaxton 3500 C46FT	Travellers, Hounslow 1.91
2	BH9602	1988	Volvo B10M-61	Plaxton 3500 C46FT	Travellers, Hounslow 1.91
3	BH9603	1988	Volvo B10M-61	Plaxton 3500 C46FT	Travellers, Hounslow 1.91
4	BH9604	1989	Volvo B10M-61	Plaxton 3500 C46FT	Travellers, Hounslow 1.91
5	BJ4891	1988	Volvo B10M-61	Plaxton 3500 C46FT	Travellers, Hounslow 8.93
6	BJ8256	1986	Volvo B10M-61	Plaxton 3500 C46FT	Ribble 1994
7	BJ8257	1986	Volvo B10M-61	Plaxton 3500 C46FT	Ribble 1994

1-4 were registered E58Q/4/5/7UHS in the UK. 7 was registered WLT391 in the U.K. and was originally C104DWR.

---

200 - 203   1993 Mercedes Benz 812D   PEW B32F

200	BJ4981	201	BJ5852	202	BJ5853	203	BJ5854

---

204 - 233   1993 ERF Trailblazer 6LXB   PEW B61F

204	BJ6020	212	BJ6147	220	BJ6353	227	BJ6471
205	BJ6021	213	BJ6157	221	BJ6405	228	BJ6512
206	BJ6066	214	BJ6205	222	BJ6414	229	BJ6521
207	BJ6970	215	BJ6245	223	BJ6419	230	BJ6525
208	BJ6080	215	BJ6255	224	BJ6439	231	BJ6542
209	BJ6079	217	BJ6258	225	BJ6450	232	BJ6594
210	BJ6112	218	BJ6313	226	BJ6460	233	BJ6595
211	BJ6137	219	BJ6341				

307	BC6557	1972	Leyland Victory Mk.I	AUT B51D

---

311 - 330   1975 Leyland Victory J Mk.I   AUT B54D
(311 was rehabilitated in 1985)

311	BD2508	319	BD2519	325	BD6253	329	BD6257
314	BD2514	322	BD2522	328	BD6256	330	BD6258
315	BD2519						

---

338 - 345

1978 Leyland Victory J Mk.I AUT B55D

338	BE3166	340	BE3168	343	BE5105	345	BE5107
339	BE3167	341	BE5103	344	BE5106		

346	BF363	1980	Leyland Victory J Mk.II	AUT	B53D
347	BF364	1981	Leyland Victory J Mk.II	AUT	B55D
348	BF365	1981	Leyland Victory J Mk.II	AUT	B53D

348 was rehabilitated in 1986.

350 - 361

1985 Leyland Victory J Mk.II AUT B57D

350	BG150	353	BG153	356	BG1256	359	BG1259
351	BG151	354	BG154	357	BG1257	360	BG1260
352	BG152	355	BG1255	358	BG1258	361	BG149

362 - 365

1986 Leyland Victory J Mk.II AUT B57D

362	BG7362	363	BG7363	364	BG7364	365	BG7365

366 - 371

1987 Leyland Victory J Mk.II AUT B57D

366	BG7366	368	BG7368	370	BG7370	371	BG7371
367	BG7367	369	BG7369				

422	BG2422	1985	Leyland Victory Mk.II	AUT	B59F
423	BG2423	1985	Leyland Victory Mk.II	AUT	B59F
424	BG2424	1985	Leyland Victory J Mk.II	AUT	B49D
425	BG2425	1985	Leyland Victory J Mk.II	AUT	B49D

422-5 were rehabilitated in 1989, 1988, 1989 & 1989 respectively

426 - 437

1989 AVM Dahmer DH825 AUT B59F

426	BH1886	439	BH1889	432	BH1892	435	BH1895
427	BH1887	430	BH1890	433	BH1893	436	BH1896
428	BH1888	431	BH1891	434	BH1894	437	BH1897

438 - 443

1989 DAF TB2105 AUT B59F

438	BH1898	440	BH1900	442	BH1902	443	BH1903
439	BH1899	441	BH1901				

447	BH5747	1990	ERF Trailblazer	PEW	B59F
451	BH5751	1990	ERF Trailblazer	PEW	B59F
452	BH9333	1991	ERF Trailblazer	PEW	B59F

453 - 465

1992 ERF Trailblazer PEW B59F (+ DP51F for international service)

453+	BJ2380	456	BJ2577	458+	BJ2451	464	BJ2713
454+	BJ2381	457+	BJ2450	459	BJ2711	465	BJ3095
455	BJ2576						

470 - 489   1993   Volvo B10M   PEW   DP51F (+ for international service)

470	BJ5558	475	BJ5643	480+	BJ5960	485	BJ6144
471	BJ5551	476	BJ5604	481+	BJ5966	486	BJ6195
472	BJ5552	477	BJ5752	482+	BJ5967	487	BJ6249
473	BJ5553	478	BJ5753	483	BJ6075	488	BJ6267
474	BJ5554	479	BJ5779	484	BJ6106	489	BJ6764

500	BJ7150	1994	ERF Super Trailblazer	PEW	DP51F
720	BG2420	1985	Leyland Victory J Mk.II	AUT	B59F
721	BG2421	1985	Leyland Victory J Mk.II	AUT	B59F
773	BF2232	1983	Leyland Victory J Mk.II	AUT	B56F

720/1 were rehabilitated in 1989

781 - 798   1984 Leyland Victory J Mk.II   AUT   B57F

781	BF8808	787	BF8914	791	BF8978	795	BF8982
783	BF8810	788	BF8915	792	BF8979	796	BF8983
784	BF8811	789	BF8975	793	BF8980	797	BF8984
785	BF8812	790	BF8977	794	BF8981	798	BF8985

799 - 819   1985   Leyland Victory J Mk.II   AUT   B53F (+ FC)

799	BF8986	804+*	BG134	809	BG139	815	BG145
800	BF8987	805+	BG135	811	BG141	816	BG146
801	BG131	806+	BG136	812	BG142	817	BG147
802+	BG132	807+	BG137	813	BG143	818	BG148
803	BG133	808+	BG138	814	BG144	819	BG691

826 - 854   1986   Leyland Victory J Mk.II   AUT   B53F
(fitted with towing hook)*

826	BG3826	834	BG3834	842*	BG8342	848*	BG8348
827	BG3827	835	BG3835	843*	BG3843	849	BG3849
828	BG3828	836	BG3836	844	BG3844	850*	BG3850
829	BG3829	837	BG3837	845	BG3845	851	BG3851
830	BG3830	838	BG3838	846	BG3846	852	BG3852
832	BG3832	839	BG3839	847	BG3847	854*	BG3854
833	BG3833	841	BG3841				

855	BG3855	1987	Leyland Victory J Mk.II	AUT	B51F (FC)
856	BG3856	1986	Leyland Victory J Mk.II	AUT	B51F (FC)

857 - 861   1987   Leyland Victory J Mk.II   AUT   B53F

857	BG3857	859	BG3859	860	BG3860	861	BG3861
858	BG3858						

862 - 880   1990   ERF Trailblazer 6LXB   PEW   B61F
(fitted with a towing hook)*

862	BH5862	867	BH5867	872	BH5872	877	BH5877
863	BH5863	868	BH5868	873	BH5873	878	BH5878
864	BH5864	869	BH5869	874*	BH5874	879*	BH5879
865	BH5865	870	BH5870	875	BH5875	880	BH5752
866	BH5866	871	BH5871	876	BH5876		

881 - 897

1991 ERF Trailblazer   PEW B61F
(*fitted with a towing hook)

881	BH9596	886	BJ446	890	BJ1194	894	BJ1284
882*	BH9697	887	BJ447	891	BJ1191	895	BJ1285
883	BH9698	888	BJ448	892	BJ1192	896	BJ1286
884	BH9599	889	BJ1193	893	BJ1283	897	BJ1287
885	BJ445						

898 - 905

1992 ERF Trailblazer   PEW B61F
(*fitted with a towing hook)

898	BJ1604	900	BJ1606	902	BJ1755	904	BJ1974
899	BJ1605	901*	BJ1754	903	BJ1756	905	BJ1975

906 - 949

1992 ERF Trailblazer   PEW B61F
(*fitted with a towing hook)

906*	BJ1976	917	BJ3203	928*	BJ3519	939	BJ3997
907*	BJ2061	918	BJ3244	929	BJ3521	940	BJ4044
908*	BJ2062	919*	BJ3245	930	BJ3600	941*	BJ4064
909*	BJ2063	920*	BJ3247	931*	BJ3604	942*	BJ4151
910*	BJ2064	921	BJ3246	932*	BJ3673	943*	BJ4161
911*	BJ2065	922	BJ3354	933	BJ3674	944*	BJ4212
912*	BJ2331	923	BJ3373	934	BJ3675	945	BJ4213
913*	BJ2332	924	BJ3387	935*	BJ3857	946	BJ4301
914	BJ2333	925	BJ3402	936	BJ3858	947*	BJ4358
915	BJ3095	926*	BJ3403	937	BJ3872	948	BJ4394
916	BJ3136	927*	BJ3461	938	BJ3971	949	BJ4438

950   BJ5517   1993 ERF Trailblazer   PEW DP51F
950 was rebuilt from an ERF Trailblazer bendibus in 1994

951	BH5748	1990	ERF Trailblazer	PEW	B59F
952	BH5749	1990	EFR Trailblazer	PEW	B59F
953	BF5750	1990	ERF Trailblazer	PEW	B59F
954	BJ2712	1992	ERF Traiblazer	PEW	B59F
955	BJ2715	1992	ERF Trailblazer	PEW	B59F
956	BJ2710	1992	ERF Trailblazer	PEW	B59F
957	BJ3094	1992	ERF Trailblazer	PEW	B59F
958	BH5744	1990	ERF Trailblazer	PEW	B59F
959	BH5745	1990	ERF Trailblazer	PEW	B59F
960	BH5746	1990	ERF Trailblazer	PEW	B59F

1002   BH2628   1972 Daimler CVG6LX-34   Met-Sec H52/33D   Kowloon Motor Bus 5.89
1002 was originally Kowloon M.B. AD7444

1013 - 1016

1972 Daimler CVG6LX-34   Met Sec H52/33D
(ex.Kowloon Motor Bus 6.89)

1013	BH2639	1014	BH2640	1015	BH2641	1016	BH2642

1013-6 were originally Kowloon M.B. AD7453/46/346/437

1019   BH2645   1972 Daimler CVG6LX-34   Met-Sec H52/33D   Kowloon Motor Bus 5.89
1019 was originally Kowloon M.B. AD7438

1025 - 1030

1972 Daimler CVG6LX-34 Met-Sec H52/33D
(ex. Kowloon Motor Bus 1.90)

1025 BH5125	1027 BH5127	1029 BH5129	1030 BH5130

1025/7/9/30 were originally Kowloon M.B. AD7390/46/3/32

1034	BH5134	1972	Daimler CVG6LX-34	Met-Sec	H52/33D	Kowloon Motor Bus 1.90
1036	BH5836	1972	Daimler CVG6LX-34	Met-Sec	H52/33D	Kowloon Motor Bus 4.90
1039	BH5839	1972	Daimler CVG6LX-34	Met-Sec	H52/33D	Kowloon Motor Bus 3.90
1040	BH5840	1972	Daimler CVG6LX-34	Met-Sec	H52/33D	Kowloon Motor Bus 4.90
1041	BH5841	1972	Daimler CVG6LX-34	Met-Sec	H52/33D	Kowloon Motor Bus 4.90
1044	BH5844	1972	Daimler CVG6LX-34	Met-Sec	H52/33D	Kowloon Motor Bus 3.90
1047	BH5847	1972	Daimler CVG6LX-34	Met-Sec	H52/33D	Kowloon Motor Bus 5.90
1050	BH5850	1972	Daimler CVG6LX-34	Met-Sec	H52/33D	Kowloon Motor Bus 4.90

1034/6/9-41/4/7/50 were originally Kowloon M.B. AD7344/54/392/41/2/397/1/39/402

1052 - 1056

1972 Daimler CVG6LX-34 Met-Sec H52/33D
(ex. Kowloon Motor Bus 7.90)

1052 BH6752	1054 BH6754	1055 BH6755	1056 BH6756
1053 BH6753			

1052-6 were originally Kowloon M.B. AD7393/5/400/348/96

2001 - 2010

1992 Dennis Dragon DDA Duple Metsec ckd H67/41F

2001 BJ3701	2004 BJ4370	2007 BJ4575	2009 BJ4618
2002 BJ4153	2005 BJ4397	2008 BJ4590	2010 BJ4915
2003 BJ4302	2006 BJ4505		

TRAILERS

PEW drawbar freight trailer

3	7	11	16
4	8	13	17
5	9	15	18
6	10		

ANCILLARY VEHICLES

001	BF2225	1983	Leyland Victory J Mk.II	AUT	B56F	Driver trainer
002	BF2228	1983	Leyland Victory J Mk.II	AUT	B56F	Driver trainer
003	BF2230	1983	Leyland Victory J Mk.II	AUT	B56F	Driver trainer
004	BF2224	1983	Leyland Victory J Mk.II	AUT	B56F	Driver trainer
005	BF8986	1984	Leyland Victory J Mk.II	AUT	B53F	Driver trainer
006	BF8981	1984	Leyland Victory J Mk.II	AUT	B57F	Driver trainer
007	BF8982	1984	Leyland Victory J Mk.II	AUT	B57F	Driver trainer

Stagecoach NORTH-WEST

Stagecoach (North West) Ltd., Tangier Street, Whitehaven CA28 7XF

Cumberland Motor Services Ltd., Tangier Street, Whitehaven CA28 7XF

Following its acquisition, Cumberland consolidated its position by purchasing several small independent operators : Kirkpatricks; W.A.Palmer, Stephenson, Vine and Yeowarts along with the local bus operations of Brownriggs. Further expansion was gained with the transfer to the company of Ribble's South Cumbria operations on 18 June 1989. Cumberland is now a division of Stagecoach (North West) Ltd.

Fleet names : Coachline; Lakeland Experience; Stagecoach Cumberland.

Livery : Stagecoach corporate livery except for the following : Coachline - Yellow & Tan; Lakeland Experience - Green & cream.

Depots : Barrow-in-Furness; Carlisle; Kendal; Lillyhall. *Outstations : Askam; Ambleside; Appleby; Grange over Sands; Haverthwaite; Millom; Orton; Penrith; Sedbergh; Ulverston; Whitehaven.*

Ribble Buses Ltd., Frenchwood Avenue, Preston PR1 4LU

Since its acquisition by the Stagecoach Group, Ribble has disposed of its Bee Line Buzz subsidiary to the Drawlane Group and its South Cumbria operations to sister company Cumberland,, compensating for these moves by its purchase of Barrow Borough Transport, Mercers of Longridge and the operations of Lancaster City Transport. In 1994 the company opened a new operating unit under the Stagecoach Manchester banner in order to set up a new high-frequency service from that city to Hazel Grove via Stockport in competition to GM Buses. Ribble is now a part of Stagecoach (North West) Ltd.

Fleet names : Stagecoach Manchester; Stagecoach Ribble; Stagecoach Ribble Zippy.

Depots : STAGECOACH RIBBLE - Blackburn; Bolton; Chorley; Clitheroe; Fleetwood; Lancaster; Morecambe; Preston. *Outstations : Burnley; Ingleton.* STAGECOACH MANCHESTER - Bredbury.

Cumberland Fleet list

31	D514RCK	1986	Mercedes Benz L608D	Reeve Burgess DP19F	Ribble 9.94
32	D539RCK	1986	Mercedes Benz L608D	Reeve Burgess B20F	Ribble 9.94
33	D547RCK	1986	Mercedes Benz L608D	Reeve Burgess B20F	Ribble 9.94

34 - 43		1986	Mercedes Benz L608D		Reeve Burgess B20F	
34	D34UAO	37	D37UAO	40	D40UAO	42	D42UAO
35	D35UAO	38	D38UAO	41	D41UAO	43	D43UAO
36	D36UAO	39	D39UAO				

44	D44UAO	1987	Mercedes Benz L608D	Reeve Burgess B20F	Ribble 9.91
45	D45UAO	1987	Mercedes Benz L608D	Reeve Burgess B20F	
46	D46UAO	1987	Mercedes Benz L608D	Reeve Burgess B20F	

47 - 50

1988 Mercedes Benz 709D   Alexander AM B25F

47	E47CHH	48	E48CHH	49	E49CHH	50	E50CHH

51 - 53

1988 Mercedes Benz 709D   Alexander AM BF25F
(ex. Hampshire Bus 11.88)

51	E510PVV	52	E511PVV	53	E512PVV

54	G178PAO	1990	Mercedes Benz 709D	Alexander AM B23F	Magicbus 8.90
55	G299TSL	1990	Mercedes Benz 709D	Alexander AM B23F	Magicbus 9.90
56	G300TSL	1990	Mercedes Benz 709D	Alexander AM B23F	Magicbus 9.90
57	G267TSL	1990	Mercedes Benz 709D	Alexander AM B25F	Stagecoach 9.90
58	G268TSL	1990	Mercedes Benz 709D	Alexander AM B25F	Stagecoach 9.90
59	G269TSL	1990	Mercedes Benz 709D	Alexander AM B25F	Stagecoach 9.90
60	G296TSL	1990	Mercedes Benz 709D	Alexander AM B23F	Magicbus 9.90

61 - 64

1990 Mercedes Benz 709D   Alexander AM B25F
(ex. Stagecoach 10.90)

61	G263TSL	62	G264TSL	63	G265TSL	64	G266TSL

65	G297TSL	1990	Mercedes Benz 709D	Alexander AM B23F	Magicbus 10.90
66	G298TSL	1990	Mercedes Benz 709D	Alexander AM B23F	Magicbus 10.90
67	G295TSL	1990	Mercedes Benz 709D	Alexander AM B23F	Inverness Traction 1.91
68	G294TSL	1990	Mercedes Benz 709D	Alexander AM B23F	Inverness Traction 2.91
70	G293TSL	1990	Mercedes Benz 709D	Alexander AM B23F	Inverness Traction 2.91

71 - 78

1993 Mercedes Benz 709D   Alexander (Belfast) B25F

71	K871GHH	73	K873GHH	75	K875GHH	77	K877GHH
72	K872GHH	74	K874GHH	76	K876GHH	78	K878GHH

79	K626UFR	1993	Mercedes Benz 709D	Alexander (Belfast) B25F	Ribble 3.94
80	K623UFR	1993	Mercedes Benz 709D	Alexander (Belfast) B25F	Ribble 3.94
81	K622UFR	1993	Mercedes Benz 709D	Alexander (Belfast) B25F	Ribble 3.94
82	K114XHG	1993	Mercedes Benz 709D	Alexander (Belfast) B25F	Ribble 5.94
83	K121XHG	1993	Mercedes Benz 709D	Alexander (Belfast) B25F	Ribble 5.94
84	L126DRN	1993	Mercedes Benz 709D	Alexander (Belfast) B25F	Ribble 5.94
85	L123DRN	1993	Mercedes Benz 709D	Alexander (Belfast) B25F	Ribble 5.94
86	K113XHG	1993	Mercedes Benz 709D	Alexander (Belfast) B25F	Ribble 5.94
90	E317BRM	1988	MCW MF150/36	MCW DP25F	Cook & Marshall, Egremont 9.88
101	109DRM	1984	Leyland TRCTL11/3R	Duple Laser C50F	

101 was originally registered A101DAO.

102	A102DAO	1984	Leyland TRCTL11/3R	Duple Laser C50F	
103	B103HAO	1984	Leyland TRCTL11/3RH	Duple Laser C50F	
105	B105HAO	1984	Leyland TRCTL11/3RH	Duple Laser C53F	
106	B106HAO	1984	Leyland TRCTL11/3RH	Duple Laser C49F	
107	B107HAO	1984	Leyland TRCTL11/3RH	Duple Laser C46F	
109	C109OHH	1986	Leyland TRCTL11/3RH	Plaxton 3200 C48F	
110	C110OHH	1986	Leyland TRCTL11/3RH	Plaxton 3200 C46FT	
111	VRR447	1985	Leyland TRCTL11/3RH	Plaxton 3200 C48F	Hampshire Bus 1.88

111 was originally registered B180RLJ.

120 - 124

1992   Volvo B10M-61   Plaxton Expressliner C46FT

120	J120AHH	122	J122AHH	123	J123AHH	124	J124AAO
121	J121AHH						

125	L125NAO	1994	Volvo B10M-60	Plaxton Premiere C46FT	
126	L126NAO	1994	Volvo B10M-60	Plaxton Premiere C46FT	
127	L127NAO	1994	Volvo B10M-60	Plaxton Premiere C46FT	
149	IIL3503	1988	Volvo B10M-61	Van Hool Alizee C49FT	East Midland 5.93
150	IIL3505	1988	Volvo B10M-61	Van Hool Alizee C49FT	East Midland 5.93
151	VLF578	1981	Volvo B10M-61	Van Hool C48F	Magicbus 10.88

149/50 were previously registered E936/42XSB prior to which they were TXI2426 & XIA257 and were originally E625/3UNE. 151 was originally registered TGD766W.

152 - 155

1982   Volvo B10M-61   Van Hool C48F
              (ex. Magicbus 10.88)

152	RUT842	153	LJC800	155	ORY640

156	B156WRN	1985	Leyland TRCTL11/3R	Duple Laser C53F	Ribble 6.89
162	B162WRN	1985	Leyland TRCTL11/3R	Duple Laser C53F	Ribble 11.91

251 - 253

1989   Leyland LX112L10ZR1   Leyland B51F

251	F251JRM	252	F252JRM	253	F253KAO

254	E709MFV	1988	Leyland LX112L10ZR1	Leyland B51F	Leyland demonstrator 6.89
255	C544RAO	1985	Leyland LX1126LXCT	Leyland B51F	Ribble 1.91

270 - 274

1993   Volvo B6   Alexander AM Dash B40F

270	L270LHH	272	L272LHH	273	L273LHH	274	L274LHH
271	L271LHH						

275	L275JAO	1994	Volvo B6	Alexander AM Dash B40F
276	L276JAO	1994	Volvo B6	Alexander AM Dash B40F
282	L282JAO	1994	Volvo B6	Alexander AM Dash B40F

420 - 437

1980   Bristol VRT/SL3/6LXB   ECW H43/31F

420	FAO420V	425	FAO425V	430	KRM430W	434	KRM434W
421	FAO421V	426	FAO426V	431	KRM431W	435	KRM435W
422	FAO422V	427	FAO427V	432	KRM432W	436	KRM436W
423	FAO423V	428	FAO428V	433	KRM433W	437	KRM437W
424	FAO424V	429	FAO429V				

505	LUA273V	1980	Leyland PSU3F/4R	Plaxton C53F	Yeowart, Whitehaven 5.88
509	E986AHH	1988	DAF SB2305DHTD585	Plaxton C53F	Yeowart, Whitehaven 5.88
511	D511RCK	1986	Mercedes Benz L608D	Reeve Burgess DP19F	Ribble 1.94

518 - 520

1986   Mercedes Benz L608D   Reeve Burgess DP19F
              (ex. Ribble 6.89)

518	D518RCK	519	D519RCK	520	D520RCK

521 - 561

1986 Mercedes Benz L608D   Reeve Burgess B20F
(ex. Ribble 6.89)

522	D522RCK	530	D530RCK	534	D534RCK	559	D559RCK
525	D525RCK	531	D531RCK	557	D557RCK	560	D560RCK
528	D528RCK	533	D533RCK	558	D558RCK	561	D561RCK
529	D529RCK						

569	LUA275V	1980	Leyland PSU3F/4R	Plaxton C51F	Kirkpatrick, Brigham 5.88
625	GRM625V	1980	Leyland PSU3E/4R	Duple Dom.II C49F	

---

699 - 738

1992 Volvo B10M-55   Alexander PS B49F

699	K699DAO	709	K709DAO	719	K719DAO	729	K729DAO
700	K700DAO	710	K710DAO	720	K720DAO	730	K730DAO
701	K701DAO	711	K711DAO	721	K721DAO	731	K731DAO
702	K702DAO	712	K712DAO	722	K722DAO	732	K732DAO
703	K703DAO	713	K713DAO	723	K723DAO	733	K733DAO
704	K704DAO	714	K714DAO	724	K724DAO	734	K734DAO
705	K705DAO	715	K715DAO	725	K725DAO	735	K735DAO
706	K706DAO	716	K716DAO	726	K726DAO	736	K736DAO
707	K707DAO	717	K717DAO	727	K727DAO	737	K737DAO
708	K708DAO	718	K718DAO	728	K728DAO	738	K738DAO

---

739 - 771

1993 Volvo B10M-55   Alexander PS B49F

739	K739DAO	748	K748DAO	756	K756DAO	764	K764DAO
740	K740DAO	749	K749DAO	757	K757DAO	765	K765DAO
741	K741DAO	750	K750DAO	758	K758DAO	766	K766DAO
742	K742DAO	751	K751DAO	759	K759DAO	767	K767DAO
743	K743DAO	752	K752DAO	760	K760DAO	768	K768DAO
744	K744DAO	753	K753DAO	761	K761DAO	769	K769DAO
745	K745DAO	754	K754DAO	762	K762DAO	770	K770DAO
746	K746DAO	755	K755DAO	763	K763DAO	771	K771DAO

---

772 - 788

1993 Volvo B10M-55   Alexander PS DP48F

772	K772DAO	777	K777DAO	781	K781DAO	785	K785DAO
773	K773DAO	778	K778DAO	782	K782DAO	786	K786DAO
774	K774DAO	779	K779DAO	783	K783DAO	787	K787DAO
775	K775DAO	780	K780DAO	784	K784DAO	788	K788DAO
776	K776DAO						

810	TRN810V	1979	Leyland LN10351B/1R	Leyland B44F	*Ribble 2.86*	
900	TSK270	1961	AEC Routemaster	Park Royal H36/28R	London Transport 5.87	
901	ALM24B	1964	AEC Routemaster	Park Royal H36/28R	London Transport 5.87	
902	ALD941B	1964	AEC Routemaster	Park Royal H36/28R	Kelvin Scottish 8.87	
903	ALD983B	1964	AEC Routemaster	Park Royal H36/28R	Kelvin Scottish 8.87	
904	ALD933B	1964	AEC Routemaster	Park Royal H36/28R	Kelvin Scottish 8.87	
905	TSK269	1961	AEC Routemaster	Park Royal H36/28R	Kelvin Scottish 8.87	
906	WLT875	1962	AEC Routemaster	Park Royal H36/28R	Kelvin Scottish 8.87	
907	TSK271	1961	AEC Routemaster	Park Royal H36/28R	Kelvin Scottish 8.87	

900/5/7 were originally registered WLT713/06/824.

RMC1515	515CLT	1962	AEC Routemaster	Park Royal O32/25RD	London Selkent 10.94	
D1102	GHV102N	1975	Daimler CRL6-30	Park Royal O44/27D	London Selkent 10.94	
DM948	GHV948N	1975	Daimler CRL6-30	Park Royal O44/27D	London Selkent 10.94	

The Routemasters and Fleetlines are all currently in store

1001	URM801Y	1982	Leyland ONLXB/1R		ECW	DPH45/30F
1002	URM802Y	1982	Leyland ONLXB/1R		ECW	H45/32F

1003 - 1011 — 1988 Leyland ONLXB/2RZ — Alexander H51/36F

1003	F803FAO	1006	F806FAO	1008	F808FAO	1010	F810FAO
1004	F804FAO	1007	F807FAO	1009	F809FAO	1011	F811FAO
1005	F805FAO						

1012 - 1019 — 1990 Leyland ON2R56G13Z4 — Alexander H51/34F

1012	H112SAO	1014	H114SAO	1016	H116SAO	1018	H118SAO
1013	H113SAO	1015	H115SAO	1017	H117SAO	1019	H119SAO

1020 - 1027 — 1991 Leyland ON2R56G13Z4 — Alexander CH47/27F

1020	J120XHH	1022	J122XHH	1024	J124XHH	1026	J126XHH
1021	J121XHH	1023	J123XHH	1025	J125XHH	1027	J127XHH

1028 - 1035 — 1992 Leyland ON2R50G13Z4 — Alexander RL CH43/27F

1028	K128DAO	1030	K130DAO	1032	K132DAO	1034	K134DAO
1029	K129DAO	1031	K131DAO	1033	K133DAO	1035	K135DAO

1090	GSO3V	1986	Leyland ONLXB/1RV	Alexander RL H47/30F	Bluebird Northern	7.91
1091	GSO4V	1986	Leyland ONLXB/1RV	Alexander RL H47/30F	Bluebird Northern	7.91
1092	GSO5V	1987	Leyland ONLXB/1RV	Alexander RL H47/30F	Bluebird Northern	7.91

1090-2 were originally registered C473/4SSO & D375XRS.

1093	D380XRS	1987	Leyland ONLXB/1RV	Alexander RL H47/30F	Bluebird Northern	1.92
1094	D381XRS	1987	Leyland ONLXB/1RV	Alexander RL H47/30F	Bluebird Northern	1.92
1103	KRN103T	1979	Leyland PSU3E/4R	Duple Dom.II C47F	Ribble	6.89
1105	KRN105T	1979	Leyland PSU3E/4R	Duple Dom.II C47F	Ribble	6.89
1113	KRN113T	1979	Leyland PSU3E/4R	Duple Dom.II C47F	Ribble	6.89
1119	KRN119T	1979	Leyland PSU3E/4R	Duple Dom.II C49F	*Ribble*	*2.86*
1140	WCK140V	1980	Leyland PSU3E/4R	Duple Dom.II C49F	*Ribble*	*2.86*
1151	B151WRN	1985	Leyland TRCTL11/2R	Duple Laser C49F	Ribble	11.91
1153	B153WRN	1985	Leyland TRCL11/2R	Duple Laser C49F	Ribble	11.91
1154	B154WRN	1985	Leyland TRCTL11/2R	Duple Laser C49F	Ribble	11.91
1155	PCK335	1985	Leyland TRCTL11/2R	Duple Laser C53F	Ribble	11.91

1155 was originally registered B155WRN

1175	MRJ275W	1981	Leyland PSU5C/4R	Plaxton C50F	Ribble	6.89
1199	FDV799V	1979	Leyland PSU3E/4RT	Plaxton C49F	Ribble	6.89
1201	F201FHH	1989	Leyland ONLXCT/5RZ	Alexander RL CH55/41F		
1202	F202FHH	1989	Leyland ONLXCT/5RZ	Alexander RL CH55/41F		
1253	HNE253V	1980	Leyland PSU5C/4R	Duple Dom.II C53F	Ribble	6.89

1928	ERV251D	1966	Leyland PDR1/1	MCCW O43/33F	Southdown	1.91
2002	CBV2S	1977	Bristol VRT/SL3/6LXB	ECW H43/31F	Ribble	2.86
2024	DBV24W	1980	Bristol VRT/SL3/6LXB	ECW H43/31F	Ribble	2.86
2032	DBV32W	1980	Bristol VRT/SL3/6LXB	ECW H43/31F	Ribble	2.86

2035 - 2038 — 1977 Bristol VRT/SL3/501 — ECW CO43/31F
(ex. Southdown 4.90)

2035	UWV610S	2036	UWV612S	2037	UWV618S	2038	UWV620S

2134	DBV134Y	1983	Leyland ONLXB/1R	ECW H45/32F	Ribble	6.89

2175 - 2177

1985 Leyland ONLXB/1R ECW CH42/30F
(ex. Ribble 6.89)

2175	C175ECK	2176	C176ECK	2177	C177ECK

| 5031 | D503RCK | 1986 | Mercedes Benz L608D | Reeve Burgess DP19F | Ribble | 6.89 |
| 5041 | D504RCK | 1986 | Mercedes Benz L608D | Reeve Burgess DP19F | Ribble | 6.89 |

ANCILLARY VEHICLES

TD5	ABV784A	1955	Leyland PD2/13	MCCW H33/28RD	Driver Trainer
3001	CMS376L	1972	Leyland PSU3/3R	Alexander AY C49F	Driver Trainer
3002	SCS359M	1974	Leyland PSU3/3R	Alexander AY C49F	Driver Trainer
3003	OGM608M	1974	Leyland PSU3/3R	Alexander AYS B53F	Driver Trainer

TD5 was acquired from Ribble in 3.91 and was previously registered 927GTA & TRN597A and was originally registered HRN32. 3001-3 were acquired from Stagecoach in 5.90, 7.90 & 3.90 respectively.

Ribble Buses   Fleet list

135 - 137

1989 Dennis Javelin Duple B63F
(ex. Hampshire Bus 8.91)

135	F135SPX	136	F136SPX	137	F137SPX

138 - 151

1993 Dennis Javelin 11SDL Plaxton Premiere 320 DP49F

138	L138BFV	142	L142BFV	145	L145BFV	149	L149BFV
139	L139BFV	143	L143BFV	146	L146BFV	150	L150BFV
140	L140BFV	144	L144BFV	148	L148BFV	151	L151BFV
141	L141BFV						

152 - 158

1994 Dennis Javelin 11SDL Plaxton Premiere 320 DP49F

152	L152BFV	154	L154BFV	156	L156BFV	158	L158BFV
153	L153BFV	155	L155BFV	157	L157BFV		

159	L159CCW	1993	Dennis Javelin 11SDL	Plaxton Premiere DP49F	
160	L160CCW	1993	Dennis Javelin 11SDL	Plaxton Premiere DP49F	
161	L161CCW	1993	Dennis Javelin 11SDL	Plaxton Premiere DP49F	
162	L101SDY	1994	Dennis Javelin 11SDL	Plaxton Premiere C47F	South Coast Buses 3.94
163	L103SDY	1994	Dennis Javelin 11SDL	Plaxton Premiere C47F	South Coast Buses 3.94
164	L104SDY	1994	Dennis Javelin 11SDL	Plaxton Premiere C47F	South Coast Buses 3.94
165	L106SDY	1994	Dennis Javelin 11SDL	Plaxton Premiere C47F	Coastline 3.94
166	L102SDY	1994	Dennis Javelin 11SDL	Plaxton Premiere C47F	East Kent 3.94
167	L105SDY	1994	Dennis Javelin 11SDL	Plaxton Premiere C47F	South Coast Buses 3.94
168	L107SDY	1994	Dennis Javelin 11SDL	Plaxton Premiere C47F	Coastline 3.94

237 - 250

1993 Volvo B6 Alexander Dash DP40F

237	L237CCW	241	L241CCK	245	L245CCK	248	L248CCK
238	L238CCW	242	L242CCK	246	L246CCK	249	L249CCK
239	L239CCW	243	L243CCK	247	L247CCK	250	L250CCK
240	L240CCW	244	L244CCK				

251 - 256   1994   Volvo B6   Alexander Dash DP40F

251	L251CCK	253	L253CCK	255	L255CCK	256	L256CCK
252	L252CCK	254	L254CCK				

257 - 265   1994   Volvo B6   Alexander Dash DP40F
(ex.Fife Scottish 3.94)

257	L667MSF	260	L660HKS	262	L662MSF	264	L664MSF
258	L668MSF	261	L661MSF	263	L663MSF	265	L665MSF
259	L659HKS						

277 - 283   1993   Volvo B6   Alexander Dash B40F
(ex.Cumberland 5.94)

277	L277JAO	279	L279JAO	281	L281JAO	283	L283JAO
278	L278JAO						

301	CHH214T	1979	Leyland LN10351B/1R	Leyland B44F	Cumberland 10.92
303	SNS825W	1981	Leyland NL116AL11/1R	Leyland B52F	Cumberland 4.93
305	HHH371V	1980	Leyland NL116L11/1R	Leyland B52F	Cumberland 6.93
311	AHH206T	1978	Leyland LN10351B/1R	Leyland B44F	Cumberland 3.93
312	CHH210T	1979	Leyland LN10351B/1R	Leyland B44F	Cumberland 4.93
318	AHH208T	1978	Leyland LN10351B/1R	Leyland B44F	Cumberland 6.93
357	KHH377W	1980	Leyland NL116L11/1R	Leyland B52F	Cumberland 6.93
358	OLS809T	1978	Leyland LN10351B/1R	Leyland B44F	Cumberland 7.93
359	KHH375W	1980	Leyland NL116L11/1R	Leyland B52F	Cumberland 6.93
367	MAO367P	1976	Leyland LN11351/1R	Leyland B52F	Cumberland 1.93
370	HHH370V	1980	Leyland NL116L11/1R	Leyland B52F	Cumberland 2.93
371	OLS807T	1978	Leyland LN10351B/1R	Leyland B44F	Cumberland 2.93
372	HHH372V	1980	Leyland NL116L11/1R	Leyland B52F	Cumberland 2.93
373	HHH373V	1980	Leyland NL116L11/1R	Leyland B52F	Cumberland 6.93
374	KHH374W	1980	Leyland NL116L11/1R	Leyland B52F	Cumberland 2.93
375	AHH209T	1979	Leyland LN10351B/1R	Leyland B44F	Cumberland 7.93
376	KHH376W	1980	Leyland NL116L11/1R	Leyland B52F	Cumberland 2.93
378	KHH378W	1980	Leyland NL116L11/1R	Leyland B52F	Cumberland 4.93
379	NHH379W	1980	Leyland NL116AL11/1R	Leyland B52F	Cumberland 3.93
380	NHH380W	1981	Leyland NL116AL11/1R	Leyland B52F	Cumberland 6.93
381	NHH381W	1981	Leyland NL116AL11/1R	Leyland B52F	Cumberland 2.93
383	RRM383X	1981	Leyland NL116AL11/1R	Leyland DP52F	Cumberland 3.93
384	CHH211T	1979	Leyland LN10351B/1R	Leyland B44F	Cumberland 1.93
385	RRM384X	1981	Leyland NL116AL11/1R	Leyland B52F	Cumberland 2.93
386	RRM386X	1981	Leyland NL116AL11/1R	Leyland B52F	Cumberland 8.93
387	SHH387X	1982	Leyland NL116AL11/1R	Leyland B52F	Cumberland 6.93
390	SHH390X	1982	Leyland NL116AL11/1R	Leyland B52F	Cumberland 4.93
391	SHH391X	1982	Leyland NL116AL11/1R	Leyland B52F	Cumberland 7.93
392	SHH392X	1982	Leyland NL116AL11/1R	Leyland B52F	Cumberland 6.93
393	SHH393X	1982	Leyland NL116AL11/1R	Leyland B52F	Cumberland 2.93
394	SHH394X	1982	Leyland NL116AL11/1R	Leyland B52F	Cumberland 6.93
395	RRM385X	1981	Leyland NL116AL11/1R	Leyland B52F	Cumberland 8.93
396	WAO396Y	1982	Leyland NL116HLXB/1R	Leyland B52F	Cumberland 4.93
397	SNS831W	1980	Leyland NL116AL11/1R	Leyland B52F	Cumberland 10.92
398	WAO398Y	1982	Leyland NL116HLXB/1R	Leyland B52F	Cumberland 4.93
399	SHH388X	1982	Leyland NL116AL11/1R	Leyland B52F	Cumberland 8.93

449	K449YCW	1992	Optare Metrorider	Optare B31F	Lancaster City Tpt. 8.93
450	K450YCW	1992	Optare Metrorider	Optare B31F	Lancaster City Tpt. 8.93

449/50 were originally registered K300/200LCT.

501 - 521
1986 Mercedes Benz L608D   Reeve Burgess DP19F

501	D501RCK	506	D506RCK	510	D510RCK	515	D515RCK
502	D502RCK	507	D507RCK	512	D512RCK	516	D516RCK
505	D505RCK	508	D508RCK	513	D513RCK	521	D521RCK

524	D524RCK	1986	Mercedes Benz L608D	Reeve Burgess B20F	Cumberland 7.90
527	D527RCK	1986	Mercedes Benz L608D	Reeve Burgess B20F	Cumberland 8.91
530	D672SHH	1986	Mercedes Benz 609D	Ribble/Cumb.Com B20F	

536 - 556
1986 Mercedes Benz L608D   Reeve Burgess B20F

536	D536RCK	542	D542RCK	548	D548RCK	552	D552RCK
537	D537RCK	544	D544RCK	549	D549RCK	554	D554RCK
540	D540RCK	545	D545RCK	550	D550RCK	555	D555RCK
541	D541RCK	546	D546RCK	551	D551RCK	556	D556RCK

562	D562RCK	1986	Mercedes Benz L608D	Reeve Burgess B20F	Cumberland 6.91
563	D563RCK	1986	Mercedes Benz L608D	Reeve Burgess B20F	
564	D564RCK	1986	Mercedes Benz L608D	Reeve Burgess B20F	
565	G665PHH	1990	Mercedes Benz 709D	Alexander AM B23F	
566	G566PRM	1990	Mercedes Benz 709D	Alexander AM B23F	

567 - 572
1990 Mercedes Benz 709D   Alexander AM DP25F

567	G567PRM	569	G569PRM	571	G571PRM	572	G572PRM
568	G568PRM	570	G570PRM				

573 - 575
1990 Mercedes Benz 709D   Alexander AM B25F

573	G573PRM	574	G574GRM	575	G575PRM

576 - 578
1990 Mercedes Benz 709D   Alexander AM B23F

576	G576PRM	577	G577PRM	578	G578PRM

579	G179PAO	1990	Mercedes Benz 709D	Alexander AM B23F	Magicbus 7.90
580	G180PAO	1990	Mercedes Benz 709D	Alexander AM B23F	Magicbus 7.90

581 - 592
1990 Mercedes Benz 709D   Alexander AM B23F
(581/2 were loaned to Inverness Traction from new until 6.90)

581	G181PAO	584	G184PAO	587	G187PAO	590	G190PAO
582	G182PAO	585	G185PAO	588	G188PAO	591	G191PAO
583	G183PAO	586	G186PAO	589	G189PAO	592	G192PAO

595 - 608
1993 Mercedes Benz 709D   Alexander (Belfast) B25F

595	K115XHG	598	K118XHG	602	L122DRN	607	L127DRN
596	K116XHG	599	L119DRN	604	K124XHG	608	L128DRN
597	K117XHG	600	K120XHG	605	L125DRN		

610 - 618   1992 Mercedes Benz 709D   Alexander (Belfast) B25F

610	K610UFR	613	K613UFR	615	K615UFR	617	K617UFR
611	K611UFR	614	K614UFR	616	K616UFR	618	K618UFR
612	K612UFR						

619 - 628   1993 Mercedes Benz 709D   Alexander (Belfast) B25F

619	K619UFR	621	K621UFR	625	K625UFR	628	K628UFR
620	K620UFR	624	K624UFR	627	K627UFR		

629 - 637   1993 Mercedes Benz 709D   Alexander (Belfast) B25F

629	L629BFV	632	L632BFV	634	L634BFV	636	L636BFV
630	L630BFV	633	L633BFV	635	L635BFV	637	K112XHG
631	L631BFV						

643	WAO643Y	1983	Leyland TRCTL11/2R	Alexander TC C47F	Cumberland 12.91
645	WAO645Y	1983	Leyland TRCTL11/2R	Alexander TC C47F	Cumberland 12.91
800	NCW800T	1979	Leyland LN113690/1R	Leyland B52F	
801	GCW461S	1978	Leyland LN10351B/1R	Leyland B44F	Cumberland 1.93
802	TRN802V	1979	Leyland LN10351B/1R	Leyland B44F	Cumberland 1.93
806	TRN806V	1979	Leyland LN10351B/1R	Leyland B44F	Cumberland 1.93
807	TRN807V	1979	Leyland LN10351B/1R	Leyland B44F	Cumberland 3.93
808	TRN808V	1979	Leyland LN10351B/1R	Leyland B44F	Cumberland 2.93
809	TRN809T	1979	Leyland LN10351B/1R	Leyland B44F	Cumberland 1.93
812	TRN812V	1979	Leyland LN10351B/1R	Leyland B44F	Cumberland 1.93
813	YRN813V	1980	Leyland NL106L11/1R	Leyland B44F	Cumberland 3.93
814	YRN814V	1980	Leyland NL106L11/1R	Leyland B44F	Cumberland 2.93

815 - 841   1980 Leyland NL106L11/1R   Leyland B44F

815	YRN815V	823	BCW823V	830	DBV830W	836	DBV836W
817	YRN817V	824	BCW824V	831	DBV831W	837	DBV837W
818	YRN818V	825	BCW825V	832	DBV832W	838	DBV838W
819	YRN819V	826	BCW826V	833	DBV833W	839	DBV839W
820	YRN820V	828	DBV828W	834	DBV834W	840	DBV840W
822	YRN822V	829	DBV829W	835	DBV835W	841	DBV841W

842	DBV842W	1980	Leyland NL106L11/1R	Leyland B44F	Cumberland 3.93
843	DBV843W	1980	Leyland NL106L11/1R	Leyland B44F	
846	JCK846W	1980	Leyland NL106AL11/1R	Leyland B44F	
847	JCK847W	1980	Leyland NL106AL11/1R	Leyland B44F	Cumberland 4.93
848	JCK848W	1980	Leyland NL106AL11/1R	Leyland B44F	
856	LFR856X	1981	Leyland NL106AL11/1R	Leyland B44F	Cumberland 1.93
857	LFR857X	1981	Leyland NL106AL11/1R	Leyland B44F	Cumberland 3.93
858	LFR858X	1981	Leyland NL106AL11/1R	Leyland B44F	
859	LFR859X	1981	Leyland NL106AL11/1R	Leyland B44F	
860	LFR860X	1981	Leyland NL106AL11/1R	Leyland B44F	Cumberland 3.93
861	LFR861X	1981	Leyland NL106AL11/1R	Leyland B44F	Cumberland 3.93
863	LFR863X	1981	Leyland NL106AL11/1R	Leyland B44F	Cumberland 6.93

866 - 871   1981 Leyland NL106AL11/1R   Leyland B44F

866	LFR866X	868	LFR868X	870	LFR870X	871	LFR871X

872	LFR872X	1981	Leyland NL106AL11/1R	Leyland B44F	Cumberland 6.93
873	LFR783X	1981	Leyland NL106AL11/1R	Leyland B44F	Cumberland 6.93

877	LFR877X	1981	Leyland NL106AL11/1R	Leyland B44F	
878	RHG878X	1982	Leyland NL116AL11/1R	Leyland B52F	
879	RHG879X	1982	Leyland NL116AL11/1R	Leyland B52F	
881	RHG881X	1982	Leyland NL116AL11/1R	Leyland B52F	Cumberland 3.93
884	RHG884X	1982	Leyland NL116AL11/1R	Leyland B52F	
886	RHG886X	1982	Leyland NL116AL11/1R	Leyland B52F	

888 - 891   1983 Leyland NL116HLXB/1R   Leyland B52F

| 888 | ARN888Y | | 889 | ARN889Y | | 890 | ARN890Y | | 891 | ARN891Y |

893	ARN893Y	1983	Leyland NL116HLXB/1R	Leyland B52F	
894	ARN894Y	1983	Leyland NL116HLXB/1R	Leyland B52F	
895	CEO720W	1980	Leyland NL116L11/1R	Leyland DP45F	Cumberland 8.93
896	CEO721W	1980	Leyland NL116L11/1R	Leyland B49F	Cumberland 8.93
897	CEO722W	1980	Leyland NL116L11/1R	Leyland B49F	Cumberland 2.93
898	CEO723W	1980	Leyland NL116AL11/1R	Leyland B49F	Cumberland 4.93

900	B900WRN	1985	Leyland TRCTL11/2R	Duple Dom. B49F	
1150	A150LFR	1984	Leyland TRCTL11/2R	Duple Dom.IV C51F	
1152	B152WRN	1985	Leyland TRCT11/2R	Duple Laser C49F	
1157	927GTA	1985	Leyland TRCTL11/3R2	Duple Laser C53F	
1158	B158WRN	1985	Leyland TRCTL11/3R2	Duple Laser C53F	
1159	LJY145	1987	Volvo B10M-61	Plaxton 3500 C48FT	Cumberland 5.93
1160	YDG616	1987	Volvo B10M-61	Plaxton 3500 C48FT	Cumberland 5.93
1163	IIL3507	1988	Volvo B10M-60	Plaxton 3500 C46FT	Cumberland 10.93
1164	M164SCK	1994	Volvo B10M-60	Plaxton Ex'liner C46FT	
1165	M165SCK	1994	Volvo B10M-60	Plaxton Ex'liner C46FT	
1166	H150CVU	1991	Volvo B10M-60	Plaxton Ex'liner C46FT	Skyliner, Mosseley 11.93
1167	H150CVU	1991	Volvo B10M-60	Plaxton Ex'liner C46FT	Skyliner, Mosseley 11.93

1157/9/60/3 were originally registered B157WRN, D205/6LWX & F410DUG.

1200	TCK200X	1982	Leyland AN68D/2R	East Lancs H50/36F	Lancaster City Tpt. 8.93
1205	LFV205X	1981	Leyland AN68C/2R	East Lancs H50/36F	Lancaster City Tpt. 8.93
1206	LFV206X	1981	Leyland AN68C/2R	East Lancs H50/36F	Lancaster City Tpt. 8.93
1212	TCK212X	1982	Leyland AN68D/2R	East Lancs H50/36F	Lancaster City Tpt. 8.93
1213	WCK213Y	1982	Leyland AN68D/2R	East Lancs H50/36F	Lancaster City Tpt. 8.93
1214	A214MCK	1984	Leyland AN68D/2R	East Lancs H50/36F	Lancaster City Tpt. 8.93
1215	WCK215Y	1982	Leyland AN68D/2R	East Lancs H50/36F	Lancaster City Tpt. 8.93
1221	BFV221Y	1983	Leyland AN68D/2R	East Lancs DPH45/32F	Lancaster City Tpt. 8.93
1222	BFV222Y	1983	Leyland AN68D/2R	East Lancs DPH45/32F	Lancaster City Tpt. 8.93
1223	A223MCK	1984	Leyland AN68D/2R	East Lancs DPH45/32F	Lancaster City Tpt. 8.93
1450	LEO735Y	1983	Leyland AN68D/1R	NCME H43/32F	Barrow B.T. 5.89
1451	LEO736Y	1983	Leyland AN68D/1R	NCME H43/32F	Barrow B.T. 5.89
1469	TRN469V	1979	Leyland AN68A/1R	ECW H43/31F	Cumberland 1.93
1476	TRN476V	1980	Leyland AN68A/1R	ECW H43/31F	Cumberland 10.92

1478 - 1485   1980 Leyland AN68A/1R   ECW H43/31F
(ex.Cumberland 1.93)

| 1478 | TRN478V | | 1481 | TRN481V | | 1484 | TRN484V | | 1485 | TRN485V |
| 1480 | TRN480V | | 1482 | TRN482V | | | | | |

2021	CBV21S	1977	Bristol VRT/SL3/501	ECW H43/31F	
2030	CBV26W	1980	Bristol VRT/SL3/6LXB	ECW H43/31F	
2034	URF662S	1977	Bristol VRT/SL3/501	ECW H43/31F	*PMT 1982*
2040	FDV813V	1980	Bristol VRT/SL3/6LXB	ECW H43/31F	Stagecoach 1.90
2042	RRP858R	1977	Bristol VRT/SL3/6LXB	ECW H43/31F	United Counties 1.90
2043	FDV817V	1980	Bristol VRT/SL3/6LXB	ECW H43/31F	Stagecoach 1.90
2044	FDV833V	1980	Bristol VRT/SL3/6LXB	ECW H43/31F	Stagecoach 1.90
2045	FDV784V	1979	Bristol VRT/SL3/6LXB	ECW H43/31F	Stagecoach 1.90

2051 - 2058

1981 Bristol VRT/SL3/6LXB ECW H43/31F
(ex.United Counties 9.93)

2051	LFJ882W	2053	LFJ858W	2055	LFJ885W	2057	LFJ861W
2052	LFJ883W	2054	LFJ859W	2056	LFJ866W	2058	LFJ884W

2075	XRR175S	1978	Bristol VRT/SL3/6LXB	ECW O43/27F	East Midland 1.94
2076	UWV622S	1978	Bristol VRT/SL3/6LXB	ECW CO43/31F	East Kent 3.94
2100	DBV100W	1980	Leyland B45.02	ECW H45/33F	
2101	GFR101W	1981	Leyland ONLXB/1R	ECW H45/32F	

2102 - 2113

1981 Leyland ONLXB/1R ECW H45/32F

2102	JFR2W	2105	JFR5W	2108	JFR8W	2111	JFR11W
2103	JFR3W	2106	JFR6W	2109	JFR9W	2112	JFR12W
2104	JFR4W	2107	JFR7W	2110	JFR10W	2113	JFR13W

2114 - 2123

1982 Leyland ONLXB/1R ECW H45/32F

2114	OFV14X	2117	OFV17X	2120	OFV20X	2122	OFV22X
2115	OFV15X	2118	OFV18X	2121	OFV21X	2123	OFV23X
2116	OFV16X	2119	OFV19X				

2124 - 2130

1983 Leyland ONLXBT/1R ECW H45/32F

2124	SCK224X	2126	SCK226X	2128	VRN828Y	2130	VRN830Y
2125	SCK225X	2127	VRN827Y	2129	VRN829Y		

2131 - 2137

1983 Leyland ONLXB/1R ECW H45/32F

2131	DBV131Y	2132	DBV132Y	2137	DBV137Y

2138 - 2152

1984 Leyland ONLXB/1R ECW H45/32F

2138	A138MRN	2143	A143MRN	2145	A145OFR	2152	B152TRN
2142	A142MRN						

2156 - 2159

1985 Leyland ONLXB ECW DPH42/30F

2156	A156OFR	2157	A157OFR	2158	A158OFR	2159	A159OFR

2170 - 2179

1986 Leyland ONLXB/1R ECW DPH42/30F

2170	C170ECK	2172	C172ECK	2174	C174ECK	2179	C179ECK
2171	C171ECK	2173	C173ECK	2178	C178ECK		

2180 - 2189

1989 Leyland ONLXB/2RZ Alexander RL DPH51/31F

2180	G180JHG	2183	G183JHG	2186	G186JHG	2188	G188JHG
2181	G181JHG	2184	G184JHG	2187	G187JHG	2189	G189JHG
2182	G182JHG	2185	G185JHG				

2191 - 2197

1990 Leyland ON2R56G13Z4 Alexander RL H51/36F

2191	H191WFR	2193	H193WFR	2195	H195WFR	2197	H197WFR
2192	H192WFR	2194	H194WFR	2196	H196WFR		

2198 - 2210   1991 Leyland ON2R56G13Z4   Alexander RL DPH47/27F

2198	J198HFR	2202	J202HFR	2205	J205HFR	2208	J208HFR
2199	J199HFR	2203	J203HFR	2206	J206HFR	2209	J209HFR
2201	J201HFR	2204	J204HFR	2207	J207HFR	2210	J210HFR

2211 - 2214   1984 Leyland ONLXB/1R   Alexander RL H45/32F
(ex. Highland Scottish 11.91)

2211	A975OST	2212	A977OST	2213	A978OST	2214	A979OST

2215 - 2223   1985 Leyland ONLXB/1R   Alexander RL H45/32F
(ex. Highland Scottish 11.91)

2215	B891UAS	2218	B894UAS	2220	B896UAS	2222	B898UAS
2216	B892UAS	2219	B895UAS	2221	B897UAS	2223	B899UAS
2217	B893UAS						

702	WSK219	1960	AEC Routemaster	Park Royal H36/28R	United Counties	10.92
707	CUV122C	1965	AEC Routemaster	Park Royal H36/28R	United Counties	10.92
716	ALM60B	1964	AEC Routemaster	Park Royal H36/28R	United Counties	10.92

702 was originally registered WLT528. 702/7/16 are currently in store awaiting disposal

---

ANCILLARY VEHICLES

T251	SCS355M	1974	Leyland PSU3/3R	Alexander AY C49F	Driver Trainer
T252	SCS357M	1974	Leyland PSU3/3R	Alexander AY C49F	Driver Trainer
T253	SCS358M	1974	Leyland PSU3/3R	Alexander AY C49F	Driver Trainer
295	CK3825	1927	Leyland PLSC1	Ribble (replica-Leyland) B31F	Preserved
296	VY957	1929	Leyland PLSC3	Ribble (replica-Roe) B32R	Preserved
1841	AAO771A	1963	Leyland PD3/5	MCCW FH41/31F	Driver Trainer/ Preserved
BD1	PED631R	1977	Leyland	Recovery wagon	
PV1	PTF728L	1973	Leyland LN1151/2R	Leyland B --D	Publicity Office
	H615VHH	1991	Mercedes Benz 310D	Lorry	
	K253KSR	1993	Ford Escort	Van	
	K254KSR	1993	Ford Escort	Van	

T251-3 were acquired from Stagecoach in 7.90, 5.90 & 6.90 respectively. 1841 was previously registered TRN841.

Stagecoach Manchester   Fleet list

249	L249CCK	1993	Volvo B6	Alexander AM Dash DP40F
250	L250CCK	1993	Volvo B6	Alexander AM Dash DP40F

401 - 427   1994 Volvo B10M-55   Alexander PS DP48F

401	L341KCK	411	M411RRN	417	M417RRN	423	M423RRN
402	L342KCK	412	M412RRN	418	M418RRN	424	M424RRN
403	L343KCK	413	M413RRN	419	M419RRN	425	M425RRN
404	L344KCK	414	M414RRN	420	M420RRN	426	M426RRN
409	L339KCK	415	M415RRN	421	Mi421RRN	427	M427RRN
410	L340KCK	416	M416RRN	422	M422RRN		

401-4/9/10 were reregistered from L606-9/14/4TDY before entering service

553	D553RCK	1986	Mercedes Benz L608D	Reeve Burgess B20F

Stagecoach Scotland Ltd., Ruthvenfield Road, Inveralmond, Perth PH1 3EE

Bluebird Buses Ltd., Guild Street, Aberdeen AB9 2DR

Formed as W.Alexander & Sons (Northern) Ltd. on 15 May 1961 as a result of the division of W.Alexander & Sons Ltd empire, the new company was renamed Northern Scottish Omnibuses Ltd. in 1985 becoming Bluebird Northern in 1992 and Bluebird Buses in 1993. Soon after its acquisition by the Stagecoach Group it took over the small business of Clark, Banchory and more recently (early in 1994) purchased Norrie of New Deer and Hardy of Aberchirder. Meanwhile, in November 1991 the company took over responsibility for Inverness Traction from its Perth-based sister, Stagecoach. Diversification was embarked upon in February 1994 with the acquisition of an Aberdeed-based express parcels delivery company, Pegasus Express. Bluebird Buses is now part of Stagecoach Scotland Ltd.

Fleet names : Bluebird; Inverness Traction; Pegasus Express (parcels vans).

Depots : BLUEBIRD BUSES - Aberdeen; Ballater; Elgin; Fyvie; MacDuff; Peterhead; Stonehaven. *Outstations : Aberchirder; Alford; Braemar; Buckie; Ellon; Forres; Fraserburgh; Inverurie; Mintlaw; Strathdon; Tyrie.* INVERNESS TRACTION - Inverness; Tain. PEGASUS EXPRESS - Aberdeen

---

Bluebird Buses   Fleet list

---

002 - 007

1981   Leyland ONLXB/1R   Alexander RL H45/32F

002	SSA2X	004	SSA4X	006	SSA6X	007	SSA7X
003	SSA3X	005	SSA5X				

---

008 - 018

1992 Leyland ON2R50G13Z4 Alexander RL DPH43/27F

008	K508ESS	010	K510ESS	015	K515ESS	018	K518ESS
009	K509ESS	011	K511ESS				

---

033 - 047

1983   Leyland ONLXB/1R   Alexander RL H45/32F

(044 - DPH43/27F)

033	YSO33Y	037	YSO37Y	042	YSO42Y	045	A45FRS
034	YSO34Y	038	YSO38Y	043	YSO43Y	046	A46FRS
035	YSO35Y	040	YSO40Y	044	A44FRS	047	A47FRS
036	YSO36Y	041	YSO40Y				

---

048 - 060

1985 Leyland ONLXB/1R   Alexander RL H45/32F

048	B348LSO	051	B351LSO	054	B354LSO	057	B357LSO
049	B349LSO	052	B352LSO	055	B355LSO	058	B358LSO
050	B350LSO	053	B353LSO				

061 - 066

1986 Leyland ONLXB/1RV   Alexander RL DPH43/27F

061	C461SSO	063	C463SSO	065	MHS5P	066	C466SSO
062	C462SSO	064	MHS4P				

064/5 originally registered C464/5SSO.

067 - 071

1986 Leyland ONLXB/1RV   Alexander RL H45/32F
(converted from H47/26D in 1991)

067	C467SSO	069	C469SSO	070	C470SSO	071	GSO1V
068	C468SSO						

071 was originally registered C471SSO

085 - 089

1987 Leyland ONLXB/1RV   Alexander RL DPH43/27F

085	D385XRS	087	D387XRS	088	D388XRS	089	D389XRS
086	D386XRS						

091	J121XHH	1991	Leyland ON2R56G13Z4	Alexander RL DPH47/27F	Div'd from Cumberland

096 - 099

1991 Leyland ON2R56G13Z4   Alexander RL H47/30F

096	J196YSS	097	J197YSS	098	J198YSS	099	J199YSS

120	SAO410R	1977	Bristol VRT/SL3/501	ECW H43/31F	Cumberland 10.91
122	SAO412R	1977	Bristol VRT/SL3/501	ECW H43/31F	Cumberland 10.91
128	RJT155R	1977	Bristol VRT/SL3/6LXB	ECW H43/31F	Stagecoach Buses 5.92

131 - 138

1977 Leyland PSU3E/4R   Duple Dominant Express C49F

131	RRS46R	133	RRS48R	135	RRS50R	138	RRS53R
132	RRS47R						

139 - 144

1979 Leyland PSU3E/4R   Alexander AT DP49F

139	CRS60T	141	CRS62T	143	CRS68T	144	CRS69T
140	CRS61T	142	CRS63T				

145 - 148

1979 Leyland PSU3E/4R   Duple Dominant I Exp. C49F

145	CRS70T	146	CRS71T	147	CRS73T	148	CRS74T

159 - 161

1980 Leyland PSU3E/4R   Duple Dominant II Exp. C49F

159	KRS529V	160	KRS531V	161	KRS532V

159-61 were previously registered CSU920-2 and originally registered HSA96-8V.

216	XRM772Y	1983	Leyland PSU5C/4R	Duple Dom. C57F	Hardie, Aberchirder 2.94
217	D523KSE	1986	Bedford YNV	Duple 320 C57F	Hardie, Aberchirder 2.94
227	D27PVS	1987	Frieght Rover Sherpa	Dormobile C16F	Norries, New Deer 1.94
229	E992MSE	1987	Toyota	Caetano Optimo C20F	Hardie, Aberchirder 2.94
230	D435RYS	1987	Mercedes Benz 609D	Scott C24F	*Airpark, Linwood 1990*
231	D436RYS	1987	Mercedes Benz 609D	Scott C24F	*Airpark, Linwood 1990*
233	E364YGB	1988	Mercedes Benz 609D	Scott C24F	*Airpark, Linwood 1990*
234	E842KAS	1988	Mercedes Benz 609D	Reeve Burgess C23F	*Carr & Robbins, Tomintoul 1990*
235	E947BHS	1988	Mercedes Benz 609D	Scott C24F	*Whitelaw, Stonehouse 1990*
236	F77HAU	1988	Mercedes Benz 609D	Scott C24F	*Skill, Nottingham 1990*
237	F164XCS	1989	Mercedes Benz 609D	Scott C24F	*Clyde Coast, Ardrossan 1990*
238	F862FWB	1989	Mercedes Benz 609D	Scott C24F	*Metcalfe, Ferryhill 1990*
239	D322MNC	1986	Mercedes Benz 609D	M to Measure DP25F	Fife Scottish 2.94
240	B875GSG	1984	Mercedes Benz L608D	Mercedes Benz C24F	Fife Scottish 2.94
241	C901HWF	1985	Mercedes Benz L608D	Reeve Burgess DP19F	Fife Scottish 2.94
242	C902HWF	1985	Mercedes Benz L608D	Reeve Burgess DP19F	Fife Scottish 2.94
248	A353ASF	1983	Mercedes Benz L608D	Devon Con. C19F	Norries, New Deer 1.94
249	C701RSS	1986	Mercedes Benz L608D	Scott C25F	Norries, New Deer 1.94
251	G251TSL	1990	Mercedes Benz 709D	Alexander AM B25F	Stagecoach 1.93
256	G256TSL	1990	Mercedes Benz 709D	Alexander AM B25F	Stagecoach 5.92
257	G257TSL	1990	Mercedes Benz 709D	Alexander AM B25F	Stagecoach 5.92
258	G258TSL	1990	Mercedes Benz 709D	Alexander AM B25F	Stagecoach 7.91
259	G259TSL	1990	Mercedes Benz 709D	Alexander AM B25F	Stagecoach 7.91
260	G260TSL	1990	Mercedes Benz 709D	Alexander AM B25F	Stagecoach 7.91
261	G261TSL	1990	Mercedes Benz 709D	Alexander AM B25F	Stagecoach 6.91
262	G262TSL	1990	Mercedes Benz 709D	Alexander AM B25F	Stagecoach 6.91
270	G270TSL	1990	Mercedes Benz 709D	Alexander AM B25F	Stagecoach 4.91
271	G271TSL	1990	Mercedes Benz 709D	Alexander AM B25F	Stagecoach 2.92
272	G272TSL	1990	Mercedes Benz 709D	Alexander AM B25F	Stagecoach 2.92
273	G273TSL	1990	Mercedes Benz 709D	Alexander AM B25F	Stagecoach 2.92
274	G274TSL	1990	Mercedes Benz 709D	Alexander AM B25F	Stagecoach 3.92
275	G275TSL	1990	Mercedes Benz 709D	Alexander AM B25F	Stagecoach 4.92
276	G276TSL	1990	Mercedes Bena 709D	Alexander AM B23F	
277	G277TSL	1990	Mercedes Benz 709D	Alexander AM B25F	Stagecoach 5.92
278	G278TSL	1990	Mercedes Benz 709D	Alexander AM B23F	
279	G279TSL	1990	Mercedes Benz 709D	Alexander AM B25F	
288	G288TSL	1990	Mercedes Benz 709D	Alexander AM B23F	Inverness Traction 7.91
289	G289TSL	1990	Mercedes Benz 709D	Alexander AM B23F	Inverness Traction 7.91
290	G290TSL	1990	Mercedes Benz 709D	Alexander AM B23F	Inverness Traction 7.91
291	G291TSL	1990	Mercedes Benz 709D	Alexander AM B23F	Inverness Traction 4.91
292	G292TSL	1990	Mercedes Benz 709D	Alexander AM B23F	Inverness Traction 4.91
301	L301JSA	1993	Mercedes Benz 709D	Alexander AM DP25F	
302	L302JSA	1993	Mercedes Benz 709D	Alexander AM DP25F	
303	L303JSA	1993	Mercedes Benz 709D	Alexander AM DP25F	
304	G193PAO	1990	Mercedes Benz 709D	Alexander AM DP25F	
307	G196PAO	1990	Mercedes Benz 709D	Alexander AM DP25F	Inverness Traction 9.91
313	G202PAO	1990	Mercedes Benz 709D	Alexander AM DP25F	Stagecoach 2.92
314	G203PAO	1990	Mercedes Benz 709D	Alexander AM DP25F	Stagecoach 2.92
315	L315JSA	1993	Mercedes Benz 709D	Alexander AM DP25F	
316	L316JSA	1993	Mercedes Benz 709D	Alexander AM DP25F	
317	M317RSO	1994	Mercedes Benz 709D	Alexander AM DP25F	
318	M318RSO	1994	Mercedes Benz 709D	Alexander AM DP25F	
319	M319RSO	1994	Mercedes Benz 709D	Alexander AM DP25F	
421	A116ESA	1983	Leyland TRBTL11/2R	Alexander P B52F	
422	A117ESA	1983	Leyland TRBTL11/2R	Alexander P B52F	
423	A118ESA	1983	Leyland TRBTL11/2R	Alexander P B52F	

424 - 430   1984   Leyland TRBLXB/2RH   Alexander P B52F

| 424 | A121GSA | 426 | A123GSA | 428 | A125GSA | 430 | A127GSA |
| 425 | A122GSA | 427 | A124GSA | 429 | A126GSA | | |

432	PSO177W	1981	Leyland TRCTL11/3R	Duple Gold.IV C53F	*Kelvin Scottish 1989*
434	PSO178W	1981	Leyland TRCTL11/3R	Duple Gold.IV C51F	*Kelvin Scottish 1989*
436	RRS225X	1982	Leyland TRCTL11/3R	Duple Gold.IV DP53F	*Kelvin Scottish 1989*
439	CSO389Y	1983	Leyland TRCTL11/2R	Duple Dom.I C49F	
440	CSO386Y	1983	Leyland TRCTL11/2R	Duple Dom.I C47F	

432 was previously registered CSU920, WGB175W & 630DYE and was originally BSG549W. 434 was previously registered CSU921, WGB176W & WLT742 and was originally BSG547W. 436/9/40 were previously registered CSU923 & TSV779/80 and were originally MSC556X & ASA9/10Y.

442 - 446   1985   Leyland TRCTL11/2RP   Alexander TC C47F

| 442 | TSV718 | 444 | TSV720 | 445 | TSV721 | 446 | TSV722 |
| 443 | TSV719 | | | | | | |

442-6 originally registered B328-32LSA.

450 - 454   1987   Leyland TRCTL11/3RH   Alexander TC C57F

| 450 | BSK744 | 452 | D438XRS | 453 | 147YFM | 454 | BSK756 |
| 451 | LSK547 | | | | | | |

450/1/3/4 were originally registered D436/7/9XRS & E640BRS

455	HSK760	1986	Leyland TRCLXC/2RH	Duple 320 C47FT	*Central Scottish 1989*
456	C111JCS	1986	Leyland TRCLXC/2RH	Duple 320 C47FT	*Central Scottish 1989*
458	WAO643Y	1983	Leyland TRCTL11.2R	Alexander TC C47F	Ribble 5.94
459	A40XHE	1983	Leyland TRCTL11.2R	Alexander TE C49F	East Midland 6.91

455 was originally registered C110JCS.

460 - 463   1984   Leyland TRCTL11/3R   Duple Laser C53F
(ex.National Welsh 5.92)

| 460 | AAX600A | 461 | AAX631A | 462 | AAX232A | 463 | AAX589A |

460-3 were originally registered A219/22/9/16VWO

464	AAX601A	1984	Leyland TRCTL11/3R	Duple Laser C53F	National Welsh 8.92
465	AAX162A	1984	Leyland TRCTL11/3R	Duple Laser C53F	National Welsh 8.92
466	NIB4138	1984	Leyland TRCTL11/3RH	Duple Laser C51F	East Midland 3.93
267	NIB5455	1984	Leyland TRCTL11/3RH	Duple Laser C51F	East Midland 3.93
468	A663WSU	1983	Leyland TRCTL11/2RP	Alexander TE DP53F	Kelvin Central 4.93

464/5 were originally registered A218/23VWO. 466/7 were originally registered A45/6YAK. 468 was previously register WLT976 and was originally A120GLS.

471	E648KCX	1988	DAF MB230LB	Van Hool C53FT	Selkent 10.94
473	J35GCX	1992	DAF SB2305DHS	Duple 340 C57F	Selkent 10.94
474	J36GCX	1992	DAF SB2304DHS	Duple 340 C57F	Selkent 10.94
475	K536RJX	1993	DAF MB230LT	Van Hool C51FT	Selkent 10.94
476	K537RJX	1993	DAF MB230LT	Van Hool C51FT	Selkent 10.94
477	K538RJX	1993	DAF MB230LT	Van Hool C51FT	Selkent 10.94
478	K539RJX	1993	DAF MB230LT	Van Hool C51FT	Selkent 10.94

518 - 522   1993   Dennis Dart 98SDL   Alexander Dash B40F
(ex.United Counties 11.93)

| 518 | K106XHG | 520 | K108XHG | 521 | K110XHG | 522 | K110XHG |
| 519 | K107XHG | | | | | | |

530 - 536   1994   Volvo B10M-60   Plaxton Premiere DP51F

530	M530RSO	532	M532RSO	534	M534RSO	536	M536RSO
531	M531RSO	533	M533RSO	535	M535RSO		

545	1412NE	1986	Volvo B10M-61	Van Hool Alizee C53F	Hardie, Aberchirder 2.94
546	TSV778	1986	Volvo B10M-61	Van Hool Alizee C53F	Hardie, Aberchirder 2.94
547	TSV779	1987	Volvo B10M-61	Van Hool Alizee C53F	East Midland 11.92
548	TSV780	1987	Volvo B10M-61	Van Hool Alizee C53F	Shearings, Wigan 11.91
549	TSV781	1987	Volvo B10M-61	Van Hool Alizee C53F	Shearings, Wigan 11.91
550	CSU920	1987	Volvo B10M-61	Van Hool Alizee C53F	East Midland 11.92
551	CSU921	1987	Volvo B10M-61	Van Hool Alizee C53F	Shearings, Wigan 11.91
552	CSU922	1987	Volvo B10M-61	Van Hool Alizee C53F	Shearings, Wigan 11.91
553	CSU923	1987	Volvo B10M-61	Van Hool Alizee C53F	Shearings, Wigan 11.91

545-53 were originally registered C325/30DND & D547-53MVR.

562 - 588   1993   Volvo B10M-60   Plaxton Premiere 320 DP51F

562	K562GSA	567	K567GSA	581	L581JSA	585	L585JSA
563	K563GSA	568	K568GSA	582	L582JSA	586	L586JSA
564	K564GSA	569	K569GSA	583	L583JSA	587	L587JSA
565	K565GSA	579	L579JSA	584	L584JSA	588	L588JSA
566	K566GSA	580	L580JSA				

589 - 593   1994   Volvo B10M-55   Alexander PS DP49F

589	M589OSO	591	M591OSO	592	M592OSO	593	M593OSO
590	M590OSO						

652	GRS343E	1967	Albion VK43	Alexander Y DP40F	*Preserved*

ANCILLARY VEHICLES

712	J764EDS	1991	Citroen C15D	Van	Mobile Inspector
713	J509ESL	1991	Citroen C15D	Van	
714	J549CSR	1991	Citroen C15D	Van	
717	K403LES	1993	Renault Traffic	Van	
718	K138LES	1993	Ford Fiesta D	Van	Mobile Inspector
725	C108RSS	1986	Ford Cargo	Stores lorry	Vehicle Examiner
726	DMS325C	1965	Leyland PSU3/3R	Towing wagon	
728	OAG535H	1970	Leyland PSU3/3E	Towing wagon	
729	XYH127T	1979	Leyland Buffalo	Recovery wagon	
730	CYM111V	1979	Leyland Buffalo	Recovery wagon	

Inverness Traction   Fleet list

026	L26JSA	1993	Volvo YN2RV18Z4	Northern Counties DPH38/30F	
027	L27JSA	1993	Volvo YN2RV18Z4	Northern Counties DPH38/30F	
028	L28JSA	1993	Volvo YN2RV18Z4	Northern Counties DPH38/30F	
039	YSO39Y	1983	Leyland ONLXB/1R	Alexander RL H45/32F	
056	B356LSO	1985	Leyland ONLXB/1R	Alexander RL H45/32F	
059	B359LSO	1985	Leyland ONLXB/1R	Alexander RL H45/32F	
060	B360LSO	1985	Leyland ONLXB/1R	Alexander RL H45/32F	
076	MAU146P	1976	Bristol VRT/SL3/6LX	ECW H39/31F	Stagecoach 3.92
082	OCY910R	1977	Bristol VRT/SL3/501	ECW H43/31F	East Midland 1.92
090	J120XHH	1991	Leyland ON2R56G13Z4	Alexander RL DPH47/30F	Div'd from Cumberland
092	J122XHH	1991	Leyland ON2R56G13Z4	Alexander RL DPH47/30F	Div'd from Cumberland
100	L110JSA	1993	Volvo YN2RV18Z4	Northern Counties DPH38/30F	
101	L101JSA	1993	Volvo YN2RV18Z4	Northern Counties DPH38/30F	
102	L102JSA	1993	Volvo YN2RV18Z4	Northern Counties DPH38/30F	
103	FDV810V	1980	Bristol VRT/SL3/6LXB	ECW H43/31F	Stagecoach 7.94
106	UWV608S	1977	Bristol VRT/SL3/6LXB	ECW CO43/31F	Southdown 6.90
108	UWV609S	1977	Bristol VRT/SL2/6LXB	ECW CO43/31F	Southdown 4.91
219	YFS98S	1977	Leyland PSU3D/4R	Alexander AYS B53F	Stagecoach 9.94
220	YFS100S	1977	Leyland PSU3E/4R	Alexander AYS B53F	Stagecoach 9.94
236	F77HAU	1988	Mercedes Benz 609D	Scott C24F	*Skill, Nottingham 1990*
250	A121XWB	1983	Mercedes Benz L608D	Whittaker C23F	Stagecoach 3.90

282 - 287   1990   Mercedes Benz 709D   Alexander AM B23

282	G282TSL	284	G284TSL	286	G286TSL	287	G287TSL
283	G283TSL	285	G285TSL				

305	G194PAO	1990	Mercedes Benz 709D	Alexander AM DP25F	
306	G195PAO	1990	Mercedes Benz 709D	Alexander AM DP25F	
308	G197PAO	1990	Mercedes Benz 709D	Alexander AM DP25F	Stagecoach 9.92
320	M320RSO	1994	Mercedes Benz 709D	Alexander AM DP25F	
321	M321RSO	1994	Mercedes Benz 709D	Alexander AM DP25F	
447	126ASV	1983	Leyland TRBTL11/2R	Alexander TE C51F	*Kelvin Scottish 1986*
448	127ASV	1983	Leyland TRBTL11/2R	Alexander TE C51F	*Kelvin Scottish 1986*
449	128ASV	1983	Leyland TRBTL11/2R	Alexander TE C51F	*Kelvin Scottish 1986*

447-9 were originally registerd BMS511/3/5Y

453	147YFM	1987	Leyland TRCTL11/3RH	Alexander TC C57F	
454	BSK756	1987	Leyland TRCTL11/3RH	Alexander TC C57F	
459	A40XHE	1983	Leyland TRCTL11/2R	Alexander TE C49F	
469	NIB5232	1985	Leyland TRCTL11/3R	Plaxton 3200 C51F	East Midland 6.93
470	NIB5233	1985	Leyland TRCTL11/3R	Plaxton 3200 C51F	East Midland 6.93

453/4/69/70 were originally registered D439XRS, E640BRS & B47/8DWE.

503 - 512   1992   Dennis Dart 9.8SDL   Alexander AM Dash B40F

503	J503FPS	506	J506FPS	509	J509FPS	511	J511FPS
504	J504FPS	507	J507FPS	510	J510FPS	512	J512FPS
505	J505FPS	508	J508FPS				

513 - 515   1993   Dennis Dart 9.8SDL   Alexander AM Dash B40F

513	K101XHG	514	K102XHG	515	K103XHG

516	K104XHG	1993	Dennis Dart 9.8SDL	Alexander AM Dash B40F	United Counties 11.93
517	K105XHG	1993	Dennis Dart 9.8SDL	Alexander AM DAsh B40F	United Counties 11.93

594 - 598   1994   Volvo B10M-55   Alexander PS   DP49F

594	M594OSO		596	M596OSO		597	M597OSO		598	M598OSO
595	M595OSO									

696	UWV605S	1977	Bristol VRT/SL3/6LXB	ECW CO43/31F	Fife Scottish 10.92

ANCILLARY VEHICLES

715	K427JSN	1992	Citroen C15D	Van	Mobile inspector
716	D824KSE	1986	Freight Rover Sherpa	B8F Shuttle	
721	G795LSS	1989	Ford Fiesta D	Van	
727	HGM431E	1967	Bristol FLF6G	Towing wagon	

Pegasus Express   Fleet list

950	A6SEG	1990	SAAB 900	Car	
951	J362XRS	1991	Ford Sierra	Estate car	
952	B874WHD	1985	Mercedes Benz 7.5T	Van	
953	M152PSS	1994	Vauxhall Combo	Van	*Leased*
954	M154PSS	1994	Vauxhall Combo	Van	*Leased*
955	M156PSS	1994	Vauxhall Combo	Van	*Leased*
956	M103RSA	1994	Vauxhall Combo	Van	*Leased*
957	M104RSA	1994	Vauxhall Combo	Van	*Leased*
589	M105RSA	1994	Vauxhall Combo	Van	*Leased*
959	M106RSA	1994	Vauxhall Combo	Van	*Leased*
960	M107RSA	1994	Vauxhall Combo	Van	*Leased*
967	J351YSA	1991	Ford Fiesta Courier	Van	
968	J339BSO	1992	DAF 400	Van	
969	J585ASA	1992	DAF 400	Van	
970	K52FSA	1992	Vauxhall Astramax	Van	
971	K53FSA	1992	Vauxhall Astramax	Van	
972	J479DSR	1991	Renault T1100D	Van	
983	K331OHW	1993	Iveco Cargo 7.5T	Van	*Leased*
984	K530MFB	1992	Iveco Cargo 7.5T	Van	*Leased*
985	L838CHD	1994	Iveco Cargo 7.5T	Van	*Leased*
986	L861HCP	1994	Ford Transit 190	Van	*Leased*
987	L43VVK	1993	Ford Transit	Hi-top van	*Leased*
988	L918ADM	1994	Ford Transit	Luton van	*Leased*
989	L743AAT	1994	Iveco Ford 17T	Van	*Leased*
990	L165ARG	1994	Ford Transit 190	Van	*Leased*
991	L127YRH	1994	Ford Transit	Luton van	*Leased*
992	L243CKH	1994	Ford Transit	Van	*Leased*

Stagecoach Scotland Ltd., Ruthvenfield Road, Inveralmond, Perth PH1 3EE

Formed in 1980 as GT Coaches, the Stagecoach name was adopted in October of that year for the company's Anglo-Scottish express coach services. Its entry into stage carriage operations came on 22 December 1980 when it acquired the Perth to Errol service of A. & C. McLennan whose entire business was ultimately taken over in 1985. Meanwhile an Edinburgh-based coach company (Adamson & Low) had been acquired in 1983 although two years later it was sold back to one of its original owners. A year later, upon deregulation, a new operation was set up in Glasgow under the title 'Magicbus' to operate a handful of local services and following the collapse of Cotters in 1987 that company's Coachline express services were acquired. After purchasing Highwayman Coaches of Errol in February 1989, Stagecoach sold its express coach operations to National Express in August of that year to leave it free to concentrate wholly on local bus services, especially in Perth where a new unit was set to up under the title of Perth Panther in order to compete with Strathtay Scottish. Later, in November, the local bus operation of the ailing Inverness Traction was purchased from the Receiver, this company passing to sister company Bluebird Northern's control in September 1991, two months after Stagecoach had taken over the Crieff area operations of Strathtay Scottish. In April 1992 the Glasgow-based Magicbus was sold to Kelvin Central Buses.

Fleet names : Stagecoach; Stagecoach Perth Panther

Depots : Perth; Crieff *Outstation : Spittalfield*

Stagecoach Buses   Fleet list

012	TSO12X	1982	Leyland ONLXB/1R	ECW H45/32F	Bluebird Northern 4.91
013	TSO13X	1982	Leyland ONLXB/1R	ECW H45/32F	Bluebird Northern 8.91
014	TSO14X	1982	Leyland ONLXB/1R	ECW H45/32F	Bluebird Northern 8.91
016	TSO16X	1982	Leyland ONLXB/1R	ECW H45/32F	Bluebird Northern 8.91
017	TSO17X	1982	Leyland ONLXB/1R	ECW H45/32F	Bluebird Northern 4.92
019	OMS910W	1981	Leyland ONLXB/1R	ECW H45/32F	Clydeside 2000 3.93
020	TSO20X	1982	Leyland ONLXB/1R	ECW H45/32F	Bluebird Northern 6.91
021	TSO21X	1982	Leyland ONLXB/1R	ECW H45/32F	Bluebird Northern 5.91
022	9492SC	1982	Leyland ONLXB/1R	ECW H45/32F	Bluebird Northern 5.91
023	TSO23X	1982	Leyland ONLXB/1R	ECW H45/32F	Bluebird Northern 6.91
024	TSO24X	1982	Leyland ONLXB/1R	ECW H45/32F	Bluebird Northern 6.91
025	TSO15X	1982	Leyland ONLXB/1R	ECW H45/32F	Clydeside 2000 3.93
029	TSO29X	1982	Leyland ONLXB/1R	ECW H45/32F	Bluebird Northern 4.92
030	TSO30X	1982	Leyland ONLXB/1R	ECW H45/32F	Bluebird Northern 10.91
031	TSO31X	1982	Leyland ONLXB/1R	ECW H45/32F	Bluebird Northern 4.92
032	TSO32X	1982	Leyland ONLXB/1R	ECW H45/32F	Bluebird Northern 4.91

022 originally registered TSO19X.

105	FDV816V	1980	Bristol VRT/SL3/6LXB	ECW H43/31F	Inverness Traction 9.94
107	FDV819V	1980	Bristol VRT/SL3/6LXB	ECW H43/31F	Inverness Traction 9.94
109	FDV840V	1980	Bristol VRT/SL3/6LXB	ECW H43/31F	Inverness Traction 9.94
110	JAK210W	1860	Bristol VRT/SL3/6LXB	ECW H43/31F	East Midland 4.94
112	JAK212W	1980	Bristol VRT/SL3/6LXB	ECW H43/31F	East Midland 4.94
152	GSO89V	1980	Leyland PU3E/4R	Alexander AYS DP49F	Bluebird Buses 8.93
153	GSO90V	1980	Leyland PSU3E/4R	Alexander AYS DP49F	Bluebird Buses 8.93
154	GSO91V	1980	Leyland PSU3E/4R	Alexander AYS DP49F	Bluebird Buses 9.93
155	GSO92V	1980	Leyland PSU3E/4R	Alexander AYS DP49F	Bluebird Buses 8.94
156	GSO93V	1980	Leyland PSU3E/4R	Alexander AYS DP49F	Bluebird Buses 11.93
157	GSO94V	1980	Leyland PSU3E/4R	Alexander AYS DP49F	Bluebird Buses 8.94
158	GSO95V	1980	Leyland PSU3E/4R	Alexander AYS DP49F	Bluebird Buses 8.93
167	4585SC	1981	Leyland PSU3G/4R	Duple Dom.II C49F	Bluebird Buses 8.93
168	145CLT	1981	Leyland PSU3G/4R	Duple Dom.II C49F	Bluebird Buses 8.93
169	OVL473	1981	Leyland PSU3G/4R	Duple Dom.II C49F	Bluebird Buses 9.93
170	LSK528	1981	Leyland PSU3G/4R	Duple Dom.II C49F	Bluebird Buses 8.93
171	866NHT	1981	Leyland PSU3G/4R	Duple Dom.II C49F	Bluebird Buses 8.93

167-71 were previously registered PSO2727-9/31/2W after being TSV718-22 and were originally ORS106-10W.

188	DWF188V	1979	Bristol VRT/SL3/6LXB	ECW H43/31F	East Midland 10.93
190	DWF190V	1979	Bristol VRT/SL3/6LXB	ECW H43/31F	East Midland 10.93
191	DWF191V	1979	Bristol VRT/SL3/6LXB	ECW H43/31F	East Midland 10.93
193	DWF193V	1979	Bristol VRT/SL3/6LXB	ECW H43/31F	East Midland 10.93

213	HNE252V	1980	Leyland PSU5C/4R	Duple Dom.II C53F	Bluebird Buses 8.94
214	HNE254V	1980	Leyland PSU5C/4R	Duple Dom.II C53F	Bluebird Buses 8.94
215	JND260V	1980	Leyland PSU5C/4R	Duple Dom.II C53F	Bluebird Buses 8.94
219	NPA229W	1981	Leyland PSU3E/4R	Plaxton Sup.IV C53F	East Midland 8.94
221	WFS135W	1980	Leyland PSU3F/4R	Alexander AYS B53F	Fife Scottish 8.94
222	WFS136W	1980	Leyland PSU3F/4R	Alexander AYS B53F	Fife Scottish 8.94
223	WFS137W	1980	Leyland PSU3F/4R	Alexander AYS B53F	Fife Scottish 8.94

252 - 255   1990   Mercedes Benz 709D   Alexander AM B25F

252	G252TSL	253	G253TSL	254	G254TSL	255	G255TSL

309 - 312   1990   Mercedes Benz 709D   Alexander AM DP25F

309	G198PAO	310	G199PAO	311	G200PAO	312	G201PAO

472	F637OHD	1989	DAF MB230LB	Van Hool Alizee C53FT	Selkent 10.94
561	K561GSA	1993	Volvo B10M-60	Plaxton Prem. DP51F	
570	K570GSA	1993	Volvo B10M-60	Plaxton Prem. DP51F	Bluebird Buses 10.93
601	UYJ654	1962	AEC Routemaster	Park Royal H36/28R	United Counties 9.92
602	EDS50A	1960	AEC Routemaster	Park Royal H36/28R	London Transport 5.85
603	NSG636A	1962	AEC Routemaster	Park Royal H36/28R	East Midland 10.92
604	YTS820A	1963	AEC Routemaster	Park Royal H36/28R	East Midland 10.92
605	USK625	1961	AEC Routemaster	Park Royal H36/28R	East Midland 10.92
607	LDS201A	1963	AEC Routemaster	Park Royal H36/28R	London Transport 5.86
608	490CLT	1962	AEC Routemaster	Park Royal H32/25RD	Selkent 11.94
609	XSL596A	1962	AEC Routemaster	Park Royal H36/28R	Hampshire Bus 10.87
614	LDS210A	1962	AEC Routemaster	Park Royal H36/28R	Hampshire Bus 10.87
616	ALD968B	1964	AEC Routemaster	Park Royal H36/28R	Hampshire Bus 10.87

601-4 originally registered 224CLT, WLT560, 164CLT, 599CLT. 605 originally registered WLT980 then USK625. 607/9/14 originally registered 607DYE, 289CLT, 245CLT.

621	J917LEM	1991	Volvo B10M-60	Plaxton 3500 C46FT	Selkent 10.94
622	J919LEM	1991	Volvo B10M-60	Plaxton 3500 C46FT	Selkent 10.94
623	J455FSR	1992	Volvo B10M-60	Plaxton 3500 C46FT	Selkent 10.94
625	G386PNV	1990	Volvo B10M-60	Plaxton 3500 C46FT	10.94
650	FES831W	1981	Volvo B58-61	Duple Dom. II B59F	
651	NMY634E	1967	AEC Routemaster	Park Royal H32/24F	Kelvin Central 8.93

ANCILLARY VEHICLES

702	RWH621S	1978	Leyland Buffalo	Recovery wagon	Ribble 9.89
705	Q910FRU	1960	AEC Matador	Recovery wagon	Hampshire Bus 5.90
710	L230RTS	1994	Ford Transit	Pick-up truck	
723	D956XSO	1987	Ford Transt	Van	

South East London & Kent Bus Co. Ltd., 180 Bromley Road, Catford, London SE6 2XA

Formed on 5 December 1988 as a result of the restructuring of London Buses Ltd., Selkent gradually adopted its own vehicle policy which led to a number of new types of bus entering the fleet. The company's Orpington area operations are maintained under the Roundabout banner. Sold to Stagecoach Holdings on 6 September 1994, as part of the sale agreement the company is required to retain a red livery. The coaching unit operated under the Selkent Travel banner was closed in October 1994 when some of its activities were transferred to Stagecoach East London.

Livery : Red (unrelieved)

Depots : Bromley (TB); Catford (TL); Orpington (OB); Plumstead (PD).

In the lists below, a 't' suffix to fleet numbers signifies a driver training vehicle. The 't' is for reference only and is not carried on the vehicles concerned.

Selkent Fleet list

DT28	49CLT	1990	Dennis Dart 8.5SDL	Carlyle	DP28F
DT30	G30TGW	1990	Dennis Dart 8.5SDL	Carlyle	DP28F
DT31	G31TGW	1990	Dennis Dart 8.5SDL	Carlyle	DP28F

DT28 was originally registered G28TGW

DT32 - DT55   1990 Dennis Dart 8.5SDL   Carlyle B28F

32	VLT240	35	G35TGW	38	G38TGW	40	G49TGW
33	G33TGW	36	G36TGW	39	G39TGW	55	WLT575
34	G34TGW	37	G37TGW				

Dt32/55 were originally registered G32/55TGW

DW59 - DW71   1991 Dennis Dart 8.8SDL   Wright B28F

59	JDZ2359	61	JDZ2361	63	JDZ2363	65	JDZ2365
60	JDZ2360	62	JDZ2362	64	JDZ2364	71	JDZ2371

FM1 - FM10   1993 Fiat 59.12   Marshall B23F

1	K521EFL	4	K524EFL	7	K527EFL	9	K529EFL
2	K522EFL	5	K525EFL	8	K528EFL	10	K530EFL
3	K523EFL	6	K526EFL				

L7 - L145

1986 Leyland ONLXB/1RH   ECW H42/26D

7	C807BYY	60	C60CHM	91	C91CHM	120	C120CHM
9	C809BYY	61	C61CHM	92	C92CHM	121	C121CHM
10	C810BYY	62	C62CHM	94	C94CHM	122	C122CHM
11	C811BYY	64	C64CHM	97	C97CHM	123	D123FYM
12	C812BYY	67	C67CHM	98	C98CHM	124	D124FYM
15	C815BYY	68	C68CHM	103	C103CHM	125	D125FYM
18	C818BYY	69	C69CHM	104	C104CHM	126	D126FYM
19	C819BYY	70	C70CHM	105	C105CHM	127	D127FYM
23	C23CHM	71	C71CHM	106	C106CHM	128	D128FYM
28	C28CHM	72	C72CHM	107	C107CHM	129	D129FYM
29	C29CHM	73	C73CHM	108	C108CHM	130	D130FYM
30	C30CHM	74	C74CHM	109	C109CHM	131	D131FYM
42	C42CHM	75	C75CHM	110	C110CHM	132	D132FYM
43	C43CHM	76	C76CHM	111	C111CHM	133	D133FYM
44	C44CHM	77	C77CHM	112	C112CHM	134	D134FYM
48	C48CHM	80	C80CHM	114	C114CHM	136	D136FYM
51	C51CHM	81	C81CHM	115	C115CHM	137	D137FYM
53	C53CHM	82	C82CHM	116	C116CHM	141	D141FYM
54	C54CHM	83	C83CHM	117	C117CHM	142	D142FYM
55	C55CHM	86	C86CHM	118	C118CHM	144	D144FYM
57	C57CHM	87	C87CHM	119	C119CHM	145	D145FYM

L260	VLT20	1987	Leyland ONLXB/1RH	Leyland CH42/26D
L262	VLT14	1987	Leyland ONLXB/1RH	Leyland CH42/26D
L263	VLT9	1987	Leyland ONLXB/1RH	Leyland CH42/26D

L260/2/3 were originally registered D260FYM & D262/3FUL

LA1 - LA16

1992 Dennis Lance   Alexander B39D

1	J101WSC	5	J105WSC	9	J109WSC	13	J113WSC
2	J102WSC	6	J106WSC	10	J110WSC	14	J114WSC
3	J103WSC	7	J107WSC	11	J411WSC	15	J115WSC
4	J104WSC	8	J108WSC	12	J112WSC	16	J116WSC

LV1 - LV12

1994 Dennis Lance   Plaxton Verde B42D

1	L201YAG	4	L204YAG	7	L207YAG	10	L210YAG
2	L202YAG	5	L205YAG	8	L208YAG	11	L211YAG
3	L203YAG	6	L206YAG	9	L209YAG	12	WLT461

LV12 was originally registered L212YAG

MA9 - MA25

1988 Mercedes Benz 811D   Alexander B28F

9	F609XMS	16	F616XMS	20	F620XMS	24	F624XMS
14	F614XMS	17	F617XMS	21	F621XMS	25	F625XMS
15	F615XMS	19	F619XMS				

MA29 - MA41

1989 Mercedes Benz 811D   Alexander B28F

29	F629XMS	30	F630XMS	31	F631XMS	41	F641XMS

MC1	WLT491	1989	Mercedes Benz 811D	Carlyle DP28F	*Demonstrator 1990*
MC2	H882LOX	1990	Mercedes Benz 811D	Carlyle B33F	
MC3	H883LOX	1990	Mercedes Benz 811D	Carlyle B33F	
MC4	WLT400	1990	Mercedes Benz 811D	Carlyle DP28F	
MC5	H885LOX	1990	Mercedes Benz 811D	Carlyle B33F	

Mc1/4 were originally registered F430BOP & H884LOX

| MR27 | E127KYW | 1987 | MCW Metrorider MF150/38 | MCW B25F |
| MR46 | E146KYW | 1987 | MCW Metrorider MF150/38 | MCW B25F |

MRL141 - MRL152 1990 Optare Metrorider   Optare B26F

141	H141UUA	144	H144UUA	147	H147UUA	150	H150UUA
142	H142UUA	145	H145UUA	148	H148UUA	151	H151UUA
143	H143UUA	146	H146UUA	149	H149UUA	152	H152UUA

MRL153 - MRL176 1991 Optare Metrorider   Optare B26F

153	H153UUA	163	H163WWT	168	H168WWT	173	H173WWT
154	H154UUA	164	H564WWR	169	H169WWT	174	H174WWT
160	H160WWT	165	H165WWT	170	H170WWT	175	H175WWT
161	H161WWT	166	H166WWT	171	H171WWT	176	H176WWT
162	H162WWT	167	H167WWT	172	H172WWT

MT4	F394DHL	1988	Mercedes Benz 709D	Reeve Burgess B20F
MW1	HDZ2601	1990	Mercedes Benz 811D	Wright B26F
MW2	HDZ2602	1990	Mercedes Benz 811D	Wright B26FL

MW3 - MW7   1990 Mercedes Benz 811D   Wright B26F

| 3 | HDZ2603 | 5 | HDZ2605 | 6 | HDZ2606 | 7 | HDZ2607 |
| 4 | HDZ2604 |

| MW8 | HDZ2608 | 1990 | Mercedes Benz 811D | Wright B26FL |

MW9 - MW13   1990 Mercedes Benz 811D   Wright B26F

| 9 | HDZ2609 | 11 | HDZ2611 | 12 | HDZ2612 | 13 | HDZ2613 |
| 10 | HDZ2610 |

MW14	HDZ2614	1990	Mercedes Benz 811D	Wright B26FL
MW15	HDZ2615	1990	Mercedes Benz 811D	Wright B26F
MW16	HDZ2616	1990	Mercedes Benz 811D	Wright B26F
RH1	C501DYM	1986	Iveco 49.10	Robin Hood DP21F
RH5	C505DYM	1986	Iveco 49.10	Robin Hood B21F
RH22	D522FYL	1986	Iveco 49.10	Robin Hood B21F

T49 - T86   1979 Leyland TNLXB/2RR   Park Royal H44/22D

| 49 | WYV49T | 56 | WYV56T | 79 | CUL79V | 86t | CUL86V |

T98 - T250   1980 Leyland TNLXB/2RR   Park Royal H44/22D

98t	CUL98V	168	CUL168V	208	CUL208V	236	EYE236V
114t	CUL114V	169	CUL169V	209	CUL209V	237	EYE237V
120t	CUL120V	179	CUL179V	215	CUL215V	238t	EYE238V
130t	CUL130V	180	CUL180V	224t	CUL224V	240	EYE240V
137t	CUL137V	189	CUL189V	225	CUL225V	244	EYE244V
142t	CUL142V	190	CUL190V	229	EYE229V	250	EYE250V
163	CUL163V	198	CUL198V	233	EYE233V

T267 - T368   1981 Leyland TNLXB/2RR   Leyland H44/24D

| 267 | GYE267W | 288 | KYN288X | 345 | KYV345X | 361 | KYV361X |
| 282 | KYN282X | 305 | KYN305X | 348 | KYV348X | 368 | KYN368X |

T397 - T674

1982 Leyland TNLXB/2RR   Leyland H44/24D

397	KYV397X	451	KYV451X	511	KYV511X	611	NUW611Y
410	KYV410X	455	KYV455X	523	KYV533X	616	NUW616Y
420	KYV420X	474	KYV474X	594	NUW594Y	618	NUW618Y
442	KYV442X	487	KYV487X	596	NUW596Y	674	NUW674Y
447	KYV447X						

T680 - T791

1983 Leyland TNLXB/2RR   Leyland H44/24D

680	OHV680Y	721	OHV721Y	762	OHV762Y	780	OHV780Y
700	OHV700Y	728	OHV728Y	770	OHV770Y	785	OHV785Y
710	OHV710Y	740	OHV740Y	771	OHV771Y	791	OHV791Y
714	OHV714Y	748	OHV748Y	772	OHV772Y		

T797 - T874

1983 Leyland TNLXB/2RR   Leyland H44/26D

797	OHV797Y	816	RYK816Y	834	A834SUL	850	A850SUL
800	OHV800Y	818	RYK818Y	836	A836SUL	854	A854SUL
801	OHV801Y	820	RYK820Y	837	A837SUL	855	A855SUL
804	OHV804Y	821	RYK821Y	838	A838SUL	856	A856SUL
805	OHV805Y	822	RYK822Y	841	A841SUL	857	A857SUL
809	OHV809Y	823	A823SUL	842	A842SUL	858	A858SUL
810	OHV810Y	824	A824SUL	843	A843SUL	859	A859SUL
812	OHV812Y	825	A825SUL	845	A845SUL	866	A866SUL
813	OHV813Y	828	A828SUL	847	A847SUL	868	A868SUL
814	OHV814Y	829	A829SUL	848	A848SUL	874	A874SUL
815	OHV815Y	830	A830SUL				

T877	A877SUL	1983	Leyland TNTL11/2RR	Leyland H44/26D
T880	A880SUL	1983	Leyland TNTL11/2RR	Leyland H44/26D

T881 - T885

1983 Letland TNTL11/2RR   Leyland H44/26D

881	A881SUL	882	A882SUL	883	A883SUL	885	A885SUL

T918 - T1125

1984 Leyland TNLXB/2RR   Leyland H44/26D

918	A918SYE	1028	A628THV	1077	A67THX	1106	B106WUV
925	A925SYE	1029	A629THV	1079	B79WUV	1108	B108WUV
926	A926SYE	1030	A630THV	1081	B81WUV	1110	B110WUV
950	A950SYE	1031	A631THV	1083	B83WUV	1112	B112WUV
951	A951SYE	1032	A632THV	1084	B84WUV	1113	B113WUV
961	A961SYE	1034	A634THV	1089	B89WUV	1114	B114WUV
976	A976SYE	1035	A635THV	1091	B91WUV	1115	B115WUV
978	A978SYE	1036	A636THV	1092	B92WUV	1116	B116WUV
988	A988SYE	1045	A645THV	1093	B93WUV	1117	B117WUV
996	A996SYE	1948	A648THV	1096	B96WUV	1118	B118WUV
999	A999SYE	1052	A652THV	1097	B97WUV	1119	B119WUV
1003	A603THV	1065	A65THX	1099	B99WUV	1121	B121WUV
1007	A607THV	1066	A66THX	1100	B100WUV	1122	B122WUV
1013	A613THV	1067	A67THX	1101	B101WUV	1124	B124WUV
1025	A625THV	1076	A76THX	1103	B103WUV	1125	B125WUV
1027	A627THV						

T1126	WDA1T	1978	Leyland TNLXB/1RF	Park Royal CH43/29F	*West Midlands PTE 1984*
T1127	WDA2T	1979	Leyland TNLXB/1RF	Park Royal CH43/29F	*West Midlands PTE 1984*
T1130	WDA5T	1979	Leyland TNLXB/1RF	Park Royal CH43/29F	*West Midlands PTE 1984*

Stagecoach (South) Ltd., Lewes Enterprise Centre, 112 Malling Street,
Lewes BN7 2RB

Sussex Coastline Buses Ltd., Lewes Enterprise Centre, 112 Malling Street,
Lewes BN7 2RB

Within a month of its purchase by Stagecoach, Southdown took over the operations of small
independent Cedar Coaches of Worthing and two months later gained further expansion by the
acquisition of Portsmouth Citybus whose services were integrated with those operated in that area
by Southdown under the Southdown Portsmouth banner. After this purchase was referred to the
Monopolies & Mergers Commission, the Portsmouth operations were sold to Transit Holdings on 18
January 1991 together with 104 vehicles. Southdown was renamed Sussex Coastline Buses Ltd.
on 4 April 1992 when it was merged with Hampshire Bus and Hastings Buses as part of
Stagecoach (South) Ltd.

Depots : Chichester; Havant; Worthing *Outstations : Henfield; Leigh Park; Littlehampton.*

Hampshire Bus Co.Ltd., Lewes Enterprise Centre, 112 Malling Street, Lewes BN7 2RB

Purchased from the National Bus Company by Skipburn Ltd. on behalf of Stagecoach together with
Pilgrim Coaches, the latter company was wound up within three weeks of its acquisition, its tiny
fleet being transferred to Hampshire Bus. Later that year the company's Southampton operations
were sold to Musterphantom Ltd. (Solent Blue Line) along with 82 vehicles. Renamed Stagecoach
(South) Ltd. on 30 March 1991 it was fully integrated with the former Southdown and Hastings
Buses operations on 4 April 1992.

Depots : Andover; Basingstoke; Winchester. *Outstations : Bishops Waltham; Marlborough;
Petersfield; Stockbridge.*

Stagecoach Hants & Surrey Ltd., Lewes Enterprise Centre, 112 Malling Street, Lewes BN7 2RB

Formed by the NBC with the merging of Aldershot & District Traction Co. Ltd., and Thames Valley
Traction Co. Ltd. and named Alder Valley, it was split into two by Frontsource Ltd. who purchased it
from the NBC. The southern part (Alder Valley) was sold to Q-Drive in 1988. Although the stage
carriage operations were sold to Stagecoach (South) Ltd. in October 1992, the Londonlink express
services were not included in the deal. The Alton outstation was transferred from Hampshire Bus in
1993.

Depots : Aldershot; Hindhead. *Outstation : Alton.*

South Coast Buses Ltd., Lewes Enterprise Centre, 112 Malling Street, Lewes BN7 2RB

Formed in March 1983 as a result of the NBC's restructuring of East Kent and Maidstone & District,
Hastings & District began its operations in May of that year. Purchased by Stagecoach Holdings in
December 1989 along with its share in Hastings Top Line Buses, Eastbourne Buses 49%

shareholding in the latter was acquired a few days later and ultimately this company was wound up. When Hastings & District was merged with Southdown and Hampshire Bus as part of Stagecoach (South) Ltd. in April 1992, changing its name to South Coast Buses in the process, it gained Southdown's eastern area operations in the Lewes/Eastbourne area.

Depots : Eastbourne; Hastings. *Outstations : Lewes; Rye; Seaford; Uckfield.*

Coastline   Fleet list

5	D935EBP	1986	Iveco 49.10		Robin Hood	B19F	Southdown 4.92
31	F61AVV	1989	Iveco 49.10		Robin Hood	B25F	Hampshire Bus 4.92
34	G34PSR	1989	Iveco 49.10		Phoenix	B23F	Southdown 4.92
45	E65BVS	1988	Iveco 49.10		Robin Hood	B23F	Southdown 4.92

120 - 126   1980 Leyland NL116L11/1R   Leyland B52F
(ex. Southdown 4.92)

120	GYJ920V	123	HFG923V	125	OUF262W	126	SYC852
122	GYJ922V	124	JNJ124V				

124/5 were previously registered DSV943 & LYJ145 and were originally HFG924V & JWV125W.
126 was originally registered JWV126W.

127	FDV830V	1980	Leyland NL116L11/1R	Leyland B52F	Hampshire Bus 5.92
128	FDV831V	1980	Leyland NL116L11/1R	Leyland B52F	Hampshire Bus 6.92

129 - 135   1982 Leyland NL116AL11/1R   Leyland B49F (*B45F)
(ex. Southdown 4.92)

129*	415DCD	131	411DCD	132*	YLJ332	135	405DCD
130	400DCD						

129-32/5 were originally registered RUF429-32/5X.

139	FDV829V	1980	Leyland NL116L11/1R	Leyland B52F	Hampshire Bus 5.92
209	G809RTS	1989	Leyland ONLXB/1R	Alexander DPH47/35F	Hampshire Bus 4.92
220	J720GAP	1992	Leyland ON2R56G13Z4	Alexander DPH47/27F	South Coast Buses .94
221	J721GAP	1992	Leyland ON2R56G13Z4	Alexander DPH47/27F	South Coast Buses .94
222	J722GAP	1992	Leyland ON2R56G13Z4	Alexander RL DP47/27F	Southdown 4.92
223	J623GCR	1991	Leyland ON2R56G13Z4	Alexander RL H47/30F	Southdown 4.92
224	J624GCR	1991	Leyland ON2R56G13Z4	Alexander RL H47/30F	Southdown 4.92
228	G708TCD	1990	Leyland ON2R56G13Z4	Alexander RL H51/34F	Hampshire Bus 5.93
229	G709TCD	1990	Leyland ON2R56G13Z4	Alexander RL H51/34F	Hampshire Bus 5.93
230	G710TCD	1990	Leyland ON2R56G13Z4	Alexander RL H51/34F	Hampshire Bus 5.93

231 - 234   1990 Leyland ON2R56G13Z4   Alexander RL H51/34F
(ex. Southdown 4.92)

231	G701TCD	232	G702TCD	233	G703TCD	234	G704TCD

237 - 240   1992 Leyland ON2R50G13Z4   Alexander RL DPH43/27F
(ex.Hants & Surrey .94)

237	K237NHC	238	K238NHC	239	K239NHC	240	K240NHC

241 - 245   1993 Volvo YN2RV18Z4   Northern Counties DPH43/25F

241	L241SDY	243	L243SDY	244	L244SDY	245	L245SDY
242	L242SDY						

304 - 309

1989 Volvo D10M NCME DPH43/33F
(ex. Southdown 4.92)

304	F304MYJ	306	F306MYJ	308	F306MYJ	309	F309MYJ
305	F305MYJ	307	F307MYJ				

336	XAP636S	1978	Bristol VRT/SL3/6LXB	ECW H43/31F	Southdown 4.92
347	AAP647T	1978	Bristol VRT/SL3/6LXB	ECW H43/31F	Southdown 4.92
351	JWV251W	1980	Bristol VRT/SL3/6LXB	ECW DPH43/31F	Southdown 4.92
355	JWV255W	1980	Bristol VRT/SL3/6LXB	ECW H43/31F	Southdown 4.92
356	JWV256W	1980	Bristol VRT/SL3/6LXB	ECW H43/31F	Southdown 4.92
359	DBV29W	1980	Bristol VRT/SL3/6LXB	ECW DPH43/31F	Southdown 4.92
362	AAP662T	1979	Bristol VRT/SL3/6LXB	ECW H43/28F	Hampshire Bus 6.93
265	DBV25W	1980	Bristol VRT/SL3/6LXB	ECW DPH43/31F	Southdown 4.92
367	JWV267W	1981	Bristol VRT/SL3/6LXB	ECW DPH43/31F	Southdown 4.92
368	JWV268W	1981	Bristol VRT/SL3/6LXB	ECW H43/31F	Southdown 4.92
372	AAP662T	1979	Bristol VRT/SL3/6LXB	ECW H43/28F	Hampshire Bus 6.93
375	JWV275W	1981	Bristol VRT/SL3/6LXB	ECW H43/31F	Southdown 4.92
376	JWV276W	1981	Bristol VRT/SL3/6LXB	ECW H43/31F	Southdown 4.92
460	G910KWF	1989	Iveco 49.10	Reeve Burgess B25F	East Midland 10.93
478	E202EPB	1987	Iveco 49.10	Robin Hood B25F	Hants & Surrey .94
479	E203EBP	1987	Iveco 49.10	Robin Hood B25F	Hants & Surrey .94

488 - 492

1990 Iveco A49.10 Phoenix B23F
(ex. Southdown 4.92)

488	G418RYJ	490	G420RYJ	491	G421RYJ	492	G422RYJ
489	G419RYJ						

551 - 579

1992 Dennis Dart 9.8SDL Alexander AM Dash B40F

551	J551GCD	557	K557NHC	562	K562NHC	567	K567NHC
552	J552GCD	558	K558NHC	563	K563NHC	568	K568NHC
553	K553NHC	559	K559NHC	564	K564NHC	569	K569NHC
554	K554NHC	560	K560NHC	565	K565NHC	574	K574NHC
555	K655NHC	561	K561NHC	566	K566NHC	579	K579NHC
556	K556NHC						

610 - 635

1994 Volvo B10M-55 Alexander PS DP48F

610	M610APN	615	M615APN	625	L625TDY	629	L629TDY
611	M611APN	621	L621TDY	626	L626TDY	630	L630TDY
612	M612APN	622	L622TDY	627	L627TDY	631	L631TDY
613	M613APN	623	L623TDY	628	L628TDY	635	L635TDY
614	M614APN	624	L624TDY				

656	L346KCK	1994	Volvo B10M-55	Alexander PS DP48F	Ribble 7.94
657	L347KCK	1994	Volvo B10M-55	Alexander PS DP48F	Ribble 7.94
658	L338KCK	1994	Volvo B10M-55	Alexander PS DP48F	Ribble 7.94
670	AAP670T	1979	Bristol VRT/SL3/6LXB	ECW H43/31F	Southdown 4.92
678	EAP978V	1979	Bristol VRT/SL3/6LXB	ECW H43/31F	Hampshire Bus 5.93

684 - 696

1980 Bristol VRT/SL3/6LXB ECW H43/31F
(ex. Southdown 4.92)

684	EAP984V	686	EAP986V	690	EAP990V	692	EAP992V
685	EAP985V	687	EAP987V	691	EAP991V	696	EAP996V

787	AET187T	1979	Bristol VRT/SL3/6LXB	ECW H43/31F		East Midland 10.93
953	VPF283S	1978	Bristol VRT/SL3/6LXB	ECW H43/31F		Hampshire Bus .94
1006	896HOD	1985	Volvo B10M-61	Plaxton 3500 C40F		Fife Scottish .91
1007	495FFJ	1985	Volvo B10M-61	Plaxton 3500 C52F		Fife Scottish .91

1006/7 were originally registered B192/3CGA.

| 1193 | YEL93Y | 1982 | Leyland PSU5E/4R | ECW C52F | | Hampshire Bus 5.93 |
| 1194 | YEL94Y | 1982 | Leyland PSU5E/4R | ECW C55F | | Hampshire Bus 5.93 |

2901 - 2904   1988 MCW MF158/9   MCW B33F
(ex. Southdown 4.92)

| 2901 | F561HPP | | 2902 | F562HPP | | 2903 | F563HPP | | 2904 | 564HPP |

2906	416DCD	1988	MCW MF158/10	MCW B31F		Southdown 4.92
2907	417DCD	1988	MCW MF158/1	MCW B31F		Hampshire Bus .94
2908	418DCD	1988	MCW MF158/3	MCW DP33F		Southdown 4.92

2906-8 were originally registered F816CWJ, F817DWG & E518YWF.

SPECIAL EVENTS VEHICLES

0135	CD7045	1922	Leyland G7	Short O27/24RO	Southdown 4.92
0424	424DCD	1964	Leyland PD3/4	NCME CO39/30F	Southdown 4.92
0813	UF4813	1929	Leyland TD1	Brush O27/24RO	Southdown 4.92

Hampshire Bus   Fleet list

21	F21PSL	1989	Iveco 49.10	Robin Hood B23F	Southdown 1.91
22	F22PSL	1989	Iveco 49.10	Robin Hood B23F	Southdown 1.91
23	F23PSL	1989	Iveco 49.10	Robin Hood B23F	Southdown 3.91
25	F25PSL	1989	Iveco 49.10	Robin Hood B23F	Southdown 12.90
26	F26PSL	1989	Iveco 49.10	Robin Hood B23F	Southdown 12.90
30	G30PSR	1989	Iveco 49.10	Robin Hood B23F	Southdown 8.91
32	F62AVV	1989	Iveco 49.10	Robin Hood B25F	United Counties 1989
33	E233JRF	1987	Iveco 49.10	Robin Hood B25F	Southdown 1.91
36	G36SSR	1989	Iveco 49.10	Phoenix B23F	Stagecoach 4.90
37	G37SSR	1989	Iveco 49.10	Phoenix B23F	Stagecoach 4.90

38 - 43   1989 Iveco 49.10   Phoenix B23F
(ex. Stagecoach 5.90)

| 38 | G38SSR | | 39 | G39SSR | | 42 | G42SSR | | 43 | G43SSR |

104	AYJ104T	1979	Leyland LN113510A/1R	Leyland B52F	South Coast Buses .94
106	DRU6T	1979	Leyland LN11351A/1R	Leyland B49F	*Hants & Dorset 1983*
119	GYJ919V	1980	Leyland NL116L11/1R	Leyland B52F	Coastline .93
121	GYJ921V	1980	Leyland NL116L11/1R	Leyland B52F	Coastline .93

133 - 138   1982 Leyland NL116AL11/1R   Leyland B49F

| 133 | 420DCD | | 136 | 406DCD | | 137 | 407DCD | | 138 | 410DCD |
| 134 | HUF451X | | | | | | | | | |

*133 was originally registered RUF433X. 134 was previously registered XLD244 and was originally
RUF434X. 136-8 were originally registered RUF436-8X.*

151	WPR151S	1978	Leyland LN11351A/1R	Leyland B49F	*Hants & Dorset 1983*
152	WPR152S	1978	Leyland LN11351A/1R	Leyland B49F	*Hants & Dorset 1983*
156	WFX256S	1978	Leyland LN11351A/1R	Leyland DP48F	*Hants & Dorset 1983*
164	VFX984S	1978	Leyland LN11351A/1R	Leyland B49F	*Hants & Dorset 1983*
166	MLJ922P	1976	Leyland LN11351/1R	Leyland B49F	*Hants & Dorset 1983*
167	MLJ917P	1976	Leyland LN11351/1R	Leyland B49F	Coastline 6.92
168	WYJ168S	1978	Leyland LN11351A/1R	Leyland B48F	Coastline 7.94
186	CBV776S	1978	Leyland LN11351A/1R	Leyland B49F	Southdown 9.90
190	TEL490R	1977	Leyland LN11351A/1R	Leyland DP48F	*Hants & Dorset 1983*
192	AYJ92T	1979	Leyland LN113510A/1R	Leyland B52F	Southdown 4.92
196	RJT146R	1977	Leyland LN11351A/1R	Leyland B49F	*Hants & Dorset 1983*

201 - 206   1988 Leyland ONLXB/2RZ   Alexander RL DPH51/36F

201	F201MSL	203	F203MSL	205	F205MSL	206	F206MSL
202	F202MSL	204	F204MSL				

207 - 214   1989 Leyland ONLXB/2RZ   Alexander RL DPH47/35F

207	G807RTS	210	G210SSL	212	G212SSL	214	G214SSL
208	G808RTS	211	G211SSL	213	G213SSL		

215 - 219   1990 Leyland ON2R56G13Z4   Alexander RL DPH51/34F

215	H815CBP	217	H817CBP	218	H818CBP	219	H819CBP
216	H816CBP						

246 - 250   1993 Volvo YN2RV18Z4   Northern Counties DPH43/25F

246	L246SDY	248	L248SDY	249	L249SDY	250	L250SDY
247	L247SDY						

315	GLJ467N	1974	Bristol VRT/SL2/6LXB	ECW H43/31F	*Hants & Dorset 1983*
321	VTV171S	1978	Bristol VRT/SL3/6LXB	ECW H43/31F	Coastline 1.94
322	VTV172S	1978	Bristol VRT/SL3/6LXB	ECW H43/31F	Coastline 1.94
323	XRR173S	1978	Bristol VRT/SL3/6LXB	ECW H43/31F	Coastline 1.94
349	AAP649T	1978	Bristol VRT/SL3/6LXB	ECW H43/31F	Coastline 8.92
353	JWV253W	1980	Bristol VRT/SL3/6LXB	ECW DPH43/31F	Coastline 7.94
358	JWV258W	1980	Bristol VRT/SL3/6LXB	ECW H43/31F	Coastline 9.92
369	JWV269W	1981	Bristol VRT/SL3/6LXB	ECW DPH43/31F	Coastline 7.94
374	JWV274W	1981	Bristol VRT/SL3/6LXB	ECW H43/31F	Coastline 2.93
377	EAP977V	1979	Bristol VRT/SL3/6LXB	ECW H43/31F	Coastline 10.92
380	EAP980V	1979	Bristol VRT/SL3/6LXB	ECW H43/31F	Coastline 10.92
382	EAP982V	1979	Bristol VRT/SL3/6LXB	ECW H43/31F	Coastline 10.92

387 - 397   1978 Bristol VRT/SL3/6LXB   ECW H43/31F
(ex. Hants & Dorset 1983)

387	VPR486S	392	VPR491S	394	HFG193T	396	YEL3T
388	VPR487S	393	VPR492S	395	YEL2T	397	YEL4T
391	VPR490S						

394 was originally registered YEL1T.

422	FDV818V	1980	Bristol VRT/SL3/6LXB	ECW H43/31F	Devon General 11.88
432	ELJ212V	1979	Bristol VRT/SL3/6LXB	ECW H43/31F	*Hants & Dorset 1983*
433	FDV834V	1980	Bristol VRT/SL3/6LXB	ECW H43/31F	Devon General 1.89
435	FDV839V	1980	Bristol VRT/SL3/6LXB	ECW H43/31F	Devon General 10.88

438 - 444

1980 Bristol VRT/SL3/6LXB   ECW H43/31F
(ex. Hants & Dorset 1983)

438	KRU838W	440	*KRU840W	441	KRU841W	444	KRU844W
439	KRU839W						

446 - 450

1981 Bristol VRT/SL3/6LXB   ECW H43/31F
(ex. Devon General 11.88)

446	LFJ874W	448	LFJ870W	449	LFJ875W	450	LFJ880W
447	LFJ881W						

524 - 540

1992 Dennis Dart 9.8SDL   Alexander AM Dash B41F (*B40F)

524	J524GCD	529	J529GCD	534	J534GCD	538*	J538GCD
525	J525GCD	530	J530GCD	535*	J535GCD	539*	J539GCD
526	J526GCD	531	J531GCD	536*	J536GCD	540*	J540GCD
527	J527GCD	532	J532GCD	537*	J537GCD		
528	J528GCD	533	J533GCD				

542 - 545

1992 Dennis Dart 9.9SDL   Alexander AM Dash B40F
(ex.Coastline 10.93)

542	J542GCD	543	J543GCD	544	J544GCD	545	J545GCD

546 - 550

1992 Dennis Dart 9.8SDL   Alexander AM Dash B40F

546	J546GCD	548	J548GCD	549	J549GCD	550	J550GCD
547	J547GCD						

580	K580NHC	1992	Dennis Dart 9.8SDL	Alexander Dash B40F	Coastline 10.93
581	J701YRM	1991	Dennis Dart 9.8SDL	Alexander Dash B40F	Cumberland 10.92
582	J703YRM	1991	Dennis Dart 9.8SDL	Alexander Dash B40F	Cumberland 10.92

841 - 843

1990 Mercedes Benz 709D   Alexander AM DP25F

841	G71APO	842	G72APO	843	G73APO

846 - 850

1990 Mercedes Benz 709D   Alexander B23F

846	G976ARV	848	G978ARV	849	H679HTP	850	H680BTP
847	G977ARV						

950	TPE156S	1978	Bristol VRT/SL3/6LXB	ECW H43/31F	Hants & Surrey 5.93
956	GGM86W	1980	Bristol VRT/SL3/6LXB	ECW H43/31F	Hants & Surrey 2.93
965	WJM825T	1979	Bristol VRT/SL3/6LXB	ECW H43/31F	Hants & Surrey 2.93
966	WJM826T	1979	Bristol VRT/SL3/6LXB	ECW H43/31F	Hants & Surrey 2.93
977	CJH117V	1980	Bristol VRT/SL3/6LXB	ECW H43/31F	Hants & Surrey 2.93
988	KKK888V	1980	Bristol VRT/SL3/6LXB	ECW H43/31F	Hants & Surrey 2.93
1017	NFX667	1982	Leyland PSU5E/4R	Plaxton Sup.V C50F	Southdown 1.91
1170	ELJ208V	1979	Leyland PSU3E/4R	Plaxton Sup.IV C53F	*Shamrock & Rambler.84*
1176	NPJ476R	1976	Leyland LN11351A/1R	Leyland B49F	Hants & Surrey 12.92
1217	KPA368P	1975	Leyland LN11351A/1R	Leyland B49F	Hants & Srrey 12.92
1221	NEL121P	1976	Leyland LN11351A/1R	Leyland B49F	East Midland 10.92
1227	KPA378P	1975	Leyland LN11351/1R	Leyland B49F	Hants & Surrey 5.93
1247	LPF605P	1976	Leyland LN11351/1R	Leyland B49F	Hants & Surrey 2.93
2701	C701FKE	1986	Ford Transit 190	Dormobile B16F	East Kent 2.94

1017 was originally registered HHC367Y

162	FRP62V	1980	Leyland LN11351A/1R	Leyland B49F	Hampshire Bus .94
189	AYJ99T	1979	Leyland LN113510A/1R	Leyland B52F	Hampshire Bus 10.92
194	AYJ94T	1979	Leyland LN11351OA/1R	Leyland B52F	South Coast Buses .94
235	K235NHC	1992	Leyland ON2R50G13Z4	Alexander DPH43/27F	
236	K236NHC	1992	Leyland ON2R50G13Z4	Alexander DPH43/27F	

469 - 476   1986 Iveco 49.10   Robin Hood B21F
(ex.Alder Valley 10.92)

| 469 | D469WPM | 471 | D471WPM | 473 | D473WPM | 476 | D476WPM |
| 470 | D470WPM | | | | | | |

477	E201EPB	1987	Iveco 49.10	Robin Hood B21F	Alder Valley 10.92
480	E204EPB	1987	Iveco 49.10	Robin Hood B21F	Alder Valley 10.92
485	F695OPA	1988	Iveco 49.10	Carlyle B23F	Alder Valley 10.92
494	G864BPD	1989	Iveco 49.10	Carlyle B23F	Alder Valley 10.92
522	J522GCD	1992	Dennis Dart 9.5	Alexander Dash B41F	Hampshire Bus 10.92
523	J523GCD	1992	Dennis Dart 9.5	Alexander Dash B41F	Hampshire Bus 10.92

570 - 588   1992 Dennis Dart 9.8 SDL   Alexander AM Dash B40F

570	K570NHC	573	K573NHC	585	K585ODY	587	K587ODY
571	K571NHC	584	K584ODY	586	K586ODY	588	K588ODY
572	K572NHC						

759	BKE859T	1979	Bristol VRT/SL3/6LXB	ECW H43/31F	South Coast Buses .94
782	AET182T	1979	Bristol VRT/SL3/6LXB	ECW H43/31F	East Midland 10.93
798	CBV798S	1978	Leyland LN11351A/1R	Leyland B49F	Hampshire Bus 10.92

853 - 880   1993 Mercedes Benz 709D   Alexander (Belfast) B25F

853	K853ODY	860	K860ODY	867	K867ODY	874	K874ODY
854	K854ODY	861	K861ODY	868	K868ODY	875	K875ODY
855	K855ODY	862	K862ODY	869	K869ODY	876	K876ODY
856	K856ODY	863	K863ODY	870	K870ODY	877	K877ODY
857	K857ODY	864	K864ODY	871	K871ODY	878	K878ODY
858	K858ODY	865	K865ODY	872	K872ODY	879	K879ODY
859	K859ODY	866	K866ODY	873	K873ODY	880	K880ODY

955	GGM85W	1980	Bristol VRT/SL3/6LXB	ECW H43/31F	Alder Valley 10.92
960	GGM80W	1980	Bristol VRT/SL3/6LXB	ECW H43/31F	Alder Valley 10.92
961	GGM81W	1981	Bristol VRT/SL3/6LXB	ECW H43/31F	Alder Valley 10.92
962	GGM82W	1980	Bristol VRT/SL3/6LXB	ECW H43/31F	Alder Valley 10.92
968	WJM828T	1979	Bristol VRT/SL3/6LXB	ECW H43/31F	Alder Valley 10.92
969	WJM829T	1979	Bristol VRT/SL3/6LXB	ECW H43/31F	Alder Valley 10.92
972	WJM832T	1979	Bristol VRT/SL3/6LXB	ECW H43/31F	Alder Valley 10.92

979 - 995   1980 Bristol VRT/SL3/6LXB   ECW H43/31F
(ex.Alder Valley 10.92)

| 979 | CJH199V | 982 | CJH142V | 985 | CJH145V | 995 | GGM105W |
| 980 | CJH120V | | | | | | |

1182 - 1188

1977 Leyland LN11351A/1R   Leyland B49F
(ex.Alder Valley 10.92)

1182 NFN82R	1183 NFN83R	1188 NFN88R

1201 - 1232

1975 Leyland LN11351/1R   Leyland B49F
(ex.Alder Valley 10.92)

1201 HPK503N	1217 KPA368P	1223 KPA374P	1228 KPA383P
1203 HPK505N	1218 KPA369P	1227 KPA378P	1232 KPA383P
1215 KPA366P			

1236 - 1261

1976 Leyland LN11351A/1R   Leyland B49F
(ex.Alder Valley 10.92)

1236 KPA387P	1238 KPA389P	1256 NPJ477R	1261 NPJ482R
1237 KPA388P	1253 NPJ474R	1259 NPJ480R	

1264 - 1273

1977 Leyland LN11351A/1R   Leyland B49F
(ex.Alder Valley 10.92)

1264 NPJ485R	1271 TPE148S	1272 TPE149S	1273 TPE150S

1276	TPE169S	1978	Leyland LN11351A/1R	Leyland B49F	Alder Valley 10.92
1279	VPF295S	1978	Leyland LN11351A/1R	Leyland B49F	Alder Valley 10.92
1298	SGS504W	1981	Leyland TRCTL11/3R	Plaxton Sup.IV C50F	Alder Valley 10.92
1299	XGS762X	1981	Leyland TRCTL11/3R	Plaxton Sup.IV C51F	Alder Valley 10.92
2712	C712FKE	1976	Ford Transit 190	Dormobile B16F	East Kent .94
7611	UWV611S	1978	Bristol VRT/SL3/6LXB	ECW CO43/31F	South Coast Buses .93

South Coast Buses   Fleet list

101	AYJ101T	1979	Leyland LN113510A/1R	Leyland B52F	Hastings & District 4.92
102	AYJ102T	1979	Leyland LN113510A/1R	Leyland B52F	Coastline 7.92
103	AYJ103T	1979	Leyland LN113510A/1R	Leyland B52F	Coastline 7.92
105	AYJ105T	1979	Leyland LN113510A/1R	Leyland B52F	Coastline 7.92
107	AYJ107T	1979	Leyland LN113510A/1R	Leyland B52F	Southdown 4.92

109 - 118

1979 Leyland LN113510A/1R   Leyland B52F

109 ENJ909V	112 ENJ912V	115 ENJ915V	117 ENJ917V
110 ENJ910V	113 ENJ913V	116 ENJ916V	118 ENJ918V
111 ENJ911V	114 ENJ914V		

140	CPO98W	1980	Leyland NL106L11/1R	Leyland B41F	Coastline 10.92
141	CPO99W	1980	Leyland NL106L11/1R	Leyland DP40F	Hastings & District 4.92
142	CPO100W	1980	Leyland NL106L11/1R	Leyland DP40F	Hastings & District 4.92

143 - 146
1981 Leyland NL106AL11/1R — Leyland B41F (ex. Hastings & District 4.92)

143	CPO115W	144	CPO116W	145	ERV117W	146	ERV118W

147	BCW827V	1980	Leyland NL106L11/1R	Leyland B44F	Ribble 3.94
148	UFG48S	1977	Leyland LN11351A/1R	Leyland B52F	Southdown 4.92
154	VOD604S	1978	Leyland LN11351A/1R	Leyland B52F	Southdown 4.92
155	VOD605S	1978	Leyland LN11351A/1R	Leyland B52F	Southdown 4.92
157	UHG757R	1977	Leyland LN11351A/1R	Leyland B49F	Hants & Surrey .94
159	YRN816V	1980	Leyland NL106L11/1R	Leyland B44F	Ribble 3.94
160	YRN821V	1980	Leyland NL106L11/1R	Leyland B44F	Ribble 3.94
163	PCD73R	1977	Leyland LN11351A/1R	Leyland B49F	Hastings & District 4.92
165	VOD625S	1978	Leyland LN11351A/1R	Leyland B52F	Southdown 4.92
169	WYJ169S	1978	Leyland LN11351A/1R	Leyland B48F	Southdown 4.92
172	PCD82R	1977	Leyland LN11351A/1R	Leyland B49F	Southdown 4.92
173	YCD73T	1978	Leyland LN11351A/1R	Leyland B52F	Southdown 4.92
174	YCD74T	1978	Leyland LN11351A/1R	Leyland B48F	Hastings & District 4.92
176	YCD76T	1978	Leyland LN11351A/2R	Leyland B48F	Southdown 4.92
177	YCD77T	1978	Leyland LN11351A/2R	Leyland B48F	Southdown 4.92
178	PCD78R	1976	Leyland LN11351A/2R	Leyland B48F	Southdown 4.92
179	PCD79R	1977	Leyland LN11351A/2R	Leyland B49F	Southdown 4.92
180	PCD80R	1977	Leyland LN11351A/1R	Leyland B49F	Southdown 4.92
182	YCD82T	1978	Leyland LN11351A/1R	Leyland B48F	Coastline 5.92
195	AYJ95T	1979	Leyland LN113510A/1R	Leyland B52F	Southdown 4.92
197	AYJ97T	1978	Leyland LN113510A/1R	Leyland B52F	Southdown 4.92
198	AYJ98T	1979	Leyland LN113510A/1R	Leyland B52F	Coastline 12.92
241	L241SDY	1993	Volvo YN2RV18Z4	Northern Counties DPH43/25F	
242	L242SDY	1993	Volvo YN2RV18Z4	Northern Counties DPH43/25F	
301	F301MYJ	1989	Volvo D10M	NCME DPH43/33F	Southdown 4.92
302	F302MYJ	1989	Volvo D10M	NCME DPH43/33F	Southdown 4.92
303	F303MYJ	1989	Volvo D10M	NCME DPH43/33F	Southdown 4.92
324	XAP644S	1978	Bristol VRT/SL3/6LXB	ECW H43/31F	Southdown 4.92
327	LHG437T	1978	Bristol VRT/SL3/6LXB	ECW H43/31F	Coastline 2.93
328	LHG438T	1978	Bristol VRT/SL3/6LXB	ECW H43/31F	Hastings & District 4.92
348	AAP648T	1978	Bristol VRT/SL3/6LXB	ECW H43/31F	Coastline 6.93
352	JWV252W	1980	Bristol VRT/SL3/6LXB	ECW H43/31F	Southdown 4.92
353	JWV253W	1980	Bristol VRT/SL3/6LXB	ECW H43/31F	Coastline .94
360	AAP660T	1978	Bristol VRT/SL3/6LXB	ECW H43/31F	Southdown 4.92
501	J501GCD	1991	Dennis Dart 9.8SDL	Alexander Dash B41F	Hastings & District 4.92

502 - 521
1992 Dennis Dart 9.8SDL — Alexander AM Dash B41F (ex.Hastings & District 4.92)

502	J502GCD	507	J507GCD	512	J512GCD	517	J517GCD
503	J503GCD	508	J508GCD	513	J513GCD	518	J518GCD
504	J504GCD	509	J509GCD	514	J514GCD	519	J519GCD
505	J505GCD	510	J510GCD	515	J515GCD	520	J520GCD
506	J506GCD	511	J511GCD	516	J516GCD	521	J521GCD

541	J541GCD	1992	Dennis Dart 9.8SDL	Alexander Dash B40F	
583	J703YRM	1991	Dennis Dart 9.8SDL	Alexander Dash B40F	Cumberland 10.92

601 - 605
1994 Volvo B10M-55 — Northern Counties DP49F

601	L601VCD	603	L603VCD	604	L604VCD	605	L605VCD
602	L602VCD						

606 - 620   1994   Volvo B10M-55   Alexander PS DP48F

606	L606TDY	609	L609TDY	617	L617TDY	619	L619TDY
607	L607TDY	616	L616TDY	618	L618TDY	620	L620TDY
608	L698TDY						

668	AAP668T	1978	Bristol VRT/SL3/6LXB	ECW H43/31F	Southdown 4.92
671	AAP671T	1978	Bristol VRT/SL3/6LXB	ECW H43/31F	Coastline 2.93
673	EAP973V	1979	Bristol VRT/SL3/6LXB	ECW H43/31F	Southdown 4.92
688	EAP988V	1980	Bristol VRT/SL3/6LXB	ECW H43/31F	Southdown 4.92
693	ELJ213V	1979	Bristol VRT/SL3/6LXB	ECW H43/31F	Hastings & District 4.92
729	WKO129S	1978	Bristol VRT/SL3/6LXB	ECW H43/31F	Hastings & District 4.92
730	WKO130S	1978	Bristol VRT/SL3/6LXB	ECW H43/31F	Hastings & District 4.92

749 - 760   Bristol VRT/SL3/6LXB   ECW H43/31F
(ex. Hastings & District 4.92)

749	BKE849T	751	BKE851T	759	BKE859T	760	BKE860T
750	BKE850T	758	BKE858T				

761	RJT151R	1977	Bristol VRT/SL3/6LXB	ECW H43/31F	Hastings & District 4.92
762	BKE862T	1979	Bristol VRT/SL3/6LXB	ECW H43/31F	Hastings & District 4.92
786	AET186T	1979	Bristol VRT/SL3/6LXB	ECW H43/31F	Eaat Midlands 10.93
830	D230UHC	1986	Mercedes Benz L608D	Alexander AM B20F	Hastings & District 4.92
844	G974ARV	1990	Mercedes Benz 709D	Alexander AM B23F	Hampshire Bus 7.94
845	G975ARV	1990	Mercedes Benz 709D	Alexander AM B23F	Hampshire Bus 7.94

881 - 888   1993   Mercedes Benz 709D   Alexander AM B25F

881	L881SDY	883	L883SDY	885	L885SDY	887	L887SDY
882	L882SDY	884	L884SDY	886	L886SDY	888	L188SDY

1214	KPA365P	1975	Leyland LN11351/1R	Leyland B49F	Hants & Surrey 7.94
2891	G91VMM	1989	Leyland LBM6T/2RA	Wad.Stringer DP34FL	Owned by E.Sussex C.C.
2892	G92VMM	1989	Leyland LBM6T/2RA	Wad.Stringer DP34FL	Owned by E.Sussex C.C.
2909	419DCD	1988	MCW MF154/16	MCW DP28F	Southdown 5.91

2909 was originally registered F565HPP

964	WJM824T	1979	Bristol VRT/SL3/6LXB	ECW H43/31F	Hants & Surrey 4.93
967	WJM827T	1979	Bristol VRT/SL3/6LXB	ECW H43/31F	Coastline H & Surrey 4.93

1001	401DCD	1983	Leyland TRCTL11/3R	Plaxton 3200 DP49F	Hastings & District 4.92
1002	402DCD	1983	Leyland TRCTL11/3R	Plaxton 3200 DP49F	Hastings & District 4.92

1001/2 were originally registered RUF430X & XUF532Y.

1008	408DCD	1981	Leyland PSU5D/4R	Plaxton 3200 C53F	Hastings & District 4.92

1008 was originally registered LPN358W

1012	412DCD	1982	Leyland PSU5E/4R	Plaxton Sup.V C50F	Hastings & District 4.92
1013	413DCD	1982	Leyland PSU5E/4R	Plaxton Sup.V C50F	Hastings & District 4.92

1012/3 were originally registered TFG222X & HHC364Y

1066	MSU466	1987	Leyland TRCTL11/3R	Duple 340 C53FT	Hastings & District 4.92

1066 was originally registered D526ESG

1084	C84PRP	1986	Leyland TRCTL11/3RZ	Plaxton 3500 C46FT	United Counties 5.93

7024	PJJ24S	1978	Bristol VRT/SL3/6LXB	ECW H43/31F	East Kent 7.94
7621	UWV621S	1978	Bristol VRT/SL3/6LXB	ECW CO43/31F	Southdown 4.92
7623	UWV623S	1978	Bristol VRT/SL3/6LXB	ECW CO43/31F	Southdown 4.92

SPECIAL EVENTS VEHICLES

0409	409DCD	1964	Leyland PD3/4	NCME CO39/30F	Southdown 4.92
0770	HKE690L	1973	Bristol VRT/SL2/6LXB	ECW O43/34F	Hastings & District 4.92
0946	MFN946F	1968	AEC Regent V	Park Royal H40/32F	Hastings & District 4.92

ANCILLARY VEHICLES

COASTLINE

L1	HUF901V	1980	Ford DO710	Lorry	
R1	STW356W	1981	DAF 2800	Recovery wagon	
R2	UHK212W	1981	DAF 2300	Recovery wagon	
V12	GCD912V	1981	Ford Transit	Van	
V18	OCD618W	1981	Ford Transit	Van	
V24	B24JFG	1985	Ford Transit	Luton van	
T265	GLS265N	1974	Leyland PSU3/3R	Alexander AYS B53F	Driver trainer
T292	FCD292D	1966	Leyland PD3/4	NCME FH39/30F	Driver trainer
0184	EUF184	1938	Leyland TD5	Towing lorry	Preserved

HAMPSHIRE BUS

R5	CNO891T	1979	DAF 2300	Recovery wagon	
R6	Q355WDT	1979	Seddon Atkinson	Recovery wagon	
V26	C946VPO	1986	Freight Rover Sherpa	Van	
T294	FCD294D	1966	Leyland PD3/4	NCME FH39/30F	Driver trainer

HANTS & SURREY

RV80	EDG586L	1972	ERF	Recovery wagon	

SOUTH COAST

L2	HUF902V	1980	Ford DO687	Lorry
L4	EUF64V	1980	Ford DO710	Lorry
R3	HDP438W	1981	DAF 2300	Recovery wagon
R4	BWP332S	1977	Leyland Buffalo	Recovery wagon
V8	C418SLO	1986	Ford Fiesta	Van
V20	VUF20Y	1983	Ford Transit	Van
V23	B223HCD	1985	Ford Transit	Van
V25	B25JFG	1985	Ford Transit	Luton van

Stagecoach East Kent Optare Delta-bodied DAF 1403 is one of several vehicles painted in a special grey & blue livery for use on the Canterbury Park & Ride scheme.   (F.W.York)

Stagecoach East Kent Ltd., Lewes Enterprise Centre, 112 Malling Street, Lewes BN7 2RB

Purchased by the NBC by its management on 5 March 1987, the company was acquired by Stagecoach Holdings in July 1993, was renamed Stagecoach East Kent Ltd, and placed under the administrative control of Stagecoach (South) Ltd.

Depots : Ashford; Dover; Folkestone; Herne Bay; Thanet. *Outstations : Canterbury; Deal; New Romsey.*

East Kent   Fleet list

---

1 - 4

		1991	Iveco 49.10		Carlyle Dailybus B23F		
1	H101EKR	2	H102EKR	3	H103EKR	4	H104EKR

6	D226VCD	1986	Iveco 40.10	Robin Hood B21F	*Brighton & Hove 1990*
10	D230VCD	1986	Iveco 49.10	Robin Hood B21F	*Brighton & Hove 1990*
11	J121LKO	1991	Iveco 49.10	Dormobile Routemaker B23F	
12	J112LKO	1991	Iveco 49.10	Carlyle Dailybus B23F	
13	J113LKO	1991	Iveco 49.10	Carlyle Dailybus B23F	
14	J114LKO	1991	Iveco 49.10	Carlyle Dailybus B23F	

---

15 - 20

		1990	Iveco 49.10		Dormobile Routemaker B23F		
15	J115LKO	17	J117LKO	19	J119LKO	20	J120LKO
16	J116LKO	18	J118LKO				

35	G35SSR	1989	Iveco 49.10	Phoenix B23F	East Midland 10.93
41	D231VCD	1986	Iveco 49.10	Robin Hood B21F	*Brighton & Hove 1990*
46	G446VKK	1990	Iveco 49.10	Carlyle Dailybus B23F	
47	G447VKK	1990	Iveco 49.10	Carlyle Dailybus B23F	

---

51 - 70

		1987	Iveco 49.10		Robin Hood B23F		
51	E151UKR	56	E156UKR	61	E161UKR	66	E166UKR
52	E152UKR	57	E157UKR	62	E162UKR	67	E167UKR
53	E153UKR	58	E158UKR	63	E163UKR	68	E168UKR
54	E154UKR	59	E159UKR	64	E164UKR	69	E169UKR
55	E155UKR	60	E160UKR	65	E165UKR	70	E170UKR

---

71 - 75

		1989	Iveco 49.10		Robin Hood B23F		
71	F71FKK	73	F73FKK	74	F74FKK	75	F75FKK
72	F72FKK						

| 76 | J416TGM | 1991 | Iveco 49.10 | | Reeve Burgess B25F | Hants & Surrey 7.94 |

80 - 87

| | | 1987 | Iveco 49.10 | | Robin Hood B19F |

| 80 | E580TKJ | 82 | E582TKJ | 84 | E584TKJ | 86 | E586TKJ |
| 81 | E581TKJ | 83 | E583TKJ | 85 | E585TKJ | 87 | E587TKJ |

91 - 94

| | | 1990 | Iveco 49.10 | | Carlyle Dailybus B23F |

| 91 | G491RKK | 92 | G492RKK | 93 | G493RKK | 94 | G494RKK |

95 - 98

| | | 1990 | Iveco 49.10 | | Phoenix B23F |

| 95 | G95SKR | 96 | G96SKR | 97 | G97SKR | 98 | G98SKR |

| 149 | JCW949W | 1981 | Leyland NL106L11/1R | Leyland B44F | South Coast Buses 7.94 |
| 161 | TRN811V | 1979 | Leyland LN11351B/1R | Leyland B44F | South Coast Buses 9.94 |

225	G705TCD	1990	Leyland ON2R56G13Z4	Alexander RL H51/34F	Coastline 8.94
226	G706TCD	1990	Leyland ON2R56G13Z4	Alexander RL H51/34F	Coastline 8.94
227	G707TCD	1990	Leyland ON2R56G13Z4	Alexander RL H51/34F	Coastline 9.94

254 - 257

| | | 1992 | Leyland ON2R50G13Z4 | Alexander RL H47/32F |
| | | | (ex.Fife Scottish 7.94) | |

| 254 | K714ASC | 255 | K715ASC | 256 | K716ASC | 257 | K717ASC |

461 - 481

| | | 1989 | Iveco 49.10 | | Reeve Burgess B25F |
| | | | (ex.East Midland 10.93) | |

| 461 | G911KWF | 464 | G914KWF | 467 | G917KWF | 481 | G921KWF |
| 463 | G913KWF | | | | | | |

482	G922KWF	1990	Iveco 49.10	Reeve Burgess B23F	East Midland .93
483	G923KWF	1990	Iveco 49.10	Reeve Burgess B23F	East Midland .93
632	L632TDY	1994	Volvo B10M-55	Alexander PS DP48F	
633	L633TDY	1994	Volvo B10M-55	Alexander PS DP48F	
634	L634TDY	1994	Volvo B10M-55	Alexander PS DP48F	
659	K789DAO	1993	Volvo B10M-55	Alexander PS DP48F	Cumberland 4.94
660	K790DAO	1993	Volvo B10M-55	Alexander PS DP48F	Cumberland 4.94
661	K791DAO	1993	Volvo B10M-55	Alexander PS DP48F	Cumberland 4.94
1064	VSV564	1983	Leyland TRCTL11/3R	Plaxton 3200 DP49F	South Coast Buses .94
1072	USV672	1983	Leyland TRCTL/3R	Plaxton 3200 DP49F	South Coast Buses .94

1064/72 were originally registered FKL171/2Y.

| 1115 | MFN115R | 1976 | Leyland LN11351A/1R | Leyland B49F | |
| 1118 | MFN118R | 1976 | Leyland LN11351A/1R | Leyland B49F | |

1181 - 1189

| | | 1977 | Leyland LN11351A/1R | Leyland DP48F |

| 1181 | NFN81R | 1083w | NFN83R | 1186 | NFN86R | 1188 | NFN88R |
| 1182 | NFN82R | 1184 | NFN84R | 1187 | NFN87R | 1189 | NFN89R |

1344 - 1346

| | | 1977 | Leyland LN10351A/1R | Leyland B41F |

| 1344 | PJJ344S | 1345 | PJJ345S | 1346 | PJJ346S |

1401 - 1403

1991 DAF SB220LC550   Optare Delta B49F

1401	J401LKO	1402	J402LKO	1403	J403LKO

1404 - 1408

1994 Dennis Lance SLF   Berkhof B40F

1404	M404OKM	1406	M406OKM	1407	M407OKM	1408	M408OKM
1405	M405OKM						

1546	GFN546N	1975	Leyland LN10351/1R	Leyland B40F
1552	GFN552N	1975	Leyland LN10351/1R	Leyland B37F
2742	C742HKK	1986	Ft.Rover Sherpa 365	Dormobile B16F

1890 - 1900

1976 Leyland LN11351A/1R   Leyland B49F

1890	JJG890P	1893	JGG893P	1898	JJG898P	1900	JJG900P
1892	JJG892P	1895	JJG895P				

7016 - 7024

1977 Bristol VRT/SL3/6LXB   Willowbrook H43/31F

7016	PJJ16S	7021	PJJ21S	7022	PJJ22S	7024	PJJ24S

7042	MFN42R	1976	Bristol VRT/SL3/6LXB	ECW H43/31F	
7043	MFN43R	1976	Bristol VRT/SL3/6LXB	ECW H43/31F	
7046	MFN46R	1976	Bristol VRT/SL3/6LXB	ECW H43/31F	
7611	UWV611S	1978	Bristol VRT/SL3/6LXB	ECW CO43/31F	Coastline 4.94

7650 - 7775

1980 Bristol VRT/SL3/6LXB   ECW H43/31F
(7655 rebodied 1983)

7650	XJJ650V	7658	XJJ658V	7664	XJJ664V	7670	XJJ670V
7651	XJJ651V	7659	XJJ659V	7665	XJJ665V	7671	BJG671V
7652	XJJ652V	7660	XJJ660V	7666	XJJ666V	7672	BJG672V
7653	XJJ653V	7661	XJJ661V	7667	XJJ667V	7673	BJG673V
7654	XJJ654V	7662	XJJ662V	7668	XJJ668V	7674	BJG674V
7655	XJJ655V	7663	XJJ663V	7669	XJJ669V	7675	BJG675V
7657	XJJ657V						

7676 - 7685

1981 Bristol VRT/SL3/6LXB   ECW H43/31F

7676	CJJ676W	7679	CJJ679W	7682	SKL682X	7684	SKL684X
7677	CJJ677W	7680	SKL680X	7683	SKL683X	7685	SKL685X
7678	CJJ678W	7681	SKL681X				

7746 - 7755

1988 MCW Metrobus Mk.2 DR132/11   MCW H46/31F

7746	E746SKR	7749	E749SKR	7752	E752SKR	7754	E754UKR
7747	E747SKR	7750	E750SKR	7753	E753SKR	7755	E755UKR
7748	E748SKR	7751	E751SKR				

7761 - 7767   1989   MCW Metrobus Mk.2 DR132/15   MCW   DPH43/27F

7761	F761EKM	7763	F762EKM	7765	F765EKM	7767	F767EKM
7762	F762EKM	7764	F764EKM	7766	F766EKM		

7771 - 7775   1989   MCW Metrobus Mk.2 DR132/14   MCW   H46/31F

7771	F771EKM	7773	F773EKM	7774	F774EKM	7775	F775EKM
7772	F772EKM						

7781	F781KKP	1989	Scania N113DRB	Alexander RH H47/33F
7782	F782KKP	1989	Scania N113DRB	Alexander RH H47/33F

7801 - 7810   1990   Leyland ON2R56C16Z4   Northern Counties H51/34F

7801	H801BKK	7804	H804BKK	7807	H807BKK	7809	H809BKK
7802	H802BKK	7805	H805BKK	7808	H808BKK	7810	H810BKK
7803	H803BKK	7806	H806BKK				

7811 - 7814   1992   Leyland ON2R50C13Z4   Northern Counties H47/30F

7811	J811NKK	7812	J812NKK	7813	J813NKK	7814	J814NKK

7821 - 7825   1993   Leyland ON2R50C13Z4   Northern Counties H47/30F

7821	K821TKP	7823	K823TKP	7824	K824TKP	7825	K825TKP
7822	K822TKP						

7826 - 7830   1993   Leyland ON2R50C13Z4   Northern Counties H47/30F

7826	L826BKK	7828	L828BKK	7829	L829BKK	7830	L830BKK
7827	L827BKK						

7982	TFN982T	1978	Bristol VRT/SL3/6LXB	Willowbrook H43/31F
7983	TFN983T	1978	Bristol VRT/SL3/6LXB	Willowbrook H43/31F
7988	TFN788T	1978	Bristol VRT/SL3/6LXB	Willowbrook H43/31F

8192	XSU912	1984	MCW Metroliner HR131/2	MCW C49FT	*Premier Travel 1988*
8211	D211VEV	1987	Scania K112CRB	Berkhof Esprite C41FT	
8243	SIB8243	1991	Volvo B10M-60	Plaxton 3500 C49FT	*Park, Hamilton 1993*

8192/243 were originally registered B192JVA & H826AHS

8245	LDZ3145	1985	MCW Metroliner HR131/1	MCW C49FT	*Premier Travel 1988*
8246	XYK976	1985	MCW Metroliner HR131/6	MCW C49FT	*Premier Travel 1988*
8399	XDU599	1983	MCW Metroliner HR131/1	MCW C49FT	*MCW, Birmingham 1988*

8245/6 were originally registered B245/6JVA. 8399 was previously registered ABM399A and was originally A543WOB.

8831	UKE831X	1982	Leyland PSU3G/4R	ECW DP47F
8837	BKR837Y	1982	Leyland PSU3G/4R	ECW DP47F

8838 - 8842   1983 Leyland TRCTL11/3R   Plaxton Paramount 3200E C53F

8838 TSU638	8840 TSU640	8841 TSU641	8842 TSU642
8839 TSU839			

(8838-42 originally registered FKK838-42Y)

8850 WSU450	1984 MCW Metroliner CR126/8	MCW C51F	
8851 WSU451	1984 MCW Metroliner CR126/8	MCW C51F	
8852 WSU452	1984 MCW Metroliner CR126/8	MCW C51F	

8850-2 were originally registered B850-2TKL

8854 E854UKR	1988 MCW Metroliner HR131/12	MCW C51F	
8855 E855UKR	1988 MCW Metroliner HR131/12	MCW C51F	
8856 J856NKK	1992 Scania K93CRB	Plaxton Para 3500 C49FT	

8901 - 8908   1989 Volvo B10M-60   Plaxton Expressliner C49FT

8901 G901PKK	8903 G903PKK	8905 G905PKK	8907 G907PKK
8902 G902PKK	8904 G904PKK	8906 G906PKK	8908 G908PKK

8909 J909NKP	1992 Volvo B10M-60	Plaxton Ex'liner C49FT	
8910 K910TKP	1993 Volvo B10M-60	Plaxton Ex'liner C49FT	
8911 M911WJK	1994 Volvo B10M-62	Plaxton Ex'liner C49FT	
8996 PFN873	1986 Bova FHD12-280	Bova Futura C49FT	*Marinair 1991*

8996 was originally registered C996FKM

Wearing a blue & white livery, Vanguard Leyland National CBV782S is seen in Coventry after arriving in the city on service 9.   (T.Carter)

United Counties Omnibus Co. Ltd., Rothersthorpe Avenue, Northampton NN4 8UT

United Counties was the third National Bus Company subsidiary to be purchased by the Stagecoach Group. Operating a wide range of local bus services, it also maintained several express services branded with the Coachlinks name and in November 1990 it introduced a new minibus network in Corby using vehicles adorned with a special livery and Magic Minis fleet name. United Counties is now a division of Stagecoach (South) Ltd.

Fleet names : Stagecoach United Counties; Coachlinks; Street Shuttle; Corby Magic Minis.

Livery : Stagecoach corporate livery except Corby Magic Minis - Black & Gold.

Depots : Bedford; Corby; Huntingdon; Kettering; Northampton. *Outstations : Biggleswade; Daventry (2); Desborough; Higham Ferrers; Husbands Bosworth; Little Paxton; Milton Keynes; Nether Heyford; Stamford; Thrapston; Uppingham; Wellingborough; Wymington; Yardley Hastings.*

United Counties   Fleet list

46 - 50		1988	Iveco 49.10			Robin Hood	B23F		
46	E46MRP		47	E47MRP		49	E49MRP	50	E50MRP

54	F491NTR	1988	Iveco 49.10		Robin Hood B25F	Hampshire Bus .88
55	F492NTR	1988	Iveco 49.10		Robin Hood B25F	Hampshire Bus .88
56	F493NTR	1988	Iveco 49.10		Robin Hood B25F	Hampshire Bus .88

57 - 66		1989	Iveco 49.10		Robin Hood B23F		
57	F57AVV	60	F60AVV	63	G63JVV	**65**	**G65JVV**
58	F58AVV	61	G61JVV	64	G64JVV	**66**	**G66JVV**
59	F59AVV	62	G62JVV				

67	G67LVV	1989	Iveco 49.10	Phoenix B23F	
68	G28PSR	1989	Iveco 49.10	Robin Hood B23F	Stagecoach 3.90
69	G29PSR	1989	Iveco 49.10	Robin Hood B23F	Stagecoach 3.90
70	G27PSR	1989	Iveco 49.10	Robin Hood B23F	Stagecoach 3.90
71	G31PSR	1989	Iveco 49.10	Robin Hood B23F	Stagecoach 3.90
72	G32PSR	1989	Iveco 49.10	Robin Hood B23F	Stagecoach 3.90
73	G33PSR	1989	Iveco 49.10	Robin Hood B23F	Stagecoach 4.90
74	G40SSR	1989	Iveco 49.10	Phoenix B23F	Stagecoach 5.90
75	G41SSR	1989	Iveco 49.10	Phoenix B23F	Stagecoach 5.90
81	C81PRP	1986	Leyland TRCTL11/3RZ	Plaxton 3500 C46FT	
82	C82PRP	1986	Leyland TRCTL11/3RZ	Plaxton 3500 C46FT	
83	83CBD	1983	Leyland TRCTL11//3R	Plaxton 3500 C48FT	Stagecioach Malawi .94
85	C85PRP	1986	Leyland TRCTL11/3RZ	Plaxton 3500 C46FT	

92	J430HDS	1992	Volvo B10M-60	Plaxton Premiere 350 C49FT	Park, Hamilton 4.93
93	J439HDS	1992	Volvo B10M-60	Plaxton Premiere 350 C49FT	Park, Hamilton 4.93
94	J445HDS	1992	Volvo B10M-60	Plaxton Premiere 350 C49FT	East Midland 4.93
95	J446HDS	1992	Volvo B10M-60	Plaxton Premiere 350 C49FT	East Midland 4.93
96	J450HDS	1992	Volvo B10M-60	Plaxton Premiere 350 C49FT	Park, Hamilton 4.93

102 - 105   1983   Leyland TRCTL11/3R   Plaxton 3200 C53F

102	NBD102Y	103	NBD103Y	104	NBD104Y	105	83CBD

105 was originally registered NBD105Y

108 - 114   1983   Leyland TRCTL11/3RH   Plaxton 3200 C50FT

108	A108TRP	110	A110TRP	112	A112TRP	114	A114TRP
109	A109TRP	111	A111TRP	113	A113TRP		

115	MSU465	1987	Leyland TRCTL11/3R	Duple 340 C46FT	Fife Scottish 2.92
116	VLT255	1985	Leyland TRCTL11.3RZ	Duple Laser 2 C44FT	Stagecoach Malawi 12.92

115/6 were originally registered D525ESG & B357KNH

120	C120PNV	1986	Leyland TRCTL11/3RZ	Plaxton 3200 C57F	
121	C121PNV	1986	Leyland TRCTL11/3RZ	Plaxton 3200 C57F	
122	C122PNV	1986	Leyland TRCTL11/3RZ	Plaxton 3200 C57F	
125	WLT908	1983	Volvo B10M-61	Plaxton 3200 C48FT	Stagecoach 5.88
126	647DYE	1983	Volvo B10M-61	Plaxton 3200 C48FT	Stagecoach 5.88

125 was previously registered A332ANH. Prior to that it was registered 4009SC and was originally A800TGG. 126 was previously registered A320ANH prior to which it was 7878SC and was originally registered A798TGG.

130 - 135   1988   Volvo B10M-61   Plaxton 3200 C53F

130	E130ORP	132	E132ORP	134	E134ORP	135	F135URP
131	E131ORP	133	E133ORP				

150 - 154   1993   Volvo B10M-60   Plaxton Premiere 320 C53F

150	K150DNV	152	K152DNV	153	K153DNV	154	K154DNV
151	K151DNV						

155 - 162   1993   Volvo B10M-60   Plaxton Premiere 320 C51F

155	L155JNH	157	L157JNH	159	L159JNH	161	L161JNH
156	L156JNH	158	L158JNH	160	L160JNH	162	L162JNH

301 - 308   1987   Iveco 49.10   Robin Hood B13F
                 (ex. Ribble 9.90)

301	D406FRV	303	D726YBV	305	D729YBV	307	D735YBV
302	D724YBV	304	D728YBV	306	D731YBV	308	D856FOT

309	D613BCK	1987	Iveco 49.10	Robin Hood B13F	Ribble 2.91
310	D610BCK	1987	Iveco 49.10	Robin Hood B13F	Ribble 2.91
311	D616BCK	1987	Iveco 49.10	Robin Hood B13F	Ribble 8.91
312	D619BCK	1987	Iveco 49.10	Robin Hood B13F	Ribble 8.91
313	D725YBV	1987	Iveco 49.10	Robin Hood B13F	Ribble 8.91
314	D938ECR	1986	Iveco 49.10	Robin Hood B13F	Stagecoach 4.92

315	D22WNH	1986	Iveco 49.10	Robin Hood B13F	
316	D771MUR	1986	Iveco 49.10	Robin Hood B13F	Luton & District 10.88
317	D26BVV	1987	Iveco 49.10	Robin Hood B13F	

350 - 359
1992 Mercedes Benz 709D   Alexander (Belfast) B25F

350	K350ANV	353	K353ANV	356	K356ANV	358	K358ANV
351	K351ANV	354	K354ANV	357	K357ANV	359	K359ANV
352	K352ANV	355	K355ANV				

360 -383
1993 Mercedes Benz 709D   Alexander (Belfast) B25F

360	L360JBD	366	L366JBD	372	L372JBD	378	L378JBD
361	L361JBD	367	L367JBD	373	L373JBD	379	L379JBD
362	L362JBD	368	L368JBD	374	L374JBD	380	L380JBD
363	L363JBD	369	L369JBD	375	L375JBD	381	L381NBD
364	L364JBD	370	L370JBD	376	L376JBD	382	L382NBD
365	L365JBD	371	L371JBD	377	L377JBD	383	L383NBD

401 - 421
1993 Volvo B6R   Alexander AM Dash B40F

401	L401JBD	407	L407JBD	413	L413JBD	418	L418JBD
402	L402JBD	408	L408JBD	414	L414JBD	419	L419JBD
403	L403JBD	409	L409JBD	415	L415JBD	420	L420JBD
404	L404JBD	410	L410JBD	416	L416JBD	421	L421JBD
405	L405JBD	411	L411JBD	417	L417JBD	422	L422MVV
406	L406JBD	412	L412JBD				

423 - 430
1994 Volvo B6R   Alexander AM Dash DP40F

423	L423XVV	425	L425XVV	427	L427XVV	429	M429BNV
424	L424XVV	426	L426XVV	428	L428XVV	430	M430BNV

500	LFR862X	1980	Leyland NL106AL11/1R	Leyland B44F	Cumberland 3.93
501	LFR864X	1980	Leyland NL106AL11/1R	Leyland B44F	Cumberland 3.93
600	F110NES	1989	Leyland ON6LXCT/5RZ	Alexander H66/44F	East Midland 10.92
601	ARP601X	1981	Leyland ONLXB/1R	ECW CH45/27F	
602	ARP602X	1981	Leyland ONLXB/1R	ECW CH41/27F	
604	ARP604X	1981	Leyland ONLXB/1R	ECW H45/32F	
605	ARP605X	1981	Leyland ONLXB/1R	ECW CH41/27F	
606	ARP606X	1981	Leyland ONLXB/1R	ECW CH41/27F	

607 - 611
1981 Leyland ONLXB/1R   ECW H45/32F

607	ARP607X	609	ARP609X	610	ARP610X	611	ARP611X
608	ARP608X						

612 - 617
1987 Leyland ONLXB/1RV   Alexander RL H47/30F
(ex. Bluebird Northern 7.91)

612	WLT528	614	WLT512	616	GSO6V	617	GSO7V
613	D383XRS	615	685DYE				

612/4/5 were originally registered D612/4XRS & D379XRS. 616/7 were originally registered D376/7XRS.

618 GSO2V 1986 Leyland ONLXB/1RV Alexander H45/32F Bluebird Buses 9.94
618 was originally registered C472SSO

---

620 - 634   1988 Leyland ONLXB/2RZ   Alexander RL H51/36F

620	F620MSL	624	F624MSL	628	F628MSL	632	F632MSL
621	F621MSL	625	F625MSL	629	F629MSL	633	F633MSL
622	F622MSL	626	F626MSL	630	F630MSL	634	F634MSL
623	F623MSL	627	F627MSL	631	F631MSL		

635 - 644   1989 Leyland ONLXB/2RZ   Alexander RL DPH51/34F

635	F635YRP	638	F638YRP	641	G641EVV	643	G643EVV
636	F636YRP	639	G639EVV	642	G642EVV	644	G644EVV
637	F637YRP	640	G640EVV				

645 - 649   1989 Leyland ONLXB/2RZ   Alexander RL CH51/31F

645	G645EVV	647	G647EVV	648	G648EVV	649	G649EVV
646	G646EVV						

650 - 654   1990 Leyland ON2R56G13Z4   Alexander RL H51/34F

650	H650VVV	652	H652VVV	653	H653VVV	654	H654VVV
651	H651VVV						

655 - 670   1992 Leyland ON2R50G13Z4   NCME H47/29F

655	K655UNH	659	K659UNH	663	K663UNH	668	K668UNH
656	K656UNH	660	K660UNH	664	K664UNH	669	K669UNH
657	K657UNH	661	K661UNH	665	K665UNH	670	K670UNH
658	K658UNH	662	K662UNH	667	K667UNH		

671 - 685   1993 Volvo Olympian   Northern Counties H47/29F

671	L671HNV	675	L675HNV	679	L679HNV	683	L683HNV
672	L672HNV	676	L676HNV	680	L680HNV	684	L684HNV
673	L673HNV	677	L677HNV	681	L681HNV	685	L685JBD
674	L674HNV	678	L678HNV	682	L682HNV		

701	HVS710	1961	AEC Routemaster	Park Royal H36/28R	London Transport 1.88
703	HVS937	1961	AEC Routemaster	Park Royal H36/28R	London Transport 1.88
705	ABD892A	1962	AEC Routemaster	Park Royal H36/28R	London Transport 1.88
706	BNK32A	1963	AEC Routemaster	Park Royal H36/28R	London Transport 1.88
708	CUV192C	1965	AEC Routemaster	Park Royal H36/28R	London Transport 1.88
709	HVS936	1959	AEC Routemaster	Park Royal H36/28R	London Transport 1.88
710	HVS935	1960	AEC Routemaster	Park Royal H36/28R	London Transport 1.88
714	BNK31A	1963	AEC Routemaster	Park Royal H36/28R	London Transport 1.88

701/3/5/6/9/10/4 were originally registered WLT512/682, 68CLT, 647DYE, VLT51/255 & 685DYE.

---

708 - 713   1992 Leyland ON2R50G1324   Alexander RL H47/32F
                        (ex.Fife Scottish 7.94)

708	J708WFS	710	K710ASC	712	K712ASC	713	K713ASC
709	K709ASC	711	K711ASC	713	K713ASC		

714	J620GCR	1991	Leyland ON2R56G13Z4	Alexander H47/30F	Bluebird Buses 9.94
715	J621GCR	1991	Leyland ON2R56G13Z4	Alexander H47/30F	Bluebird Buses 9.94
716	J622GCR	1991	Leyland ON2R50G13Z4	Alexander H47/30F	Bluebird Buses 9.94
721	LFJ862W	1981	Bristol VRT/SL3/6LXB	ECW H43/31F	Devon General 1.89
722	LFJ863W	1981	Bristol VRT/SL3/6LXB	ECW H43/31F	Devon General 2.89
723	LFJ853W	1981	Bristol VRT/SL3/6LXB	ECW H43/31F	Devon General 1.89
724	LFJ852W	1981	Bristol VRT/SL3/6LXB	ECW H43/31F	Devon General 2.89
725	LFJ854W	1981	Bristol VRT/SL3/6LXB	ECW H43/31F	Devon General 2.89
726	LFJ855W	1981	Bristol VRT/SL3/6LXB	ECW H43/31F	Devon General 2.89
727	LFJ879W	1981	Bristol VRT/SL3/6LXB	ECW H43/31F	Devon General 5.89
731	FDV809V	1980	Bristol VRT/SL3/6LXB	ECW H43/31F	Devon General 10.88
732	FDV838V	1980	Bristol VRT/SL3/6LXB	ECW H43/31F	Devon General 10.88
733	LFJ868W	1981	Bristol VRT/SL3/6LXB	ECW H43/31F	Devon General 10.88
734	FDV812V	1980	Bristol VRT/SL3/6LXB	ECW H43/31F	Devon General 11.88
735	LFJ864W	1981	Bristol VRT/SL3/6LXB	ECW H43/31F	Devon General 11.88
736	LFJ865W	1981	Bristol VRT/SL3/6LXB	ECW H43/31F	Devon General 11.88
737	FDV811V	1980	Bristol VRT/SL3/6LXB	ECW H43/31F	Devon General 11.88
738	FDV335V	1980	Bristol VRT/SL3/6LXB	ECW H43/31F	Devon General 11.88
739	LFJ869W	1981	Bristol VRT/SL3/6LXB	ECW H43/31F	Devon General 11.88
740	FDV832V	1980	Bristol VRT/SL3/6LXB	ECW H43/31F	Devon General 12.88
744	LFJ866W	1981	Bristol VRT/SL3/6LXB	ECW H43/31F	Devon General 12.88
750	FAO417V	1980	Bristol VRT/SL3/6LXB	ECW H43/31F	Cumberland 8.92
751	FAO418V	1980	Bristol VRT/SL3/6LXB	ECW H43/31F	Cumberland 8.92
752	FAO419V	1980	Bristol VRT/SL3/6LXB	ECW H43/31F	Cumberland 8.92
794	GRP794L	1973	Bristol VRT/SL2/6G	ECW H39/31F	
839	LBD839P	1975	Bristol VRT/SL3/501	ECW H43/31F	
849	OVV849R	1976	Bristol VRT/SL3/501	ECW H43/31F	
856	OVV856R	1976	Bristol VRT/SL3/501	ECW H43/31F	
862	RRP862R	1977	Bristol VRT/SL3/6LXB	ECW H43/31F	
863	RRP863R	1977	Bristol VRT/SL3/6LXB	ECW H43/31F	

870 - 873   1977 Bristol VRT/SL3/6LXB   ECW H43/31F

870	TNH870R	871	TNH871R	872	TNH872R	873	TNH873R

875 - 891   1978 Bristol VRT/SL3/6LXB   ECW H41/31F

875	WBD875S	879	XNV879S	886	XNV886S	889	XNV889S
876	WBD876S	880	XNV880S	887	XNV887S	890	XNV890S
878	XNV878S	885	XNV885S	888	XNV888S	891	XNV891S

900	BAU178T	1978	Bristol VRT/SL3/6LXB	ECW H43/31F	East Midland 4.93
901	BAU179T	1978	Bristol VRT/SL3/6LXB	ECW H43/31F	East Midland 4.93

902 - 919   1979 Bristol VRT/SL3/6LXB   ECW H43/31F (+DPH40/28F)

902	CBD902T	909	FRP909T	912	FRP912T	916	HBD916T
903	CBD903T	910	FRP910T	914	HBD914T	917	HBD917T
908	FRP908T	911	FRP911T	915	HBD915T	919+	HBD919T

920 - 926   1980 Bristol VRT/SL3/6LXB   ECW H43/31F

920	LRP920V	921	LRP921V	923	LRP923V	926	ONH926V

930 - 967

1981 Bristol VRT/SL3/6LXB ECW H43/31F

930	SNV930W	940	URP940W	950	VVV950W	962	VVV962W
931	SNV931W	941	URP941W	952	VVV952W	963	VVV963W
935	SNV935W	944	URP944W	953	VVV953W	965	VVV965W
936	SNV936W	945	URP945W	954	VVV954W	966	VVV966W
937	SNV937W	948	VVV948W	961	VVV961W	967	VVV967W
939	URP939W	949	VVV949W				

970 - 974

1980 Bristol VRT/SL3/6LXB ECW H43/31F
(ex. Hampshire Bus 9.88)

970	KRU843W	972	KRU846W	973	KRU847W	974	KRU852W
971	KRU845W						

ANCILLARY VEHICLES

1001	PRX200B	1964	Leyland PD3/4	NCME FCO39/30F	Driver Trainer
1002	PRX191B	1964	Leyland PD3/4	NCME FCO39/30F	Driver Trainer
1034	JHD334J	1971	Daimler CRG6LX	Alexander H -- F	Exhibition Unit

1001/2 were originally registered 418DCD & 404DCD and were acquired from Cumberland in 10.88.
JHD334J was new to Yorkshire Woollen District Transport.

One of Stagecoach Malawi's Plaxton Paramount-bodied Volvo B10M coaches imported secondhand from the U.K., former Travellers of Hounslow no.1 (BH9601) is seen fitted with a heavy front bumper unit and displaying Coachline fleet names. (Stagecoach International)

Stagecoach
WELLINGTON

Wellington City Transport Ltd., 45 Onepu Road, Kilbirnie, Wellington, New Zealand

After acquiring the Wellington Tramway Company in 1900 expansion was gained in 1927 with the purchase of the Wellington Suburban Motor Bus Company. The present trolleybus system dates from 1949 whilst the last trams ran on 2 May 1964. In addition to purchasing Wellington City Transport and its two subsidiaries - Cityline (NZ) Ltd and North City Bus Ltd., Stagecoach also gained a controlling interest in Harbour City Cable Car Ltd. which operates the Kelburn cable tramway and in 1994 gained further expansion with the acquisition of the Wellington-based Eastbourne Bus Company.

Depots : WELLINGTON CITY TRANSPORT - Karori; Kilbirnie.   CITYLINE AUCKLAND - Papakura. CITYLINE HUTT VALLEY - Lower Hutt; Stokes Valley.

Stagecoach Wellington   Fleet list

---

120 - 139   1984 Volvo B10M / Ansaldo   New Zealand Motor Bodies B40D

120	de-reg'd	125	de-reg'd	130	de-reg'd	135	de-reg'd
121	de-reg'd	126	de-reg'd	131	de-reg'd	136	de-reg'd
122	de-reg'd	127	de-reg'd	132	de-reg'd	137	de-reg'd
123	de-reg'd	128	de-reg'd	133	de-reg'd	138	de-reg'd
124	de-reg'd	129	de-reg'd	134	de-reg'd	139	de-reg'd

141 - 160   1987 M.A.N SL202   Coachwork International B40D

141	NF2109	146	NH2756	151	NL9377	156	NL9460
142	NF2117	147	NH2755	152	NL9393	157	NL9461
143	NH2634	148	NI5642	153	NL9414	158	NL9531
144	NH2652	149	NI5704	154	NL9420	159	NL9540
145	NH2754	150	NI5718	155	NL9466	160	NL7566

161 - 166   1988 M.A.N. SL202   Coachwork International B40D

161	OB1550	163	PA6879	165	NZ8003	166	NZ8266
162	NT9387	164	NZ8004				

167 - 170   1989 M.A.N. SL202   Coachwork International B40D

167	OG8397	168	OG898	169	OG8399	170	OG8551

171 - 180   1990 M.A.N. 16.200 UOCL   Coachwork International B39D

171	ON525	174	PL5273	177	PL5823	179	PP5206
172	PL5003	175	PL5274	178	PL5824	180	PP5205
173	PL5272	176	PL5822				

181 PP5219 1990 M.A.N. 16.240 UOCL Coachwork International B39D
201 KA9102 1981 Volvo B58 / Brown Boveri Hawke B40D

202 - 233   1983 Volvo B58 / Brown Boveri   Hawke B40D

202	KA9108	210	KA9109	218	KA7233	226	KD7487
203	PE8106	211	KA9110	219	KA7234	227	KH4274
204	JM7127	213	KA9111	220	KA7235	228s	KH4357
205	JM7125	213	KA9184	221	KD7490	229s	KH4358
206	JY6549	214	KA9185	222	KD7488	230s	KH4360
207	JY5832	215w	de-reg'd	223	KD7485	231s	KH4359
208	JY5831	216	KA9192	224	KD7486	232	KJ8245
209	KA9103	217	NA87	225	KH4273	233	KJ8244

234 LQ2643 1984 Volvo B58 / Brown Boveri Hawke B40D

235 - 268   1985/6 Volvo B58 / Brown Boveri   Hawke B40D

235	LW6465	244	ME9236	253	MJ2171	261	MS1706
236	MA8821	245	ME2504	254	MJ2172	262	MS1705
237	MA5210	246	MJ2012	255	MO1322	203	MS1704
238	MA5209	247	MJ2016	256	MO1321	264	MS1703
239	MB7635	248	MJ2015	257	MO1391	265	MS1814
240	MB7638	249	MJ2014	258	MO1390	266	MS1813
241	MB7636	250	MJ2013	259	MO1397	267	MS1812
242	MB7637	251	MJ2168	260	MS1707	268	MS1815
243	ME9235	252	MJ2169				

270 MC6399 1985 Hino AC140 Micanta C23F

290 - 293   1990 Renault S75-110   Coachwork International B23F

290	PD1037	291	PD1038	292	PD1036	293	PE5096

374s EV6923 1963 AEC Reliance 2MU2RAE NZ Motor Bodies B40D

401 - 416   1976/7 Leyland PSU3C/2R   Hawke B40D

401	HZ2712	405	FL350	410	PW8450	414	IK7802
402	HI1974	406	HE2656	411	HQ3939	415	IL4461
403	GA6806	408	HQ3899	413	IL4518	416	IK7801
404	FL349	409	HQ3907				

418 - 478   1978/9 Leyland PSU3E/2R   Hawke B40D

418	IU9433	436	IU9932	451	JD197	465	IU9928
420	IU9431	437	IU9929	452	JF1903	466	KP7998
421	IX7733	438	JC2430	453	JF1909	467	JA1188
422	IX7732	439	JC2430	454	JFI908	468	LH1322
423	IX3304	440	JA1187	455	JF1910	469	JA1184
425	IX3781	441	JA1185	456	JF1911	470	JA1197
426	IX3660	442	JA1198	457	JF1913	471	JA2261
427	IX3783	443	JC2506	458	JF1914	472	JC2505
429	IX3807	444	JC2568	459	IX3806	473	NR3918
430	IX3808	445	JC2569	460	IK3814	474	JD181
431	IX3817	446	JC2570	461	IX3815	475	JC2520
432	PA6877	447	JDI84	462	IX7767	476	JD199
433	IX7765	448	JDI83	463	IX7766	477	JF1902
434	IX7763	449	JD182	464	IU9930	478	JF1912
435	IU9931	450	JD196				

479	IX3303	1978	Leyland PSU3E/2R	Hawke B40D	*Goldstar, Frankton 3.92*
480	IX7734	1978	Leyland PSU3E/2R	Hawke B40D	*Goldstar, Frankton 3.92*
481	LA5234	1983	Leyland PSU3E/2R	NZ Motor Bodies B44D	*Invercargill City Tpt. 3.92*

501 - 520   1994 M.A.N. 11.190   Designline B39D

501	SS5537	506		511		516	
502		507		512		517	
503		508		513		518	
504		509		514		519	
505		510		515		520	

These are the first of a batch of 80 for delivery completion in 1995 which will replace a similar number of the 401-81 series of Leyland Leopards

---

NON-OPERATIONAL VEHICLES

39	EV6714	1955	BUT ETB/1	WCT/NZ Motor Bodies B42D	*Preserved*
49	de-reg'd	1958	BUT RETB/1	MCW B43D	*Preserved*
88	de-reg'd	1964	BUT RETB/1	MCW B42D	*Preserved*
90	de-reg'd	1964	BUT RETB/1	MCW B42D	*Preserved*
119	de-reg'd	1964	BUT RETB/1	NZ Motor Bodies B42D	*Preserved*
255	de-reg'd	1953	Leyland OPSU3/3	NZ Motor Bodies B39D	*Preserved*
322	EV6871	1958	AEC Reliance MU2RAE	MCW B40D	*Preserved*
397	de-reg'd	1968	Leyland PSU3/2R	NZ Motor Bodies B41D	*Preserved*

ANCILLARY VEHICLES

914	276PL	Trailer
919	47CNO	Tractor
928	IT4901	Forklift
954	KZ4888	Hino truck
963	MA8824	Hino truck
979	NH9693	Ford Trader
986	760NZ	Trailer Concrete
993	239WC	Trailer
995	OK873	Toyota Lite Ace

Cityline Auckland   Fleet list

5731	JP5614	1980	Bedford NFM/6BD1	Emslie B37D
5907	1055IC	1980	Hino BG300	Emslie C41F
5997	JX9716	1980	Bedford NFM/6BD1	NZ Motor Bodied B37D
6004	JZ5550	1980	Bedford NFM/6BD1	NZ Motor Bodies B37D
6008	JZ6947	1981	Bedford NFM/6BD1	NZ Motor Bodies B37D
6009	JZ6948	1981	Bedford NFM/6BD1	NZ Motor Bodies B37D
6890	MI8415	1985	Hino RK176	Coachwork International B45D
7193	NA6078	1987	Hino RK176	Coachwork International B45D

7232 - 7239   1987 Hino RK176   Coachwork International B47D

| 7232 | NA7350 | 7233 | NA7351 | 7239 | NA7361 |

7255 - 7535

1988 Hino RK177 — Coachwork International B47D

7242	NL7824	7263	NL7791	7271	NL8273	7533	NX9509
7255	NL7823	7264	NL7792	7278	NX9467	7534	NX9507
7256	NL7790	7267	NL7793	7532	NX9510	7535	NX9508
7259	NL7797						

7540 - 7556

1989 Hino RK177 — Coachwork International B47D

7540	OB4215	7545	OE7913	7549	OG5328	7555	OG5343
7542	OB4213	7546	OE7916	7551	OG5327	7556	OG5344
7543	OB4212	7548	OE7917				

Cityline Hutt Valley   Fleet list

294	RM4511	1992	Toyota	Toyota C15F	Wellington City Tpt. 3.93
407	HE2657	1976	Leyland PSU3C/2R	Hawke B40D	Wellington City Tpt. 3.93
412	IL4519	1977	Leyland PSU3C/2R	Hawke B40D	Wellington City Tpt. 3.93

419 - 428

1978 Leyland PSU3B/2R — Hawke B40D
(ex.Wellington City Transport 3.93)

417	IU9434	419	IU9432	424	IX3302	428	IX3782

482	JT684	1979	Leyland PSU3C/2R	Hawke B40D	Cesta Travel 2.93
5908	1056IC	1980	Hino BG300	Emslie C41F	
5989	JX9248	1980	Bedford NFM/6BD1	NZ Motor Bodies B37D Wellington City Tpt. 3.93	

5991 - 5996

1980 Bedford NFM/6BD1 — New Zealand Motor Bodies B38D

5991	JE5454	5994	JE5457	5995	JX9714	5996	JX9715
5992	JE5455						

7197 - 7201

1987 Hino RK176 — Coachwork International B45D

7197	NA6060	7199	NA6946	7200	NA6945	7201	NA6507
7198	NA6947						

7231 - 7238

1987 Hino RK176 — Coachwork I*nternational B47D

7231	NA7353	7236	NA7357	7237	NA7358	7238	NA7359

7244 - 7253   1988   Hino RK176   Coachwork International B47D

7244 NL7825	7247 NL7828	7250 NL7831	7252 NL7833
7245 NL7826	7248 NL7829	7251 NL7832	7253 NL7834
7246 NL7827	7249 NL7830		

7258 - 7539   1988   Hino RK177   Coachwork International B47D

7258 NL7796	7266 NL8272	7273 NL8267	7536 NX9516
7260 NL7799	7268 NL8264	7274 NL8268	7537 NX9517
7261 NL7794	7269 NL8265	7276 NX9485	7538 OB4207
7265 NL7798	7270 NL8266	7279 NX9488	7539 OB4208

7544 - 7554   1989   Hino RK177   Coachwork International B47D

| 7544 OB4214 | 7547 OE7912 | 7553 OG5341 | 7554 OG5342 |

Twenty Mercedes Benz L608D minibuses have been acquired from Stagecoach U.K. companies for use by Cityline Hutt Valley and Cityline Auckland as replacements for their Bedfords.

(C799SDY)	1986	Mercedes Benz L608D	Alexander AM	B20F	*South Coast Buses 11.94*
(C801SDY)	1986	Mercedes Benz L608D	Alexander AM	B20F	*South Coast Buses 11.94*
(C803SDY)	1986	Mercedes Benz L608D	Alexander AM	B20F	*Red & White 10.94*
(C804SDY)	1986	Mercedes Benz L608D	Alexander AM	B20F	*South Coast Buses 11.94*
(C807SDY)	1986	Mercedes Benz L608D	Alexander AM	B20F	*Red & White 10.94*
(C809SDY)	1986	Mercedes Benz L608D	Alexander AM	B20F	*Red & White 10.94*
(C810SDY)	1986	Mercedes Benz L608D	Alexander AM	B20F	*Red & White 10.94*
(C811SDY)	1986	Mercedes Benz L608D	Alexander AM	B20F	*South Coast Buses 7.94*
(C813SDY)	1986	Mercedes Benz L608D	Alexander AM	B20F	*Red & White 10.94*
(C814SDY)	1986	Mercedes Benz L608D	Alexander AM	B20F	*Red & White 10.94*
(C815SDY)	1986	Mercedes Benz L608D	Alexander AM	B20F	*Red & White 8.94*
(C816SDY)	1986	Mercedes Benz L608D	Alexander AM	B20F	*South Coast Buses 8.94*
(C818SDY)	1986	Mercedes Benz L608D	Alexander AM	B20F	*Coastline 7.94*
(D225UHC)	1986	Mercedes Benz L608D	Alexander AM	B20F	*South Coast Buses 8.94*
(D231UHC)	1986	Mercedes Benz L608D	Alexander AM	B20F	*South Coast Buses 8.94*
(D947UDY)	1986	Mercedes Benz L608D	Alexander AM	DP19F	*Red & White 8.94*
(D948UDY)	1986	Mercedes Benz L608D	Alexander AM	DP19F	*Red & White 7.94*
(D951UDY)	1986	Mercedes Benz L608D	Alexander AM	DP19F	*Red & White 8.94*
(D952UDY)	1986	Mercedes Benz L608D	Alexander AM	DP19F	*Red & White 8.94*

One additional vehicle has still to be delivered

Kelburn Cable Car   Fleet list

---

1 - 2   1979   Habegger   Single deck, dual door each side

1   2

Eastbourne Buses   Fleet list

1	FL4297	1976	Ford R226	Hawke DP49F
2	NA4281	1987	Isuzu MR1113	DP28F
3	FL4281	1973	Ford R192	B41F
4	NA4279	1987	Isuzu MR1113	DP28F
5	NA3943	1987	Isuzu MR1113	DP28F
6	SK700	1986	Isuzu ECR570	B45F
7	FL4279	1972	Ford R192	B41F
8	NY58	1988	Isuzu ECR570	B45F
9	MQ8716	1986	Isuzu ECR	B50F
10	JR48	1980	Ford R1114/Hess/Isuzu	DP49F
11	ON223	1989	Isuzu ECR570	B46F
12	PT2685	1991	Hino RG197	B37F
13	JR47	1980	Ford R1114/Hess/Isuzu	DP49F
14	IN2551	1977	Ford R226	DP49F
15	JZ7041	1981	Ford R1114/Hess/Isuzu	DP49F
16	OB1552	1988	Isuzu ECR570	B50F
17	JR2616	1980	Mercedes Benz 0303	C42F
18	JW8024	1980	Mercedes Benz 0303	C42F
19	LE4641	1983	Hino BX341	B49F
20	MC609	1985	Isuzu ECR570	B50F

Adorned with Perth Panther fleet names is Stagecoach Buses former Bluebird Northern ECW-bodied Leyland Olympian 020 seen here in Perth city centre.   (K.A.Jenkinson)

Stagecoach WEST

Stagecoach West Ltd., 3/4 Bath Street, Cheltenham GL50 1YE

Cheltenham & Gloucester Omnibus Co. Ltd., 3/4 Bath Street, Cheltenham GL50 1YE

Separated from Bristol Omnibus Co. in September 1983 as part of the National Bus Company's restructuring plans, Cheltenham & Gloucester adopted individual liveries and fleet names for each of its depots, the liveries being applied in a corporate fashion. Purchased in October 1986 from the NBC by its management team who formed a new company Western Travel Ltd. for this purpose, the Cheltenham & Gloucester companies each retained its individual appearance until their sale to Stagecoach Holdings in November 1994.

Fleet names : Stagecoach Gloucester Citybus; Stagecoach Stroud Valleys. Stagecoach Metro

Livery : Stagecoach corporate livery replacing Gloucester blue & yellow (Gloucester Citybus) green & yellow (Stroud Valleys) and silver with a blue & red stripe (Metro).

Depots : Gloucester (Gloucester Citybus); Stroud (Stroud Valleys) *Outstation : Cirencester (Stroud Valleys)*

Cheltenham District Traction Co. Ltd., 3/4 Bath Street, Cheltenham GL50 1YE

Cheltenham District Traction Co. Ltd. was registered as a separate company by Western Travel Ltd. on 27 July 1993.

Fleet names : Stagecoach Cheltenham District; Stagecoach Metro

Livery : Stagecoach corporate livery replacing red & Cream (Cheltenham District) and silver with a blue & red stripe (Metro)

Depot : Cheltenham

Swindon & District Bus Co. Ltd., 3/4 Bath Street, Cheltenham GL50 1YE

Swindon & District Bus Co. Ltd. was registered as a separate company by Western Travel Ltd. on 12 November 1991.

Fleet name : Stagecoach Swindon & District

Livery : Stagecoach corporate livery replacing red & cream

Depot : Swindon

Midland Red (South) Ltd., Railway Terrace, Rugby CV21 3HS

Formed in 1981 upon the division by the NBC of the giant Midland Red Omnibus Co., Midland Red (South) in December 1987 left state ownership when it was purchased by Western Travel Ltd. The services operated in Stratford-upon-Avon were maintained by vehicles wearing a blue livery adorned with Stratford Blue fleet names. Expansion was gained in 1989 with the purchase of Tanners, Sibford Gower; G & G of Leamington and Vanguard of Bedworth, the latter two being continued as separate subsidiaries.

Fleet name : Stagecoach Midland Red

Livery : Stagecoach corporate livery replacing red, grey & white (Midland Red) and blue & white (Stratford Blue)

Depots : Banbury; Coventry; Leamington Spa (Shared with G & G); Nuneaton; Rugby; Stratford-upon-Avon *Outstations : Bicester; Chipping Norton.*

G & G Travel Ltd., Station Approach; Leamington Spa CV31 3SA

Livery : Stagecoach corporate livery replacing blue, grey & cream

Depot : Leamington Spa (shared with Midland Red South)

Vanguard Coaches Ltd., Croft Fields, Park Road, Bedworth CV21 3HS

Livery : Stagecoach corporate livery replacing blue, maroon & cream.

Depot : Bedworth

Red & White Services Ltd., 1 St.David's Road, Cwmbran NP44 1QX
Aberdare Bus Co. Ltd., 1 St.David's Road, Cwmbran NP44 1QX
The Valleys Bus Co. Ltd., 1 St.David's Road, Cwmbran NP44 1QX
Eastern Valley Bus Co. Ltd., 1 St.David's Road, Cwmbran NP44 1QX
Western Valleys Bus Co. Ltd., 1 St.David's Road, Cwmbran NP44 1QX

Following financial difficulties, National Welsh was sold off in parts at the start of the 1990s, its eastern sction being purchased by Western Travel Ltd who formed a new company, Red & White Services Ltd. for this purpose on 31 January 1991. A month later, a further company was registered under the title The Valleys Bus Co. Ltd. to run Red & White's services in the Merthyr Tydfil and Ross on Wye areas whilst in August 1992 the Aberdare Bus Compant was registered for a similar purpose. 24 December 1992 saw the advent of Western Valleys Bus Co. Ltd. and Eastern Valley Bus Co. Ltd. as further Red & White divisions although all the vehicles used on their services have retained their Red & White fleet name.

Fleet name : Stagecoach Red & White

Livery : Stagecoach corporate livery replacing red, white & grey

Depots : RED & WHITE - Chepstow; Ross-on-Wye (shared with The Valleys). ABERDARE BUS - Aberdare; THE VALLEYS - Merthyr Tydfil; Pengam; Ross-on-Wye (shared with Red & White); EASTERN VALLEY - Abergavenny; Brecon; Cwmbran. WESTERN VALLEYS - Brynmawr; Cross Keys.

Gloucester Citybus Fleet list

---

112 - 123   1982 Leyland ONLXB/1R   Roe H47/29F
(ex.Bristol 9.83)

| 112 | JHU899X | | 121 | LWS39Y | | 122 | LWS40Y | | 123 | LWS41Y |
| 114 | JHU912X |

213	REU311S	1977	Bristol VRT/SL3/6LXB	ECW H43/28F	*Bristol 9.83*
217	VOD593S	1978	Bristol VRT/SL3/6LXB	ECW H43/31F	*Devon General .87*
223	TWS913T	1979	Bristol VRT/SL3/6LXB	ECW H43/28F	*Bristol 9.83*
224	TWS914T	1979	Bristol VRT/SL3/6LXB	ECW H43/28F	*Bristol 9.83*
229	EWS746W	1981	Bristol VRT/SL3/6LXB	ECW H43/31F	*Bristol 9.83*

302	YFB973V	1979	Leyland LN11351A/1R	Leyland B52F		*Bristol 9.83*
303	TAE641S	1978	Leyland LN11351A/1R	Leyland B52F		*Bristol 9.83*
305	PHW989S	1977	Leyland LN11351A/1R	Leyland B52F		*Bristol 9.83*
307	SAE752S	1978	Leyland LN11351A/1R	Leyland B52F		*Bristol 9.83*
308	TAE642S	1978	Leyland LN11351A/1R	Leyland B52F		*Bristol 9.83*
309	SAE754S	1978	Leyland LN11351A/1R	Leyland B52F		*Bristol 9.83*
310	VEU231T	1979	Leyland LN11351A/1R	Leyland B52F		*Bristol 9.83*
311	SAE756S	1978	Leyland LN11351A/1R	Leyland B52F		*Bristol 9.83*
313	TAE639S	1978	Leyland LN11351A/1R	Leyland B52F		*Bristol 9.83*
323	HEU120N	1975	Leyland LN11351/1R	Leyland B52F		*Bristol 9.93*
332	NFB602R	1976	Leyland LN11351A/1R	Leyland B52F		*Bristol 9.83*
500	VAE499T	1979	Leyland LN10351B/1R	Leyland B44F		*Bristol 9.83*
503	VAE507T	1979	Leyland LN10351B/1R	Leyland B44F		*Bristol 9.83*
630	C630SFH	1985	Ford Transit 190	Alexander B16F		
647	C591SHC	1986	Mercedes Benz L608D	PMT B20F		South Coast Buses 12.93

656 - 662   1986   Mercedes Benz L608D   Alexander B20F

656	C656XDF	658	C658XDF	660	C660XDF	662	C662XDF
657	C657XDF	659	C659XDF	661	C661XDF		

680 - 684   1989   Mercedes Benz 709D   PMT B25F

680	G680AAD	681	G681AAD	682	G682AAD	684	G684AAD

687 - 703   1994   Mercedes Benz 709D   Alexander (Belfast) B25F

687	L687CDD	699	M699EDD	702	M702EDD	703	M703EDD
688	L688CDD	701	M701EDD				

831 - 842   1994   Volvo B6   Alexander Dash B40F

831	L831CDG	834	L834CDG	837	L837CDG	840	L840CDG
832	L832CDG	835	L835CDG	838	L838CDG	841	L841CDG
833	L833CDG	835	L835CDG	839	L839CDG	842	L842CDG

Stroud Valleys   Fleet list

115 - 120   1982   Leyland ONLXB/1R   Roe H47/29F
(ex.Bristol 9.83)

115	LWS33Y	116	LWS34Y	118	LWS36Y	120	LWS38Y

211	REU309S	1977	Bristol VRT/SL3/6LXB	ECW H43/28F		*Bristol 9.83*
215	XDV620S	1978	Bristol VRT/SL3/6LXB	ECW H43/31F		*Devon General .87*

225 - 230   1981   Bristol VRT/SL3/6LXB   ECW H43/31F
(ex.Bristol 9.83)

225	DHW350W	227	EWS740W	228	EWS743W	230	EWS748W
226	DHW352W						

334	NOE584R	1976	Leyland LN11351A/1R	Leyland B49F	*Midland Red South .91*
337	NOE555R	1976	Leyland LN11351A/1R	Leyland B49F	*Midland Red South .91*
338	NOE554R	1976	Leyland LN11351A/1R	Leyland B49F	*Midland Red South .91*
339	PHW986S	1977	Leyland LN11351A/1R	Leyland B52F	*Bristol 9.83*
340	PHW987S	1977	Leyland LN11351A/1R	Leyland B52F	*Bristol 9.83*
341	SAE751S	1978	Leyland LN11351A/1R	Leyland B52F	*Bristol 9.83*
342	SAE755S	1978	Leyland LN11351A/1R	Leyland B52F	*Bristol 9.83*

347 - 350

1979 Leyland LN11351A/1R   Leyland B52F
(ex.Bristol 9.83)

347	VEU228T	348	VEU229T	349	VEU230T	350	VEU232T

362	HIL6075	1980	Leyland NL116L11/1R	Leyland B52F	*Bristol 9.83*
363	511OHU	1980	Leyland NL116L11/1R	Leyland B52F	*Bristol 9.83*
368	YJV806	1980	Leyland NL116L11/1R	Leyland B52F	*Bristol 9.83*

362/3/8 were originally registered AAE646/7/58V

376	ARN892Y	1983	Leyland NL116HLXB/1R	Leyland B52F	Ribble 11.94
377	RHG880X	1982	Leyland NL116AL11/1R	Leyland B52F	Ribble 11.94
378	NHH382W	1981	Leyland NL116L11/1R	Leyland DP52F	Ribble 11.94
379	SHH389X	1982	Leyland NL116AL11/1R	Leyland B52F	Ribble 11.94
600	A871KDF	1984	Mercedes Benz L608D	PMT DP18F	
621	C621SFH	1985	Ford Transit 190	Alexander B16F	
631	C631SFH	1985	Ford Transit 190	Alexander B16F	
632	C632SFH	1985	Ford Transit 190	Alexander B16F	
644	C644SFH	1985	Ford Transit 190	Alexander B16F	*Cheltenham District 8.94*
645	C645SFH	1985	Ford Transit 190	Alexander B16F	*Cheltenham District 8.94*
651	C651XDF	1986	Mercedes Benz L608D	Alexander B20F	
655	C655XDF	1986	Mercedes Benz L608D	Alexander B20F	
677	F677PDF	1988	Mercedes Benz 709D	PMT B25F	
678	F311DET	1988	Mercedes Benz 709D	Reeve Burgess B25F	*Demonstrator .89*
679	G679AAD	1989	Mercedes Benz 709D	PMT B25F	
683	G683AAD	1989	Mercedes Benz 709D	PMT B25F	
685	L685CDD	1994	Mercedes Benz 709D	Alexander (Belfast) B25F	
686	L686CDD	1994	Mercedes Benz 709D	Alexander (Belfast) B25F	

803 - 806

1993 Mercedes Benz 811D   Marshall B33F

803	L803XDG	804	L804XDG	805	L805XDG	806	L806XDG

807	L330CHB	1993	Mercedes Benz 811D	Marshall B33F	Red & White 12.94

Cheltenham District   Fleet list

117	LWS35Y	1982	Leyland ONLXB/1R	Roe H47/29F	*Bristol 9.83*
119	LWS37Y	1982	Leyland ONLXB/1R	Roe H47/29F	*Bristol 9.83*
201	JOU160P	1975	Bristol VRT/SL3/6LXB	ECW H43/28F	*Bristol 9.83*
202	MUA872P	1975	Bristol VRT/SL3/6LXB	ECW H43/31F	*Bristol 9.83*
204	MOU739R	1976	Bristol VRT/SL3/6LXB	ECW H43/28F	*Bristol 9.83*
205	NHU670R	1977	Bristol VRT/SL3/6LXB	ECW H43/28F	*Bristol 9.83*
212	REU310S	1977	Bristol VRT/SL3/6LXB	ECW H43/28F	*Bristol 9.83*
301	467WYA	1978	Leyland LN11351A/1R	Leyland B25DL	*Bristol 9.83*
304	PHW985S	1977	Leyland LN11351A/1R	Leyland B52F	*Bristol 9.83*
306	PHW988S	1977	Leyland LN11351A/1R	Leyland B52F	*Bristol 9.83*
312	TAE644S	1978	Leyland LN11351A/1R	Leyland B52F	*Bristol 9.83*

331	JHW103P	1975	Leyland LN11351/1R	Leyland B52F	*Bristol 9.83*
335	NOE585R	1977	Leyland LN11351A/1R	Leyland B49F	*Midland Red South .91*
336	NOE587R	1977	Leyland LN11351A/1R	Leyland B49F	*Midland Red South .91*
344	UHW101T	1978	Leyland LN11351A/1R	Leyland B52F	*Bristol 9.83*
345	TAE643S	1978	Leyland LN11351A/1R	Leyland B52F	*Bristol 9.83*
463	TTC532T	1978	Leyland LN11351A/1R	Leyland B52F	*Bristol 9.83*
351	YBF972V	1979	Leyland LN11351A/1R	Leyland B52F	*Bristol 9.83*

301 was originally registered TAE645S

361 - 375

1980 Leyland NL116L11/1R   Leyland B52F
(ex.Bristol 9.83)

| 361 | AAE644V | 365 | AAE649V | 367 | AAE651V | 374 | BHY998V |
| 364 | AAE648V | 366 | AAE650V | 370 | AAE660V | 375 | BOU6V |

533 - 548

1990 Volvo B10M-60   Plaxton 3500 C48FT
(ex.Wallace Arnold 1993)

| 533 | G533LWU | 546 | G546LWU | 547 | G547LWU | 548 | G548LWU |
| 534 | G534LWU | | | | | | |

617 - 643

1985 Ford Transit 190   Alexander B16F

617	C617SFH	637	C637SFH	640	C640SFH	642	C642SFH
633	C633SFH	639	C639SFH	641	C641SFH	643	C643SFH
636	C636SFH						

| 648 | C594SHC | 1986 | Mercedes Benz L608D | PMT B20F | *South Coast Buses 12.93* |

649 - 654

1986 Mercedes Benz L608D   Alexander B20F

| 649 | C649XDF | 652 | C652XDF | 653 | C653XDF | 654 | C654XDF |
| 650 | C650XDF | | | | | | |

663 - 669

1987 MCW Metrorider MF150   MCW B25F

| 663 | E663JAD | 666 | E666JAD | 668 | E668JAD | 669 | E669JAD |
| 665 | E665JAD | 667 | E667JAD | | | | |

| 670 | E670JDG | 1988 | MCW Metrorider MF150 | MCW DP25F |
| 671 | E671JDG | 1988 | MCW Metrorider MF150 | MCW DP25F |

689 - 698

1994 Mercedes Benz 709D   Alexander (Belfast) B25F

689	L689CDD	692	L692CDD	695	L695CDD	697	M697EDD
690	L690CDD	693	L693CDD	696	L696CDD	698	M698EDD
691	L691CDD	694	L694CDD				

Swindon & District   Fleet list

101 - 105

1990 Leyland ONLXB/2RZ   Alexander RL H51/36F

| 101 | G101AAD | 103 | G103AAD | 104 | G104AAD | 105 | G105AAD |
| 102 | G102AAD | | | | | | |

106 - 111

1979 Leyland TNLXB/1RF   Park Royal H47/26F
(ex.Thames Transit 1990)

106	GNF6V	109	GNF9V	110	GNF10V	111	GNF11V
108	GNF8V						

113	UWW7X	1982	Leyland ONLXB/1R	Roe H47/29F	*Yorkshire Rider .87*
124	NTC132Y	1983	Leyland ONLXB/1R	Roe H47/29F	*Bristol 9.83*
208	NWS288R	1977	Bristol VRT/SL3/6LXB	ECW H43/28F	*Bristol 9.83*
209	NWS289R	1977	Bristol VRT/SL3/6LXB	ECW H43/28F	*Bristol 9.83*
210	PEU515R	1977	Bristol VRT/SL3/6LXB	ECW H43/31F	*Bristol 9.83*
214	RFB617S	1978	Bristol VRT/SL3/6LXB	ECW H43/31F	*Bristol 9.83*
216	XDV606S	1978	Bristol VRT/SL3/6LXB	ECW H43/31F	*Devon General .87*
218	VOD596S	1978	Bristol VRT/SL3/6LXB	ECW H43/31F	*Devon General .87*
219	VOD597S	1978	Bristol VRT/SL3/6LXB	ECW H43/31F	*Devon General .87*
220	VOD598S	1978	Bristol VRT/SL3/6LXB	ECW H43/31F	*Devon General .87*
221	TWS903T	1978	Bristol VRT/SL3/6LXB	ECW H43/28F	*Bristol 9.83*
222	TWS906T	1979	Bristol VRT/SL3/6LXB	ECW H43/31F	*Bristol 9.83*
333	NFB603R	1976	Leyland LN11351A/1R	Leyland B52F	*Bristol 9.83*

369 - 373

1980 Leyland NL116L11/1R   Leyland B52F
(ex.Bristol 9.83)

369	AAE659V	371	AAE665V	372	BHY996V	373	BHY997V

626	C626SFH	1985	Ford Transit 190	Alexander B16F
664	E664JAD	1987	MCW Metrorider	MCW B25F
672	E672KDG	1988	MCW Metrorider	MCW B25F
673	E673KDG	1988	MCW Metrorider	MCW B25F
674	E674KDG	1988	MCW Metrorider	MCW B25F
675	E675KDG	1988	MCW Metrorider	MCW DP25F
676	E676KDG	1988	MCW Metrorider	MCW DP25F
801	K801OMW	1993	Mercedes Benz 811D	Wright B33F
802	K802OMW	1993	Mercedes Benz 811D	Wright B33F

Midland Red South   Fleet list

1	A75NAC	1983	Leyland TCRTL11/2R	Plaxton 3200 DP47F	
2	A76NAC	1983	Leyland TRCTL11/2R	Plaxton 3200 DP47F	
3	Q275UOC	1976	Leyland PSU3C/4R	(1983) Plaxton 3200 DP49F	
4	230HUE	1980	Leyland PSU3E/4R	Plaxton Sup.IV DP49F	*Midland Red North 1981*
5	331HWD	1980	Leyland PSU3E/4R	Plaxton Sup.IV DP49F	*Midland Red North 1981*
6	3273AC	1980	Leyland PSU3E/4R	Plaxton Sup.IV DP49F	*Midland Red North 1981*
9	BVP791V	1980	Leyland PSU3E/4R	Plaxton Sup.IV DP49F	*Midland Red 1981*
10	BVP801V	1980	Leyland PSU3E/4R	Plaxton Sup.IV DP49F	*Midland Red 1981*
15	NPA230W	1981	Leyland PSU3E/4R	Plaxton Sup.IV DP47F	East Midland 2.94
28	NAK28X	1981	Leyland PSU3F/4R	Duple Dom.IV DP47F	East Midland 2.94

1/2 were previously registered 420/91GAC and were originally A190/1GVC. 3-6 were originally registered JOX453P & BVP786-8V.

60 - 65

1990 Volvo B10M-60   Plaxton 3500 C48FT
(ex.Wallace Arnold 1993)

60	G528LWU	62	G530LWU	64	G532LWU	65	G535LWU
61	G529LWU	63	G531LWU				

70	BIW4977	1984	Leyland TRCTL11/3R	Plaxton 3200 DP49F	
90	5520HU	1983	Leyland TRCTL11/3R	Plaxton 3200 DP57F	*Cheltenham & Glos. 1990*
91	CDG213Y	1983	Leyland TRCTL11/3R	Plaxton 3200 DP46FT	*Cheltenham & Glos. 1991*
92	420GAC	1983	Leyland TRCTL11/3R	Plaxton 3200 C53F	*Cheltenham & Glos 1991*

70/2 & 90/2 were originally registered A70KDU, B73OKV, A201RHT & A211SAE.

300	E433YHL	1988	Mercedes Benz 709D	Reeve Burgess B25F	Lofty, Bridge Trafford .93
301	G301WHP	1989	Mercedes Benz 709D	PMT B25F	
302	G302WHP	1989	Mercedes Benz 709D	PMT B25F	
303	G303WHP	1989	Mercedes Benz 709D	PMT B25F	
304	J304THP	1992	Mercedes Benz 709D	Alexander AM B25F	
305	J305THP	1992	Mercedes Benz 709D	Alexander AM B25F	
306	K306ARW	1992	Mercedes Benz 709D	Wright B25F	
307	L307SKV	1993	Mercedes Benz 709D	Wright B25F	

308 - 330

1994 Mercedes Benz 709D   Alexander (Belfast) B23F

308	L308YDU	314	L314YDU	320	L330YDU	326	L326YDU
309	L309YDU	315	L315YDU	321	L321YDU	327	L327YDU
310	L310YDU	316	L316YDU	322	L322YDU	328	L328YDU
311	L311YDU	317	L317YDU	323	L323YDU	329	L329YDU
312	L312YDU	318	L318YDU	324	L324LDU	330	L330YDU
313	L313YDU	319	L319YDU	325	L325YDU		

352 - 360

1985 Ford Transit 190D   Alexander B16F
(ex.Cheltenham & Gloucester 1990)

352	C619SFH	354	C622SFH	356	C642SFH	360	C647SFH
353	C620SFH	355	C623SFH	359	C646SFH		

361 - 365

1986 Ford Transit 190D   Dormobile B16F
(ex.East Kent 1990/1)

361	C702FKE	363	C713FKE	364	C714FKE	365	C720FKE
362	C703FKE						

366 - 370

1986 Ford Transit 190D   Carlyle B16F
(ex.Alder Valley 1991)

366	D313WPE	368	D315WPE	369	D320WPE	370	D321WPE
367	D314WPE						

371	C729JJO	1986	Ford Transit 190D	Carlyle B20F	*City of Oxford 1991*
373	F718FKE	1986	Ford Transit 190D	Dormobile BI6F	*East Kent 1991*
376	C706FKE	1986	Ford Transit 190D	Dormobile B16F	*East Kent 1992*
382	C719FKE	1986	Ford Transit 190D	Dormobile B16F	*East Kent 1992*
383	C618SFH	1985	Ford Transit 190D	Alexander B16F	Stroud Valleys 7.94
384	C627SFH	1985	Ford Transit 190D	Alexander B16F	Cheltenham & Glos. **7.94**
385	C629SFH	1985	Ford Transit 190D	Alexander B16F	Cheltenham & Glos. **7.94**
387	C634SFH	1985	Ford Transit 190D	Alexander B16F	Cheltenham &,Glos. **7.94**
388	C635SFH	1985	Ford Transit 190D	Alexander B16F	Cheltenham & Dist. **7.94**
389	C638SFH	1985	Ford Transit 190D	Alexander B16F	Cheltenham & Dist. **7.94**
390	C705FKE	1986	Ford Transit 190D	Dormobile B16F	Stroud Valleys **7.94**
391	C715FKE	1986	Ford Transit 190D	Dormobile B16F	Stroud Valleys **7.94**
392	C742FKE	1986	Ford Transit 190D	Dormobile B16F	Swindon & District **7.94**
400	F71LAL	1988	Mercedes Benz 811D	Alexander AM DP33F	*Skills, Nottingham 1991*
401	H401MRW	1991	Mercedes Benz 811D	Wright B31F	
402	H402MRW	1991	Mercedes Benz 811D	Wright DP31F	
403	H403MRW	1991	Mercedes Benz 811D	Wright B31F	
404	H404MRW	1991	Mercedes Benz 811D	Wright DP31F	
405	H495MRW	1991	Mercedes Benz 811D	Wright B31F	
406	H406MRW	1991	Mercedes Benz 811D	Wright B31F	

407 - 412   1991   Mercedes Benz 811D   Wright DP33F

407	J407PRW	409	J409PRW	411	J411PRW	412	J412PRW
408	J408PRW	410	J410PRW				

413	J413PRW	1991	Mercedes Benz 811D	Wright B31F	
414	J414PRW	1991	Mercedes Benz 811D	Wright DP33F	
415	J415PRW	1991	Mercedes Benz 811D	Wright DP33F	
416	J416PRW	1991	Mercedes Benz 811D	Wright DP33F	
417	J417PRW	1991	Mercedes Benz 811D	Wright B31F	
418	J418PRW	1991	Mercedes Benz 811D	Wright B31F	
419	G115OGA	1989	Mercedes Benz 811D	Alexander AM DP33F	*Beaton, Blantyre 1992*

420 - 425   1993   Mercedes Benz 811D   Wright B31F

420	K420ARW	422	K422ARW	424	K424ARW	425	K425ARW
421	K421ARW	423	K423ARW				

426	F846TLU	1989	Mercedes Benz 811D	Optare StarRider C29F	*Brents, Watford 1993*

453 - 456   1994   Volvo B6R   Alexander AM Dash B40F

453	L453YAC	454	L454YAC	455	L455YAC	456	L456YAC

483	D273OOJ	1987	Ft Rover Sherpa 365	Carlyle B20F	*Carlyle demonstrator 1988*
485	D735OOG	1987	Ft Rover Sherpa 365	Carlyle B20F	*Carlyle demonstrator 1988*
487	D755JUB	1986	Ft Rover Sherpa 374	Dormobile B20F	*Yorkshire Rider 1990*
502	JOX503P	1976	Leyland LN11351A/1R	Leyland B49F	*Midland Red 1981*
503	JOX503P	1976	Leyland LN11351A/1R	Leyland B49F	*Midland Red 1981*
504	JOX504P	1976	Leyland LN11351A/1R	Leyland B49FL	*Midland Red 1981*
505	JOX505P	1976	Leyland LN11351A/1R	Leyland B49F	*Midland Red 1981*
506	JOX506P	1976	Leyland LN11351A/1R	Leyland B49F	*Midland Red 1981*
567	NOE567R	1976	Leyland LN11351A/1R	Leyland B49F	*Midland Red 1981*
568	NOE568R	1976	Leyland LN11351A/1R	Leyland B49F	*Midland Red 1981*
570	NOE570R	1976	Leyland LN11351A/1R	Leyland B49F	*Midland Red 1981*

577 - 589   1976   Leyland LN11351A/1R   Leyland B49F
(ex.Midland Red 1981)

577	NOE577R	579	NOE579R	582	NOE582R	589	NOE589R
578	NOE578R	581	NOE581R	586	NOE586R		

590	NOE590R	1977	Leyland LN11351A/1R	Leyland B49FL	*Midland Red 1981*
591	YEU446Y	1981	Leyland LN10351B/1R	Leyland B44F	Cheltenham & Glos. 10.94
592	NOE551R	1976	Leyland LN11351A/1R	Leyland B49F	Cheltenham & Dist. 7.94
593	KHT122P	1976	Leyland LN11351/1R	Leyland B52F	Cheltenham & Dist. 7.94
594	VAE502T	1979	Leyland LN10351B/1R	Leyland B44F	Cheltenham & Glos. 7.94
595	GOL426N	1975	Leyland LN11351/1R	Leyland B49F	Cheltenham & Glos. 7.94
596	GOL413N	1975	Leyland LN11351/1R	Leyland B49F	Stroud Valleys 7.94
599	WFR392V	1979	Leyland LN10351B/1R	Leyland B44F	Ribble 10.94

602 - 664   1977   Leyland LN11351A/1R   Leyland B49F (*B45F)
(ex.Midland Red 1981)

602	NOE602R	606	NOE606R	624	PUK624R	628	PUK628R
603	NOE603R	621	PUK621R	625	PUK625R	629	PUK629R
604	NOE604R	622	PUK622R	626*	PUK626R	664	SOA664S
605	NOE605R	623	PUK623R	627	PUK627R		

707 - 710

1978 Leyland LN11351A/1R   Leyland B49F
(ex.Midland Red 1981)

707	TOF707S	708	TOF708S	709	TOF709S	710	TOF710S

753 - 760

1979 Leyland LN11351A/1R   Leyland B49F
(ex.Midland Red 1981)

753	XOV753T	755	XOV755T	756	XOV756T	760	XOV760T
754	XOV754T						

771	BVP771V	1980	Leyland LN11351A/1R	Leyland B49F	*Midland Red 1981*
772	BVP772V	1980	Leyland LN11351A/1R	Leyland B52F	*Midland Red 1981*

834 - 847

1986 Iveco 49.10   Robin Hood City Nippy B19F
(ex.Rhondda 1992/3)

834	D34KAX	843	D43KAX	845	D45KAX	847	D47KAX

851 - 862

1986 Iveco 49.10   Robin Hood City Nippy B19F (*B21F)

851	D851CKV	854	D854CKV	857	D857CKV	860	D860CKV
852*	D852CKV	855	D855CKV	858	D858CKV	861	D861CKV
853	D853CKV	856	D856CKV	859	D859CKV	862	D862CKV

864 - 868

1988 Iveco 49.10   Robin Hood City Nippy B19F

864	F864PAC	866	F866PAC	867	F867PAC	868	F868PAC
865	F865PAC						

871	F871UAC	1989	Iveco 49.10	Robin Hood B25F	
872	F872UAC	1989	Iveco 49.10	Robin Hood B25F	
873	G26XBK	1990	Iveco 49.10	Phoenix B25F	*Lofty, Bridge Trafford 1993*
882	D882CKV	1986	Iveco 49.10	Robin Hood DP21F	
883	D883CKV	1986	Iveco 49.10	Robin Hood DP21F	

884 - 888

1986 Iveco 49.10   Robin Hood City Nippy DP19F

884	D884CKV	886	D886CKV	887	C887CKV	888	C888CKV
885	D885CKV						

904 - 907

1983 Leyland ONLXB/1R   RCW H45/32F

904	A544HAC	905	A545HAC	906	A546HAC	907	A547HAC

910	B910ODU	1984	Leyland ONLXB/1R	ECW H45/32F	
911	B911ODU	1984	Leyland ONLXB/1R	ECW H45/32F	
912	B912ODU	1984	Leyland ONLXB/1R	ECW H45/32F	
928	LHT725P	1979	Bristol VRT/SL3/6LXB	ECW H39/31F	Swindon & District 10.94
929	NHU672R	1979	Bristol VRT/SL3/6LXB	ECW H43/27D	Cheltenham & Glos. 10.94
931	CBV11S	1977	Bristol VRT/SL3/501	ECW H43/31F	Ribble 4.94
932	CBV16S	1977	Bristol VRT/SL3/501	ECW H43/31F	Ribble 4.94
933	CBV20S	1977	Bristol VRT/SL3/501	ECW H43/31F	Ribble 4.94
935	DBV31W	1980	Bristol VRT/SL3/6LXB	ECW H43/31F	Ribble 4.94
936	URF661S	1977	Bristol VRT/SL3/501	ECW H43/31F	Ribble 4.94
937	DWF195V	1980	Bristol VRT/SL3/6LXB	ECW H43/31F	East Midland 2.94
939	DWF194V	1980	Bristol VRT/SL3/6LXB	ECW H43/31F	East Midland 2.94

940	PEU511R	1977	Bristol VRT/SL3/6LXB	ECW DPH43/31F	Badgerline 12.93
943	GTX754W	1980	Bristol VRT/SL3/501	ECW H43/31F	Red & White 12.93
944	HUD475S	1977	Bristol VRT/SL3/6LXB	ECW H43/27F	City of Oxford 12.93
945	HUD480S	1977	Bristol VRT/SL3/6LXB	ECW H43/27F	City of Oxford 12.93
946	HUD479S	1977	Bristol VRT/SL3/6LXB	ECW H43/27F	City of Oxford 12.93
947	AET181T	1979	Bristol VRT/SL3/6LXB	ECW H43/27F	East Midland 12.93
948	VTV170S	1978	Bristol VRT/SL3/6LXB	ECW H43/27F	East Midland 12.93
949	DWF189V	1979	Bristol VRT/SL3/6LXB	ECW H43/27F	East Midland 12.92
952	OUC44R	1976	Leyland FE30AGR	MCCW H44/29F	*Stevenson, Spath 1989*
953	OJD241R	1977	Leyland FE30AGR	MCCW H44/29F	*Stevenson, Spath 1989*
954	OUC42R	1976	Leyland FE30AGR	MCCW H44/29F	*Stevenson, Spath 1990*
955	OJD136R	1976	Leyland FE30AGR	Park Royal H44/29F	*Stevenson, Spath 1990*
959	YNA363M	1974	Daimler CRG6LXB	NCME H43/32F	*GM Buses 1988*
960	B960ODU	1984	Leyland ONLXB/1R	ECW DPH42/30F	
961	B961ODU	1984	Leyland ONLXB/1R	ECW DPH42/30F	
962	C962XVC	1986	Leyland ONLXB/1RH	ECW DPH42/29F	
963	C963XVC	1986	Leyland ONLXB/1RH	ECW DPH42/29F	
964	C964XVC	1986	Leyland ONLXB/1RH	ECW DPH42/29F	
1008	KHP649N	1975	Leyland PSU3B/4R	Duple Dom. C53F	*Tanners Internat. 1989*
1009	NGU602P	1976	Bedford YMT	Plaxton Sup.III C53F	*Tanners Internat. 1989*
1010	NGU605P	1976	Bedford YMT	Plaxton Sup.III C53F	*Tanners Internat. 1989*
1015	YWK3S	1978	Bedford YMT	Plaxton Sup.III C53F	*Tanners Internat. 1989*
1051	KIB8140	1978	Leyland LN10351A/2R	Leyland B36DL	*London Buses 1991*
1052	AIB4053	1978	Leyland LN10351A/2R	Leyland B36FL	*London Buses 1991*
1053	PIB8019	1978	Leyland LN10351A/1R	Leyland B36DL	*London Buses 1991*

1008 was previously registered AIB4053 and wa originally HNU123N. 1051-3 were originally THX249/186/19S

2013	LOA838X	1982	Leyland PSU3F/4R	Willowbrook 003 C49F	Vanguard .94
	NHU671R	1976	Bristol VRT/SL3/6LXB	ECW H43/28F	Cheltenham & Glos. 9.94

G & G   Fleet list

571	NOE571R	1976	Leyland LN11351A/1R	Leyland B49F	Midland Red South 7.94
902	A542HAC	1983	Leyland ONLXB/1R	ECW H45/32F	Midland Red South 7.94
903	A543HAC	1983	Leyland ONLXB/1R	ECW H45/32F	Midland Red South 7.94
934	DBV23W	1980	Bristol VRT/SL3/6LXB	ECW H43/31F	Ribble 4.94
1019	A848VML	1979	Leyland PSU3E/4R	(1983) Duple Dom.IV DP53F	*Grey Green 1987*
1020	TVC504W	1981	Leyland PSU3E/4R	Duple Dom.IV DP53F	
1030	NAK30X	1981	Leyland PSU3F/4R	Duple Dom.IV DP47F	East Midland 2.94
1058	9984PG	1980	Leyland PSU3B/4R	Duple Dom.II DP53F	*Grey Green 1988*
1059	E630KCX	1988	DAF SB2305DHTD585	Duple 320 C53F	*Gray, Hoyland Cmn. 1990*
1068	WSU293	1990	Volvo B10M-60	Plaxton 3200 C53F	*Cheltenham & Glos. .93*
1086	CSV219	1984	MCW Metroliner	MCW CH55/19FT	*Go-Ahead Northern 1992*
1087	498FYB	1983	Leyland TRCTL11/3R	Plaxton 3200 C50F	*Cheltenham & Glos. 93*
1088	A8GGT	1983	Leyland TRCTL11/1R	Plaxton 3200 C57F	*Cheltenham & Glos. .93*
1089	A7GGT	1984	Leyland TRCTL11/3RH.	Plaxton 3200 C51F	*Midland Red South .92*

1058/86-9 were originally registered FYX815W, B231XEU, CDG207Y, A202RHT & B720KV

1427	H912XGA	1990	Mercedes Benz 814D	Reeve Burgess DP33F	Midland Red South 7.94
1451	L451YAC	1994	Volvo B6	Alexander Dash B40F	
1452	L452YAC	1994	Volvo B6	Alexander Dash B40F	
1484	D271OOJ	1987	Ft Rover Sherpa 365	Carlyle B20F	Midland Red South 7.94
1486	D736OOG	1987	Ft Rover Sherpa 365	Carlyle B20F	Midland Red South 7.94
1489	E77PUH	1987	Ft Rover Sherpa 405	Carlyle Citybus B20F	*Red & White 1991*
1490	E95OUH	1987	Ft Rover Sherpa 405	Carlyle Citybus B20F	*Red & White 1991*
1491	E99OUH	1987	Ft Rover Sherpa 405	Carlyle Citybus B20F	*Red & White 1991*
1820	F660PWK	1988	Leyland LX112L10ZR1R	Leyland B51F	
1821	F661PWK	1988	Leyland LX112L10ZR1R	Leyland B51F	

Displaying corporate livery and Stagecoach Midland Red fleet names at a bus rally in the summer of 1994 is Midland Red South Leyland National 755.   (Campbell Morrison)

Ribble is busy replacing its Mercedes Benz L608D minibuses with new 709Ds. One of the old brigade, 526 is seen here complete with Zippy fleet names at Blackburn bus station. (K.A.Jenkinson)

1930	LHT724P	1976	Bristol VRT/SL3/6LXB	ECW H43/31F	*Swindon & District 1992*
1931	MAU145P	1976	Bristol VRT/SL3/6LXB	ECW H43/31F	*Bluebird Buses 10.93*
1932	ONH646P	1976	Bristol VRT/SL3/6LXB	ECW H43/31F	*Bluebird Buses 10.93*
1933	PEU516R	1977	Bristol VRT/SL3/6LXB	ECW H43/31F	*Swindon & District 1992*
1956	SDA651S	1978	Leyland FE30AGR	Park Royal H45/33F	*West Midlands 1990*
1957	SDA715S	1978	Leyland FE30AGR	MCCW H43/33F	*West Midlands 1990*
1958	WDA994T	1979	Leyland FE30AGR	MCCW H43/33F	*West Midlands 1990*

Vanguard   Fleet list

377	C707FKE	1986	Ford Transit 190D	Dormobile B16F	Midland Red South .94
597	HEU122N	1975	Leyland LN11351/1R	Leyland B52F	Stroud Valleys .94
598	KHT124P	1976	Leyland LN11351/1R	Leyland B52F	Swindon & District .94
938	DWF197V	1980	Bristol VRT/SL3/501	ECW H43/31F	East Midland 2.94
941	GTX746W	1980	Bristol VRT/SL3/501	ECW H43/31F	Midland Red South .94
2007	4012VC	1980	Leyland PSU3E/4R	Plaxton Sup.IV DP53F	*Premier Travel 1991*
2016	YBO16T	1979	Leyland PSU3E/2R	East Lancs B51F	G & G, Leamington .93
2018	YBO18T	1979	Leyland PSU3E/2R	East Lancs B51F	G & G, Leamington .93
2026	ELJ209V	1979	Leyland PSU3E/4R	Plaxton Sup.IV DP49F	East Midland 2.94
2035	A35XBO	1984	Dennis Lancet SD515	East Lancs B47F	*National Welsh 1992*
2036	A36XBO	1984	Dennis Lancet SD515	East Lancs B47F	*National Welsh 1992*
2037	A37XBO	1984	Dennis Lancet SD515	East Lancs B47F	*National Welsh 1992*
2066	3063VC	1990	Volvo B10M-60	Plaxton 3500 C49F	*Wallace Arnold 1993*
2067	9258VC	1990	Volvo B10M-60	Plaxton 3500 C49F	*Wallace Arnold 1993*
2074	4828VC	1985	Leyland TRCTL11/3R	Plaxton 3500 C51F	*Sovereign 1990*
2075	9737VC	1985	Leyland TRCTL11/3R	Plaxton 3500 C51F	*Sovereign 1990*
2076	6253VC	1986	Leyland TRCTL11/3R	Plaxton 3200 C51F	*Thames Transit 1991*
2077	6804VC	1986	Leyland TRCTL11/3R	Plaxton 3200 C51F	*Thames Transit 1991*

2007/66/7/74/5 were originally registered KUB546V, G543/4LWU & C211/2PPE. 2076 was previously registered YDK917 & JPU817 and was originally C472CAP. 2077 was previously registered WVT618 and was originally C473CAP.

2345	C102HKG	1986	Ford Transit 190D	Robin Hood B16F	*Red & White 1993*
2507	XGR728R	1977	Leyland LN11351A/1R	Leyland B49F	*United 1993*
2508	THX155S	1978	Leyland LN10351A/2R	Leyland B36D	*Scorpio, Harrow 1991*
2509	THX231S	1978	Leyland LN10351A/2R	Leyland B36D	*London Buses 1991*
2510	CBV780S	1978	Leyland LN11351A/1R	Leyland B49F	*Thames Transit 1991*
2511	CBV783S	1978	Leyland LN11351A/1R	Leyland B49F	*Thames Transit 1991*
2512	EMB365S	1978	Leyland LN11351A/1R	Leyland B49F	*Crosville Wales 1991*
2513	LMA411T	1979	Leyland LN11351A/1R	Leyland B49F	*Crosville Wales 1991*
2808	BVP808V	1980	Leyland NL116L11/1R	Leyland B49F	*North Western 1991*
2809	SVV589W	1980	Leyland NL116TL11/1R	Leyland B49F	*Luton & District 1991*

Red & White   Fleet list

10-14

| | | 1988 | Renault S56 | NCME DP25F | |
| | | | (ex.Cynon Valley 1992) | | |

| 10 | E291TAX | 12 | E293TAX | 13 | E294TAX | 14 | E295TAX |
| 11 | E292TAX | | | | | | |

15-18

1987   Dodge S56   East Lancs   B29F
(ex.Cynon Valley 1992)

15	E896SDW	16	E897SDW	17	E898SDW	18	E899SDW

20-24

1988   Renault S56   NCME   B25F
(ex.Cynon Valley 1992)

20	E931UBO	21	E932UBO	23	E929UBO	24	E930UBO

30	E275BRG	1987	Renault S56	Alexander AM DP19F	*Go-Ahead Northern 1992*
75	D63OKG	1987	Freight Rover Sherpa	Carlyle B18F	*National Welsh 1991*
94	D67OKG	1987	Freight Rover Sherpa	Carlyle B18F	*National Welsh 1991*

96-139

1987   Freight Rover Sherpa   Carlyle Citybus 2   B20F
(ex.National Welsh 1991)

96	E96OUH	100	E100OUH	119	E119RAX	122	E122RAX
97	E97OUH	115	E115RAX	120	E120RAX	139	E139RAX

158-202

1988   Freight Rover Sherpa   Carlyle Citybus 2   B20F
(ex.National Welsh 1991)

158	E158RNY	200	F200YKG	201	F201YKG	202	F202YKG

203	F203YKG	1988	Freight Rover Sherpa	Carlyle B18F	*National Welsh 1991*
206	F206YKG	1989	Freight Rover Sherpa	Carlyle B18F	*National Welsh 1991*
234	F234BAX	1989	Freight Rover Sherpa	Carlyle B18F	*National Welsh 1991*
237	C514BFB	1985	Ford Transit 190D	Dormobile B16F	*Badgerline 1993*
238	B458WTC	1985	Ford Transit 190D	Dormobile B16F	*Badgerline 1993*
239	C294MEG	1985	Ford Transit 190D	Dormobile B16F	*National Welsh 1991*
240	C293MEG	1985	Ford Transit 190D	Dormobile B14F	*National Welsh 1991*
242	C361OFL	1986	Ford Transit 190D	Dormobile B16F	*National Welsh 1991*
243	C318OFL	1986	Ford Transit 190D	Dormobile B16F	*National Welsh 1991*
244	B456WTC	1985	Ford Transit 190D	Dormobile B16F	*Badgerline 1993*
245	C351GFJ	1986	Ford Transit 190D	Robin Hood B16F	*North Devon 1991*
247	C362GFJ	1986	Ford Transit 190D	Dormobile B16F	*North Devon 1991*
248	C364GFJ	1986	Ford Transit 190D	Dormobile B16F	*North Devon 1991*

255-258

1986   Ford Transit 190D   Robin Hood   B16F
(ex.National Welsh 1992)

255	C101HKG	256	C103HKG	257	C107HKG	258	C108HKG

261-266

1986   Ford Transit 190D   Robin Hood   B16F
(ex.Rhondda 1992)

261	C118HUH	262	C111HKG	263	C113HUH	266	C106HKG

267-270

1986   Ford Transit 190D   Dormobile   B16F
(ex.Bristol City Line 1993)

267	C434BHY	268	C466BHY	269	C471BHY	270	C474BHY

272	C557TUT	1986	Ford Transit 190D	Rootes B16F	*Stevenson, Spath 1993*

280	D948UDY	1986	Mercedes Benz L608D	Alexander AM DP19F	South Coast Buses 1.94
281	D950UDY	1986	Mercedes Benz L608D	Alexander AM DP19F	South Coast Buses 1.94
284	C595SHC	1986	Mercedes Benz L608D	PMT B20F	Stagecoach South 1.94
285	C808SDY	1986	Mercedes Benz L608D	Alexander AM B20F	Hampshire Bus 1.94
287	C820SDY	1986	Mercedes Benz L608D	Alexander AM B20F	Coastline 1.94
288	C593SHC	1986	Mercedes Benz L608D	PMT B20F	Hants & Surrey 4.94
289	C596SHC	1986	Mercedes Benz L608D	PMT B20F	South Coast Buses 4.94
295	F958HTO	1988	Iveco 49.10	Robin Hood B23F	East Midland 9.94
296	G912KWF	1989	Iveco 49.10	Robin Hood B25F	East Midland 5.94
297	G919KWF	1989	Iveco 49.10	Robin Hood B25F	East Midland 5.94
298	G920KWF	1990	Iveco 49.10	Robin Hood B25F	East Midland 5.94
299	G924KWF	1990	Iveco 49.10	Robin Hood B25F	East Midland 5.94
300	H370PNY	1991	Iveco 49.10	Carlyle B25F	*Cynon Valley 1992*
301	H301PAX	1991	Mercedes Benz 709D	PMT C25F	
302	J302TUH	1991	Mercedes Benz 709D	PMT B25F	
303	J303TUH	1991	Mercedes Benz 709D	PMT B25F	

304-318

1992 Mercedes Benz 811D   Wright B33F

304	J304UKG	308	K308YKG	312	K312YKG	316	K316YKG
305	J305UKG	309	K309YKG	313	K313YKG	317	K317YKG
306	J306UKG	310	K310YKG	314	K314YKG	318	K318YKG
307	J307UKG	311	K311YKG	315	K315YKG		

319	K319YKG	1992	Mercedes Benz 709D	Alexander AM B25F
320	K320YKG	1992	Mercedes Benz 709D	Alexander AM B25F
321	K321YKG	1992	Mercedes Benz 709D	Alexander AM B25F

322-325

1992 Mercedes Benz 811D   Wright B33F

| 322 | K322YKG | 323 | K323YKG | 324 | K324YKG | 325 | K325YKG |

326-331

1993 Mercedes Benz 811D   Marshall B33F

| 326 | L326CHB | 328 | L328CHB | 329 | L329CHB | 331 | L331CHB |
| 327 | L327CHB | | | | | | |

| 332 | H556TUG | 1990 | Mercedes Benz 709D | Dormobile C29F | Davies, Tredegar 1.94 |

334-343

1994 Mercedes Benz 709D   Alexander (Belfast) B25F

334	L334FWO	337	L337FWO	340	L340FWO	342	L342FWO
335	L385FWO	338	L338FWO	341	L341FWO	343	L343FWO
336	L336FWO	339	L339FWO				

344-360

1994 Mercedes Benz 709D   Alexander B25F

344	M344JBO	349	M349JBO	353	M353JBO	357	M357JBO
345	M345JBO	350	M350JBO	354	M354JBO	358	M358JBO
346	M346JBO	351	M351JBO	355	M355JBO	359	M359JBO
347	M347JBO	352	M352JBO	356	M356JBO	360	M360JBO
348	M348JBO						

362	WUH179T	1978	Leyland PSU3E/4R	Plaxton Sup.III C49F	*National Welsh 1991*
368	WUH185T	1978	Leyland PSU3E/4R	Plaxton Sup.III C49F	*National Welsh 1991*
391	GMB146N	1974	Bristol RESL6L	ECW B44F	*Cynon Valley 1992*
392	HTG354N	1975	Bristol RESL6L	ECW B44F	*Cynon Valley 1992*
393	GMB148N	1974	Bristol RESL6L	ECW B44F	*Cynon Valley 1992*
394	D109NDW	1987	Leyland LX112TL11	Leyland B48F	*Cynon Valley 1992*
395	E113RBO	1987	Leyland LX112TL11	Leyland B48F	*Cynon Valley 1992*

Ribble ECW-bodied Leyland Olympian 2111 was painted into a silver version of the corporate livery to commemorate the 75th anniverasry of its Preston-based owner. (Travelscene)

Now transferred to Ribble, Alexander Dash-bodied Volvo B6 243 is seen here at Stockport whilst operating for Stagecoach Manchester in the spring of 1994. (K.A.Jenkinson)

Bluebird 535, a Plaxton Premiere Interurban-bodied Volvo B10M leaves Inverness bus station on the 27 service to Strathpeffer in November 1994.   (B.Newsome)

Typifying Stagecoach at Perth is former London Routemaster 607 seen here at Kinnoull Street followed by one of the company's Alexander-bodied Mercedes Benz minibuses.

396	E114SDW	1987	Leyland LX112TL11	Leyland B48F	*Cynon Valley 1992*			
397	E115SDW	1988	Leyland LX112TL11	Leyland B48F	*Cynon Valley 1992*			
398	F74DCW	1989	Leyland LX2R11C	Leyland DP45F	*Cynon Valley 1992*			
413	KDW359P	1975	Leyland LN11351/1R	Leyland DP48F	*National Welsh 1991*			

420-434
1977 Leyland LN11351A/1R   Leyland DP48F
(ex.National Welsh 1991)

420	NWO454R	427	NWO461R	432	NWO466R	434	NWO468R
423	NWO457R						

435	LDW361P	1975	Leyland LN10351/1R	Leyland B44F	*Cynon Valley 1992*
439	RHB307R	1977	Leyland LN10351A/1R	Leyland B44F	*Cynon Valley 1992*

440-444
1978 Leyland LN10351A/1R   Leyland B44F
(ex.Cynon Valley 1992)

440	UTX724S	441	UTX725S	442	UTX726S	444	UTX728S

447	DDW432V	1979	Leyland LN10351A/1R	Leyland B44F	*Cynon Valley 1992*
448	DDW433V	1979	Leyland LN10351A/1R	Leyland B44F	*Cynon Valley 1992*
449	DDW434V	1980	Leyland LN10351A/1R	Leyland B44F	*Cynon Valley 1992*
469	YBO144T	1979	Leyland LN10351A/1R	Leyland B44F	*National Welsh 1991*
472	YBO147T	1979	Leyland LN10351A/1R	Leyland B44F	*National Welsh 1991*
482	BUH203V	1979	Leyland LN10351A/1R	Leyland B44F	*National Welsh 1991*
500	YSX934W	1981	Leyland NL106L11/1R	Leyland B44F	Fife Scottish 7.94
501	RSG814V	1980	Leyland NL116L11/1R	Leyland B52F	Fife Scottish 7.94
502	YSX932W	1981	Leyland NL106L11/1R	Leyland B44F	Fife Scottish 7.94
503	YSX933W	1981	Leyland NL106L11/1R	Leyland B44F	Fife Scottish 7.94
504	MSO13W	1980	Leyland NL116L11/1R	Leyland B52F	Fife Scottish 7.94
505	RSG815V	1980	Leyland NL116L11/1R	Leyland B52F	Fife Scottish 7.94
506	YSX926W	1981	Leyland NL106L11/1R	Leyland B44F	Fife Scottish 11.94
507	WAS717V	1980	Leyland NL116L11/1R	Leyland B52F	Fife Scottish 7.94
508	MSO14V	1980	Leyland NL116L11/1R	Leyland B52F	Fife Scottish 7.94
	RSG824V	1980	Leyland NL116L11/1R	Leyland B52F	Fife Scottish 11.94
	RSG825V	1980	Leyland NL116L11/1R	Leyland B52F	Fife Scottish 11.94
	YSX935W	1981	Leyland NL106L11/1R	Leyland B44F	Fife Scottish 11.94
559	NWO475R	1976	Leyland LN11351A/1R	Leyland B52F	*National Welsh 1991*
570	NWO486R	1976	Leyland LN11351A/1R	Leyland B49F	*National Welsh 1991*
578	NWO494R	1977	Leyland LN11351A/1R	Leyland B52F	*National Welsh 1991*

584-604
1977 Leyland LN11351A/1R   Leyland B49F
(ex.National Welsh 1991)

584	• NWO500R	597	SKG907S	598	SKG908S	604	SKG914S

605	SKG915S	1978	Leyland LN11351A/1R	Leyland B49F	*National Welsh 1991*
609	PKG741R	1977	Leyland LN11351A/1R	Leyland B49F	*National Welsh 1991*

619-635
1978 Leyland LN11351A/1R   Leyland B49F
(ex.National Welsh 1991)

619	SKG923S	633	WUH166T	634	WUH167T	635	WUH168T

642-649
1979 Leyland LN11351A/1R   Leyland B49F
(ex.National Welsh 1991)

642	BUH207V	646	BUH211V	647	BUH212V	649	BUH214V
645	BUH210V						

650	HEU121N	1975	Leyland LN11351/1R	Leyland B52F	*Badgerline 1991*
651	NOE552R	1976	Leyland LN11351A/1R	Leyland B49F	*Cheltenham & Glos. 1991*
652	NOE573R	1976	Leyland LN11351A/1R	Leyland B49F	*Midland Red South 1992*
653	NOE572R	1977	Leyland LN11351A/1R	Leyland B49F	*Midland Red South 1992*
654	NOE576R	1976	Leyland LN11351A/1R	Leyland B49F	*Midland Red South 1992*
655	SGR555R	1976	Leyland LN11351A/1R	Leyland B49F	*GO-Ahead Northern 1992*
657	MGR948T	1979	Leyland LN11351A/1R	Leyland B49F	*Go-Ahead Northern 1992*
658	BPT903S	1978	Leyland LN11351A/1R	Leyland B49F	*Go-Ahead Northern 1992*
659	NWS903R	1977	Leyland LN113510A/1R	Leyland B49F	*Bristol City Line 1992*
660	XVV540S	1978	Leyland LN113510A/1R	Leyland B49F	*Bristol City Line 1993*
661	MFN114R	1976	Leyland LN11351A/1R	Leyland B49F	*Bristol City Line 1993*
662	HHY813N	1975	Leyland LN11351/1R	Leyland B49F	*Bristol City Line 1993*
	G21CSG	1989	Renault S56	Reeve Burgess B25F	Fife Scottish 11.94
	G24CSG	1989	Renault S56	Reeve Burgess B25F	Fife Scottish 11.94
	L685CDD	1994	Mercedes Benz 709D	Alexander AM B25F	Stroud Valleys 12.94

701-712

1994 Volvo B6 — Alexander Dash B40F

701	L701FWO	704	L704FWO	707	L707FWO	710	L710FWO
702	L702FWO	705	L705FWO	708	L708FWO	711	L711FWO
703	L703FWO	706	L706FWO	709	L709FWO	712	L712FWO

803	SKG896S	1977	Bristol VRT/SL3/6L	ECW H43/31F	*National Welsh 1991*
814	XBO116T	1979	Bristol VRT/SL3/6L	ECW H43/31F	*National Welsh 1991*
825	TWS909T	1979	Bristol VRT/SL3/6LXB	ECW H42/28F	*Cheltenham & Glos 1992*
826	HPT86N	1975	Bristol VRT/SL3/6LX	ECW H43/31F	*Cheltenham & Glos 1992*
827	A541HAC	1983	Leyland ONLXB/1R	ECW H45/32F	*Midland Red South 1993*
828	A548HAC	1983	Leyland ONLXB/1R	ECW H45/32F	*Midland Red South 1993*
829	A549HAC	1983	Leyland ONLXB/1R	ECW H45/32F	*Midland Red South 1993*
830	AET185T	1979	Bristol VRT/SL3/6LXB	ECW H43/31F	East Midland 12.93
831	DAK201V	1980	Bristol VRY/SL3/6L	ECW H43/31F	East Midland 1.94
832	CBV6S	1977	Bristol VRT/SL3/6L	ECW H43/31F	Ribble 4.94
833	DBV36W	1980	Bristol VRT/SL3/6LXB	ECW H4331F	Ribble 4.94
834	BUH232V	1980	Bristol VRT/SL3/6L	ECW H43/31F	*National Welsh 1991*
835	BUH237V	1980	Bristol VRT/SL3/6L	ECW H43/31F	*National Welsh 1991*
836	GTX738W	1980	Bristol VRT/SL3/6LXB	ECW H43/31F	*National Welsh 1991*

837-844

1980 Bristol VRT/SL3/6L — ECW H43/31F
(ex.National Welsh 1991)

837	GTX742W	839	GTX744W	841	GTX748W	844	GTX753W
838	GTX743W	840	GTX747W	843	GTX750W		

845	CBV8S	1977	Bristol VRT/SL3/6LXB	ECW H43/31F	Ribble 8.94

861-864

1977 Bristol VRT/LL3/6L — Alexander AL H49/38F
(ex.National Welsh 1991)

861	OSR206R	862	OSR207R	863	OSR208R	864	OSR209R

897-902

1983 Leyland TRCTL11/3R — Plaxton 3200 C51F
(ex.National Welsh 1991)

897	AAX312A	899	AAX451A	901	AAX466A	902	AAX483A
898	AAX450A	900	AAX465A				

897-902 were originally registered SDW913-8Y

One of a large quantity of Leyland Titans inherited by the Stagecoach Group through its acquisition of two London Buses companies, Selkent's T176 is seen here at Victoria before having its London-style roundels and fleet names removed. (K.A.Jenkinson)

Stagecoach East Kent Northern Counties-bodied Leyland Olympian 7813 awaits its passengers in Canterbury bus station followed by MCW Metrobus 7767 which still wears East Kent's pre-Stagecoach colours. (F.W.York)

South Coast Buses Northern Counties-bodied Volvo B10M 601 passes through Hastings on 26 October 1994 whilst working Coastliner service 711 from Folkestone to Brighton. (T.S.Blackman)

One of a massive order for Alexander-bodied Mercedes Benz 709D minibuses, this example was allocated to the United Counties fleet in which it is numbered 370 and carries Street Shuttle fleet names.   (J.A.Godwin)

906-915   1983   Leyland TRCTL11/3R   Plaxton 3200 C46FT
(ex.National Welsh 1991)

906	AAL544A	910	AAL518A	912	AAX489A	914	AAX516A
907	AAL575A	911	AAL516A	913	AAX515A	915	AAX529A
909	AAL538A						

906/7/9-15 were originally registered SDW922/3/5-31Y

925-934   1984   Leyland TRCTL11/3R   Duple Laser C49FT
(ex.National Welsh 1991)

| 925 | AKG197A | 927 | AKG214A | 931 | AKG271A | 934 | AKG296A |

925/7/31/4 were originally registered A225/7/31/4VWO

935   A277MDD   1984   Leyland TRCTL11/3R   Plaxton 3200 C53F   Swindon & District 5.94
935 was previously registered YJV806, A873MRW & 552OHU and was originally A71KDU.

Weaving its way through the streets of Inverness in November 1994 is Inverness Traction 449, an Alexander-bodied Leyland Tiger acquired by Northern Scottish from Kelvin Scottish in 1986. (B.Newsome)

Western Scottish Omnibuses Ltd., Nursery Avenue, Kilmarnock, KA1 3JD

Having been divided in 1985 by the separation of its northern territory to form a new company, Clydeside Scottish, reunited in 1989 and divided again in October 1991 Western Scottish was acquired by Stagecoach Holdings on 1 August 1994, further consolidating the Group's activities in Scotland. Expansion was gained on 1 October 194 with the acquisition of the Arran Transport & Trading Co. Ltd.

Fleet Names : Stagecoach Western Scottish; Citylink.

Livery : Stagecoach corporate livery replacing white, black, red & grey. Citylink coaches - BITwo tone blue & yellow.

Depots : Ayr (A); Cumnock (C); Dumfries (D); Dunoon (O); Isle of Arran (N); Kilmarnock (K); Rothesay (R); Stranraer (S). *Outstation : Annan; Girvan; Whitehorn*

Western Scottish   Fleet list

R101	XSJ656T	1978	Leyland FE30AGR	NCME O44/31F	
R102	HDS566H	1970	Daimler CRG6LX	Alexander AD O44/31F	*Clydeside Scottish 1989*

R102 was previously registered 703DYE and was originally SMS402H.

H105	VLT81	1986	Duple 425	Duple C51FT	
H106	VLT206	1986	Duple 425	Duple C51FT	
H107	VLT54	1986	Duple 425	Duple C55FT	
H108	J8WSB	1992	Plaxton 425	Lorraine C53F	
N111	VLT154	1991	Dennis Javelin 11SDL	Plaxton 3500 C50F	*Wallace Arnold 1992*
N113	J13WSB	1992	Dennis Javelin 11SDL	Plaxton 3200 C53F	
N114	J14WSB	1992	Dennis Javelin 11SDL	Plaxton 3200 C53F	
N115	J15WSB	1992	Dennis Javelin 11SDL	Plaxton Premiere C53F	

H105-7 & N111 were originally registered C205-7HSD and H661UWR.

N116 - N120   1987 Dennis Dorchester SDA811   Alexander TC C55F

N116	WLT526	N118 WLT415	N119 VLT73	N120 WLT447
N117	FSU737			

N116-N120 were originally registered D216-20NCS

N142	VLT272	1985	Dennis Dorchester	Plaxton 3500 C55F	
L170	G262EHD	1989	DAF SB2305DHTD	Plaxton 3200 C57F	Arran Transport 10.94
L172	13CLT	1987	Leyland TRCTL11/3RZ	Duple 340 C48FT	*Kelvin Central 1990*
L173	WLT546	1987	Leyland TRCTL11/3RZ	Duple 340 C48FT	*Kelvin Central 1990*
V191	VCS391	1985	Volvo B10M-61	Plaxton 3500 C44FT	
V196	WLT465	1985	Volvo B10M-61	Plaxton 3500 C51FT	*Clydeside Scottish 1989*
V197	WLT697	1985	Volvo B10M-61	Plaxton 3500 C46FT	*Clydeside Scottish 1989*
V198	WLT720	1985	Volvo B10M-61	Berkhof Esprite C53F	

N142, L172/3, V191 & V196-8 were originally registered B202CGA, D317/8SGB and B191/6-8CGA.

F200	B764DEG	1985	Ford Transit 150	Dormobile B16F

The first new buses to be purchased for the Stagecoach Wellington fleet are M.A.N. midibuses of which 80 are on order. The first of these, 501 is seen here before its entry into service in the autumn of 1994.   (Stagecoach International)

Delivered to National Welsh as its first minibus in 1986, Robin Hood-converted Ford Transit C101HKG is now numbered 255 in the Red & White fleet and is seen here in May 1994 soon after gaining Stagecoach corporate livery.   (John Probert)

Leaving Ayr bus station in September 1994 at the start of its journey to Stranraer is Western Scottish Volvo B10M SV431 which began life as a coach and in August 1994 was given new East Lancs bodywork.   (K.A.Jenkinson)

G & G's former National Welsh Freight Rover Sherpa 1491 is seen here at Warwick preparing to leave for Leamington in August 1994.   (F.W.York)

Z201 - Z218   1986 Mercedes Benz L608D   Alexander B21F
(ex.Kelvin Scottish 1987)

Z201	C101KDS	Z207	D107NUS	Z211	D111NUS	Z215	D115NUS
Z204	C104KDS	Z208	D108NUS	Z212	D112NUS	Z216	D116NUS
Z205	C105KDS	Z209	D109NUS	Z213	D113NUS	Z217	D117NUS
Z206	C106KDS	Z210	D110NUS	Z214	D114NUS	Z218	D118NUS

Z219	L882LFS	1993	Mercedes Benz 709D	Alexander AM B25F	
Z220	L883LFS	1993	Mercedes Benz 709D	Alexander AM B25F	
Z221	G574FSD	1989	Mercedes Benz 709D	Reeve Burgess B25F	Arran Transport 10.94

D222 - D260   1987 Dodge S56   Alexander B25F (*DP25F)

D222	D222NCS	D232	D232NCS	D242	D242NCS	D252	D252NCS
D223	D223NCS	D233	D233NCS	D243	D243NCS	D253	D253NCS
D224	D224NCS	D234	D234NCS	D244	D244NCS	D254	D254NCS
D225	D225NCS	D235	D235NCS	D245	D245NCS	D255	D255NCS
D226	D226NCS	D236	D236NCS	D246	D246NCS	D256	D256NCS
D227	D227NCS	D237	D237NCS	D247	D247NCS	D257	D257NCS
D228	D228NCS	D238	D238NCS	D248	D248NCS	D258*	D258NCS
D229	D229NCS	D239	D239NCS	D249	D249NCS	D259	D259NCS
D230	D230NCS	D240	D240NCS	D250	D250NCS	D260	D260NCS
D231	D231NCS	D241	D241NCS	D251	D251NCS		

Z262 - Z270   1986 Mercedes Benz L608D   Alexander B21F
(ex.Kelvin Scottish 1987)

Z262	D122NUS	Z264	D134NUS	Z268	D128NUS	Z270	D130NUS
Z263	D113NUS	Z266	D136NUS	Z269	D129NUS		

Z271	D121NUS	1986	Mercedes Benz L608D	Alexander AM DP21F	*Kelvin Scottish 1987*
Z272	E638YUS	1988	Mercedes Benz 609D	Reeve Burgess CI9F	Arran Transport 10.94
T273	D94EKV	1987	Talbot Freewayaa	Talbot B12FL	*Carriageways, Wolfstein 1992*
T274	F334JHS	1989	Talbot Freeway	Talbot DP12FL	
T275	F335JHS	1989	Talbot Freeway	Talbot DP12FL	
T276	F336JHS	1989	Talbot Freeway	Talbot DP12FL	
T277	G825VGA	1990	Talbot Freeway	Talbot DP12FL	
T278	G831VGA	1990	Talbot Freeway	Talbot DP12FL	
Z279	L577NSB	1993	Mercedes Benz 709D	Dormobile B21FL	Arran Transport 10.94
Z280	L578NSB	1994	Mercedes Benz 709D	Dormobile B21FL	Arran Transport 10.94
D281	D301SDS	1987	Dodge S56	Alexander DP25F	*Clydeside 1989*

D282 - D289   1987 Dodge S56   Alexander B25F
(ex.Clydeside Scottish 1989)

D282	D302SDS	D284	D304SDS	D286	D306SDS	D289	D309SDS
D283	D303SDS	D285	D305SDS	D287	D307SDS		

D290 - D296   1987 Dodge S46   Dormobile B25F
(ex.Fife Scottish 9.94)

D290	E634DCK	D292	E637DCK	D294	E643DCK	D296	E646DCK
D291	E636DCK	D293	E640DCK	D295	E644DCK		

N301 - N310   1992   Dennis Dart 98SDL   Alexander AM Dash B40F

N301 J301BRM	N304 J304BRM	N307 J307BRM	N309 J309BRM
N302 J302BRM	N305 J305BRM	N308 J308BRM	N310 J310BRM
N303 J303BRM	N306 J306BRM		

V312 - V341   1994   Volvo B6   Alexander AM Dash DP40F

V312 M772BCS	V322 M722BCS	V332 M732BSJ	V337 M737BSJ
V313 M773BCS	V323 M723BCS	V733 M733BSJ	V338 M738BSJ
V318 M718BCS	V324 M724BCS	V334 M734BSJ	V339 M739BSJ
V319 M719BCS	V325 M725BCS	V335 M735BSJ	V340 M740BSJ
V320 M720BCS	V326 M726BCS	V336 M736BSJ	V341 M741BSJ
V321 M721BCS	V327 M727BCS		

V312/3 were reregistered from M429/30BNV prior to being licenced

V351 - V358   1994   Volvo B6R   Alexander AM Dash B40F

V351 M674SSX	V353 M676SSX	V355 M678SSX	V357 M680SSX
V352 M675SSX	V354 M677SSX	V356 M679SSX	V358 M681SSX

N399 L208PSB	1994	Dennis Dart	Marshall B39F	Arran Transport 10.94	

N403 703DYE	1983	Dennis Dorchester	Plaxton 3200 C49F	
N404 VLT104	1983	Dennis Dorchester	Plaxton 3200 C49F	*Clydeside Scottish 1989*
N405 WLT727	1983	Dennis Dorchester	Plaxton 3200 C49F	*Clydeside Scottish 1989*
N406 WLT794	1983	Dennis Dorchester	Plaxton 3200 C49F	

N403-6 were originally registered TSD153-6Y.

N407 - N410   1983   Dennis Dorchester SDA801   Plaxton 3200 C49F
               (ex.Clydeside Scottish 1989)

N407 WLT830	N408 VCS376	N409 WLT444	N410 WLT874

N407 was originally registered TSD157Y. N408 was previously registered WLT652 and was originally TSD158Y. N409/10 were originally registered TSD159/2Y.

N411 WLT441	1985	Dennis Dorchester	Plaxton 3500 C55F
N412 VLT226	1985	Dennis Dorchester	Plaxton 3500 C55F
N413 YSV730	1985	Dennis Dorchester	Plaxton 3500 C51F
N414 YSV735	1985	Dennis Dorchester	Plaxton 3500 C51F
N415 VLT245	1985	Dennis Dorchester	Plaxton 3500 C55F

N411-15 were originally registered B201/0/3/4/199CGA.

N416 - N420   1985   Dennis Dorchester   Plaxton 3500 C55F
               (ex.Clydeside 2000 1993)

N416 B987EGG	N418 B985EGG	N419 B981EGG	N420 B979EGG
N417 B986EGG			

N416-20 were previously registered WLT471, 32CLT, WLT364, 407CLT & VLT204 and were originally B401-3/7/9OSB

N421 D221NCS	1987	Dennis Dorchester	Alexander TIC C55F
V423 WLT439	1981	Volvo B10M-61	Duple Dom.IV C51F
V424 WLT416	1981	Volvo B10M-61	Duple Dom.IV C55F *Clydeside Scottish 1989*
V427 TOS550X	1982	Volvo B10M-61	1994 East Lancs DP51F
V428 FSU739	1982	Volvo B10M-61	Duple Dom.IV C46FT
V429 VLT219	1981	Volvo B10M-61	Duple Dom.IV C46FT *Clydeside Scottish 1989*

Painted in Scottish Citylink livery is Western Scottish Plaxton Premiere-bodied Volvo B10M KN115 seen here leaving Buchanan bus station, Glasgow enroute to Ayr.   (K.A.Jenkinson)

In similar fashion to the Stagecoach Group, Mainline operates a large fleet of Alexander PS-bodied Volvo B10Ms, one of which - 617 - is seen here in Sheffield.   (P.T.Stokes)

One of a large number of Volvos operated by Strathclyde's Buses, Alexander-bodied A119 was new in 1989 and is seen here passing Buchanan bus station. (K.A.Jenkinson)

Wearing KCB Network's new livery is Alexander-bodied MCW Metrobus 1667 seen here approaching Buchanan bus station, Glasgow in September 1994. (K.A.Jenkinson)

V431 WGB646W 1982 Volvo B10M-61   1994 East Lancs DP51F
V423/4 were originally registered NCS123/14W; V427 was previously registered FSU737 and was
originally GGE127X; V428/9 were originally registered GGE128X & NCS119W; V431 was previously
registered WLT415 and was originally NCS121W.

S434	DSD934V	1979	Seddon Pennine 7	Alexander AT C49F	
S435	DSD935V	1979	Seddon Pennine 7	Alexander AT C49F	
S436	DSD935V	1979	Seddon Pennine 7	Alexander AT C49F	*Clydeside Scottish 1988*
S437	DSD937V	1979	Seddon Pennine 7	Alexander AT C49F	*Clydeside Scottish 1988*
S439	WGA908V	1979	Seddon Pennine 7	Alexander AT C49F	*Clydeside Scottish 1988*
S440	DSD940V	1979	Seddon Pennine 7	Alexander AT C49F	*Clydeside Scottish 1988*

S439 was previously registered WLT652 and was originally DSD939V.

S442 - S456   1979 Seddon Pennine 7   Alexander AT C49F

S442	DSD942V	S447	DSD947V	S451	DSD951V	S454	DSD954V
S443	DSD943V	S448	DSD948V	S452	DSD952V	S455	DSD955V
S444	DSD944V	S449	DSD949V	S453	DSD953V	S456	DSD956V
S445	DSD945V	S450	DSD450V				

S457	DSD957V	1979	Seddon Pennine 7	Alexander AT C49F	*Clydeside Scottish 1988*
S460	DSD960V	1979	Seddon Pennine 7	Alexander AT C49F	*Clydeside Scottish 1989*
S462	DSD962V	1979	Seddon Pennine 7	Alexander AT C49F	*Clydeside Scottish 1988*
S464	DSD964V	1979	Seddon Pennine 7	Alexander AT C49F	*Clydeside Scottish 1989*
S470	DSD970V	1980	Seddon Pennine 7	Alexander AT B53F	*Clydeside Scottish 1989*
S472	DSD972V	1980	Seddon Pennine 7	Alexander AT C49F	*Clydeside Scottish 1989*

S473 - S478   1980 Seddon Pennine 7   Alexander AT C49F

S473	DSD973V	S475	DSD975V	S477	DSD977V	S478	DSD978V
S474	DSD974V	S476	DSD976V				

S479	DSD979V	1980	Seddon Pennine 7	Alexander AT C49F	*Clydeside Scottish 1989*
S480	DSD980V	1980	Seddon Pennine 7	Alexander AT C49F	
S481	DSD981V	1980	Seddon Pennine 7	Alexander AT C49F	
S482	DSD982V	1980	Seddon Pennine 7	Alexander AT C49F	
V486	ESU435	1982	Volvo B10M-61	Duple Goldl'r IV C46FT	
V487	GSU950	1982	Volvo B10M-61	Duple Goldl'r IV C46FT	
V488	WLT538	1983	Volvo B10M-61	Duple Goldl'r IV C53F	
V489	WLT774	1983	Volvo B10M-61	Duple Goldl'r IV C53F	
V490	WLT809	1983	Volvo B10M-61	Duple Goldl'r IV C46FT	
V491	WLT915	1983	Volvo B10M-61	Duple Goldl'r IV C46FT	
L499	PGA829V	1980	Leyland PSU3F/4R	Alexander AT C49F	*Kelvin Scottish 1988*

V486-91 were originally registered GGE130/1X and TSD148-51Y.

S518 - S523   1978 Seddon Pennine 7   Alexander AY B53F

S518	YSD818T	S520	YSD820T	S522	YSD822T	S523	YSD813T
S519	YSD819T						

S525	ASD825T	1979	Seddon Pennine 7	Alexander AY B53F
S526	ASD826T	1979	Seddon Pennine 7	Alexander AY C49F

S527 - S546   1979 Seddon Pennine 7   Alexander AY B53F

S527w	ASD827T	S532w	ASD832T	S536w	ASD836T	S544w	ASD844T
S528w	ASD828T	S533w	ASD833T	S537w	ASD837T	S545w	DSD983V
S529	ASD829T	S534w	ASD834T	S542w	ASD842T	S546w	DSD984V
S531w	ASD831T	S535w	ASD935T	S543w	ASD843T		

S551	BSD551T	1979	Seddon Pennine 7	Alexander AY C49F
S552	BSD852T	1979	Seddon Pennine 7	Alexander AY C49F

S556 - S564   1979   Seddon Pennine 7   Alexander AY C49F

S556w	BSD856T	S559w	BSD859T	S562w	BSD962T	S564w	BSD864T
S558w	BSD858T	S560w	BSD860T	S563w	BSD863T		

E571	HCS350N	1975	Bedford YRQ	Plaxton Der't B45F	Arran Transport 10.94
E572	CCS459T	1979	Bedford YMT	Duple Dom. C53F	Arran Transport 10.94
E573	MCS138W	1981	Bedford YLQ	Duple Dom.II C45F	Arran Transport 10.94
E574	MCS139W	1981	Bedford YMQ	Duple Dom.II C53F	Arran Transport 10.94
E575	FCY284W	1981	Bedford YMQ	Duple Dom. B45F	Arran Transport 10.94
E576	FCY286W	1981	Bedford YMQ	Duple Dom. B45F	Arran Transport 10.94
E577	FCY296W	1981	Bedford YMQ	Duple Dom. B45F	Arran Transport 10.94
E578	HVY132X	1982	Bedford YNT	Plaxton Bust'r B55F	Arran Transport 10.94
E579	D167TRA	1986	Bedford YMT	Duple Dom. B55F	Arran Transport 10.94
E580	D917GRU	1987	Bedford YMT	Plaxton Der't B53F	Arran Transport 10.94
E581	D799USB	1987	Bedford YMT	Duple Dom. B55F	Arran Transport 10.94
E582	D918GRU	1987	Bedford YMT	Plaxton Der't B53F	Arran Transport 10.94
E583	E849AAO	1987	Bedford YNV	Plaxton 3200 C57F	Arran Transport 10.94
L601	C802KBT	1986	Leyland CU435	Optare B33F	Arran Transport 10.94
L629	GMS285S	1978	Leyland PSU3E/4R	Alexander AYS B53F	*Kelvin Scottish 1987*
L630	GMS292S	1978	Leyland PSU3D/4R	Alexander AYS B53F	*Kelvin Scottish 1987*
L633	GCS33V	1980	Leyland PSU3E/4R	Alexander AYS B53F	*Clydeside Scottish 1989*
L637	GCS37V	1980	Leyland PSU3E/4R	Alexander AYS C49F	

L638 - L665   1980   Leyland PSU3E/4R   Alexander AY B53F

L638	GCS38V	L647	GCS47V	L653	GCS53V	L661	GCS61V
L641	GCS41V	L648	GCS48V	L657	GCS57V	L662	GCS62V
L645	GCS45V	L649	GCS49V	L658	GCS58V	L665	GCS65V
L646	GCS46V	L651	GCS51V	L660	GCS60V		

L667	TSJ67S	1977	Leyland PSU3E/4R	Alexander AYS B53F
L669	GCS69V	1980	Leyland PSU3E/4R	Alexander AYS B53F

L670 - L685   1977   Leyland PSU3D/4R   Alexander AY B53F

L670	TSJ70S	L676	TSJ76S	L679	TSJ79S	L685	TSJ85S
L671	TSJ71S	L678	TSJ78S	L680	TSJ80S		

L691	TSJ31S	1978	Leyland PSU3D/4R	Alexander AYS B53F	
L692	TSJ32S	1978	Leyland PSU3D/4R	Alexander AYS B53F	
L693	TSJ33S	1978	Leyland PSU3D/4R	Alexander AYS B53F	
L695	BSJ895T	1979	Leyland PSU3E/4R	Alexander AYS B53F	*Clydeside 1989*
L696	BSJ896T	1979	Leyland PSU3E/4R	Alexander AYS B53F	*Clydeside 1989*
L697	BSJ917T	1979	Leyland PSU3E/4R	Alexander AYS B53F	*Clydeside 1989*
L698	BSJ930T	1979	Leyland PSU3E/4R	Alexander AYS B53F	
L699	BSJ931T	1979	Leyland PSU3E/4R	Alexander AYS B53F	
L701	UIB3541	1979	Leyland LN11351A/1R	Leyland B48F	*Kelvin Central 1989*
L702	UIB3542	1978	Leyland LN11351A/3R	Leyland B48F	*British Airways 1993*
L703	UIB3543	1978	Leyland LN11351A/3R	Leyland B48F	*British Airways 1993*
L704	OIW7024	1979	Leyland LN11351A/3R	Leyland B48F	*British Airways 1993*
L705	OIW7025	1979	Leyland LN11351A/3R	Leyland B48F	*British Airways 1993*
L706	UIB3076	1978	Leyland LN11351A/3R	Leyland B48F	*British Airways 1993*

L701-6 were originally registered EGB89T, EGT451T, WGY589S, GLP433/27T & EGT458T

L707	MHD336L	1973	Leyland LN1151/1R	Leyland B52F	Arran Transport 10.94
L708	PTF732L	1973	Leyland LN1151/1R	Leyland B52F	Arran Transport 10.94
L709	NHA256M	1974	Leyland LN1151/1R	Leyland B52F	Arran Transport 10.94

L771	WAS771V	1980	Leyland NL116L11/1R	Leyland B52F	*Kelvin Scottish 1988*
L773	RFS583V	1980	Leyland NL116L11/1R	Leyland B52F	*Kelvin Scottish 1988*
L774	YFS304W	1980	Leyland NL116L11/1R	Leyland B52F	*Kelvin Scottsh 1988*
L775	MDS865V	1980	Leyland NL116L11/1R	Leyland B48F	*Kelvin Scottish 1988*
L776	MDS866V	1980	Leyland NL116L11/1R	Leyland B48F	*Kelvin Scottish 1988*
L777	MDS859V	1980	Leyland NL116L11/1R	Leyland B48F	*Kelvin Scottish 1988*

L778 - L784   1980   Leyland NL116L11/1R   Leyland B52F
(ex.Kelvin Scottish 1988)

| L778 | MDS858V | L780 | YFS308W | L782 | RFS582V | L784 | RFS584V |
| L779 | RFS579V | L781 | MSO18W | L783 | NLS983W | | |

L785	NLS985W	1980	Leyland NL116L11/1R	Leyland B48F	*Kelvin Scottish 1988*
L786	SNS826W	1980	Leyland NL116L11/1R	Leyland B52F	*Kelvin Scottish 1988*
L787	MSO17W	1980	Leyland NL116L11/1R	Leyland B48F	*Kelvin Scottish 1988*
L788	WAS768W	1980	Leyland NL116L11/1R	Leyland B48F	*Kelvin Scottish 1988*
L789	NLS986W	1980	Leyland NL116L11/1R	Leyland B48F	*Kelvin Scottish 1988*
L790	YFS310W	1981	Leyland NL116L11/1R	Leyland B48F	*Kelvin Scottish 1988*
L791	YFS309W	1981	Leyland NL116L11/1R	Leyland B48F	*Kelvin Scottish 1988*
L792	KRS540V	1980	Leyland NL106L11/1R	Leyland B41F	*Bluebird Buses 1993*
L793	KRS542V	1980	Leyland NL106L11/1R	Leyland B41F	*Bluebird Buses 1993*
L795	MSO10W	1980	Leyland NL106L11/1R	Leyland B41F	*Bluebird Buses 1993*
L796	NLP388V	1980	Leyland NL116L11/3R	Leyland B48F	*British Airways 1993*
L797	JTF971W	1981	Leyland NL116L11/1R	Leyland B52F	*Mitchell, Plean 1994*

A800 - A803   1977   Leyland AN68A/1R   Park Royal H43/32F
(ex.GM Buses 1991)

| A800 | UNA853S | A801 | UNA863S | A802 | WVM884S | A803w | WVM877S |

A804	ANA211T	1978	Leyland AN68A/1R	NCME H43/32F	*GM Buses 1991*
A805	BNC936T	1979	Leyland AN68A/1R	Park Royal H43/32F	*GM Buses 1991*
A806	RJA702R	1977	Leyland AN68A/1R	NCME H43/32F	*GM Buses 1991*
A807	UNA772S	1979	Leyland AN68A/1R	NCME H43/32F	*GM Buses 1991*
A808	RJA801R	1977	Leyland AN68A/1R	Park Royal H43/32F	*GM Buses 1992*
A809	VBA161S	1978	Leyland AN68A/1R	NCME H43/32F	*GM Buses 1992*
A810	UNA824S	1977	Leyland AN68A/1R	Park Royal H43/32F	*GM Buses 1992*
A811	UNA840S	1977	Leyland AN68A/1R	Park Royal H43/32F	*GM Buses 1992*
A812	WVM888S	1978	Leyland AN68A/1R	Park Royal H43/32F	*GM Buses 1992*

R832 - R837   1978   Leyland FE30AGR   ECW H43/32F
(ex.Northern Scottish 1987)

| R832 | ASA22T | R834 | ASA24T | R836 | ASA26T | R837 | ASA27T |
| R833 | ASA23T | | | | | | |

R839	ULS669T	1978	Leyland FE30AGR	ECW H43/32F	*Kelvin Central 1989*
R840	ULS660T	1978	Leyland FE30AGR	ECW H43/32F	*Kelvin Central 1989*
R848	XSJ648T	1978	Leyland FE30AGR	NCME H44/31F	

R851 - R858   1979   Leyland FE30AGR   NCME H44/31F

| R851 | XSJ651T | R854 | XSJ654T | R857 | XSJ657T | R858 | XSJ658T |
| R853 | XSJ653T | R855 | XSJ655T | | | | |

R859 - R876   1979   Leyland FE30AGR   NCME H44/31F
(ex.Clydeside Scottish 1988)

R859 XSJ859T	R863 XSJ663T	R867 XSJ667T	R870 BCS870T
R860 XSJ660T	R865 XSJ665T	R868 XSJ668T	R871 BCS871T
R861 XSJ661T	R866 XSJ666T	R869 XSJ669T	R876 ECS876V
R862 XSJ662T			

R877	ECS877V	1979	Leyland FE30AGR	NCME H44/31F	
R878	ECS878V	1979	Leyland FE30AGR	NCME H44/31F	
R879	ECS879V	1979	Leyland FE30AGR	NCME H44/31F	*Clydeside Scottish 1989*
R880	ECS880V	1979	Leyland FE30AGR	NCME H44/31F	*Clydeside Scottish 1988*
R882	ECS882V	1979	Leyland FE30AGR	NCME H44/31F	
R883	ECS883V	1979	Leyland FE30AGR	NCME H44/31F	
R885	ECS885V	1979	Leyland FE30AGR	NCME H44/31F	*Clydeside Scottish 1988*
R887	ECS887V	1979	Leyland FE30AGR	NCME H44/31F	*Clydeside Scottish 1989*
R888	BCS865T	1979	Leyland FE30AGR	NCME H44/31F	*Clydeside Scottish 1989*
R889	BCS869T	1979	Leyland FE30AGR	NCME H44/31F	*Clydeside Scottish 1989*
V894	E864RCS	1984	Volvo B10M-50	Alexander CH41/29F	
V295	E865RCS	1984	Volvo B10M-50	Alexander CH45/35F	
V896	E866RCS	1984	Volvo B10M-50	Alexander CH45/35F	
V897	E867RCS	1984	Volvo B10M-50	Alexander CH43/33F	
V898	B175FFS	1984	Volvo B10M-50	Alexander CH42/28F	*Fife Scottish 1987*
V899	B660EGG	1984	Volvo B10M-50	Alexander CH42/28F	*Fife Scottish 1987*

PRESERVED VEHICLES

W1059 UCS659	1963	Albion Lowlander LR3	Alexander H39/32F	Orig. N1795
W1974 YYS174	1960	Bedford C5Z1	Duple C21F	*ex.MacBrayne*
W1081 YSD350L	1973	Leyland PSU3/3R	Alexander AY B41F	Orig. L600
W1082 RCS382	1961	Leyland PD3A/3	Alexander L35/32RD	Orig. D1684
W1083 Q138RDS		AEC Matador	Recovery wagon	Orig. W1014

ANCILLARY VEHICLES

W1024 CAG444C	1965	Leyland PSU3/3R	Towing wagon	
W1030 KCS156F	1968	Leyland PSU3/3R	Towing wagon	
W1035 OAG535H	1970	Leyland PSU3/3R	Towing wagon	
W1036 XSD503T	1977	Seddon Pennine 7	Alexander	Display unit
W1037 OSJ631R	1977	Leyland PSU3C/3R	Alexander B52F	Driver trainer
W1038 OSJ637R	1977	Leyland PSU3C/3R	Alexander B52F	Driver trainer
W1041 OSJ641R	1977	Leyland PSU3C/3R	Alexander B52F	Driver trainer
W1045 CAG438C	1965	Leyland PSU3/3R	Towing wagon	
W1065 EDS486A	1962	Leyland PSU3/3R	Towing wagon	

W1065 was originally registered VCS391

Mainline Group Ltd., 8 Riverside Court, Newhall Road, Sheffield S9 2TJ

Formed as South Yorskhire PTE on 1 April 1974 by the merging of the bus operations of Sheffield, Rotherham and Doncaster Corporations, expansion was gained with the acquisition of several independent operators inluding Booth & Fisher of Halfway and Felix, Hatfield in 1976, Blue Ensign of Doncaster in 1978, Wilson, Store and Severn - all of Stainforth - in 1979 and Rossie of Rossington in 1980. Restructured under the title South Yorkshire Transport in 1986, further expansion was achieved in 1989 when SUT, Sheafline and Sheffield & District Transport Ltd. were acquired and were placed under the control of two low-cost units which were named SUT and Sheafline, these later being merged together under the Sheafline title. Following the acquisition of Skills, Sheffield in 1991 a new low-coast minibus unit was created under the title of Don Valley Buses. After being remaned yet again, Mainline was purchased by its management in November 1993. Under the conditions of sale, Mainline was not permitted to sell more than 20% of its business to another company until five years after privatisation although it excercised its right on 4 July 1994 when it sold a 20% share-holding to Stagecoach.

Fleet names : Mainline; Coachline; Don Valley Buses; Eager Beavers; Fastline; Nipper; Sheafline

Liveries : MAINLINE - Yellow & red. COACHLINE - White, yellow, red & brown. DON VALLEY BUSES - White & green; EAGER BEAVERS - Yellow, red & blue; SHEAFLINE - White, red & blue

Depots : Doncaster (Mainline); Dunscroft (Mainline); Greenland Road, Sheffield (Mainline & Sheafline); Halfway (Mainline); Olive Grove, Sheffield (Mainline & Sheafline); Petre Street, Sheffield (Don Valley); Rotherham (Mainline & Coachline).

Mainline   Fleet list

19	JKW219W	1981	Leyland PSU3G/4R	Duple Dom. DP53F	
20	JKW220W	1981	Leyland PSU3G/4R	Duple Dom. C53F	
22	KWA22W	1980	Leyland NL116L11/1R	Leyland B22DL	
23	KWA23W	1980	Leyland NL116L11/1R	Leyland B22DL	
26	KWA26W	1980	Leyland NL116L11/1R	Leyland B52F	
29	KWA29W	1980	Leyland NL116L11/1R	Leyland B52F	
45w	B45FET	1985	Dennis Domino	Optare B25F	
48w	C48HDT	1985	Dennis Domino	Optere B25F	
49w	C49HDT	1985	Dennis Domino	Optare B25F	
50w	C50HDT	1985	Dennis Domino	Optare B25F	
62	YPD122Y	1983	Leyland TRCTL11/2R	Duple Dom.IV C53F	*Sheafline 1990*
63	YPD103Y	1983	Leyland TRCTL11/2R	Duple Dom.IV C53F	*Sheafline 1990*
98	FWA498V	1980	Leyland PSU3C/4R	Duple Dom. DP53F	

1686 - 1702   1979 Leyland AN68A/1R   Alexander AL H45/29D

| 1686 | CWG686V | 1695 | CWG695V | 1697 | CWG697V | 1701 | CWG701V |
| 1693 | CWG693V | 1696 | CWG696V | 1700 | CWG700V | 1702 | CWG702V |

1750 - 1773   1979 Leyland AN68A/1R   Roe H45/29D

| 1750 | CWG750V | 1755 | CWG755V | 1766 | CWG766V | 1772 | CWG772V |
| 1752 | CWG752V | 1756 | CWG756V | 1771 | CWG771V | 1773 | CWG771V |

1777 - 1806   1981 Leyland AN68B/1R   Alexander AL H45/29D

1777	JKW277W	1781	JKW281W	1800	JKW300W	1803	JKW303W
1778	JKW278W	1782	JKW282W	1801	JKW301W	1805	JKW305W
1780	JKW280W	1784	JKW284W	1802	JKW302W	1806	JKW306W

1807 - 1832   1981 Leyland AN68B/1R   Marshall H45/29D (*H41/29D)

1807	JKW307W	1819	JKW319W	1825	JKW325W	1830	JKW330W
1808	JKW308W	1820	JKW320W	1826	JKW326W	1831	JKW331W
1812*	JKW312W	1821	JKW321W	1828	JKW328W	1832	JKW332W
1818	JKW318W	1823	JKW323W	1829	JKW329W		

1854 - 1883   1981 MCW Metrobus DR104   MCW H46/31F

1854	JHE154W	1859	JHE159W	1866	JHE166W	1876	JHE176W
1855	JHE155W	1861	JHE161W	1868	JHE168W	1883	JHE183W
1858	JHE158W	1865	JHE165W	1874	JHE174W		

1901 - 1904   1983 MCW Metrobus DR104   MCW H47/33F

| 1901 | UKY901Y | 1902 | UKY902Y | 1903 | UKY903Y | 1904 | UKY904Y |

1905 - 1920   1984 MCW Metrobus DR104   MCW H47/33F

1905	A105XWE	1909	A109XWE	1913	A113XWE	1917	A117XWE
1906	A106XWE	1910	A110XWE	1914	A114XWE	1918	A118XWE
1907	A107XWE	1911	A111XWE	1915	A115XWE	1919	A119XWE
1908	A108XWE	1912	A112XWE	1916	A116XWE	1920	A120XWE

1921 - 1940   1985 MCW Metrobus DR104   MCW H47/33F

1921	B921CDT	1926	B926CDT	1931	B931CDT	1936	B936CDT
1922	B922CDT	1927	B927CDT	1932	B932CDT	1937	B937CDT
1923	B923CDT	1928	B928CDT	1933	B933CDT	1938	B938CDT
1924	B924CDT	1929	B929CDT	1934	B934CDT	1939	B939CDT
1925	B925CDT	1930	B930CDT	1935	B935CDT	1940	B940CDT

1941 - 1946   1985 MCW Metrobus DR102   MCW CH42/28F

| 1941 | B941FET | 1943 | B943FET | 1945 | B945FET | 1946 | B946FET |
| 1942 | B942FET | 1944 | B944FET | | | | |

1947 - 1960   1986 MCW Metrobus DR102   MCW CH42/28F

1947	C947HWF	1951	C951LWJ	1955	C955LWJ	1958	C958LWJ
1948	C948HWF	1952	C952LWJ	1956	C956LWJ	1959	C959LWJ
1949	C949HWF	1953	C953LWJ	1957	C957LWJ	1960	C960LWJ
1950	C950HWF	1954	C954LWJ				

2001 - 2010

1985 Leyland DAB   Leyland DAB AB60T

2001 C101HDT	2004 C104HDT	2007 C107HDT	2009 C109HDT
2002 C102HDT	2005 C105HDT	2008 C108HDT	2010 C110HDT
2003 C103HDT	2006 C106HDT		

2011 C111HDT	1985 Leyland-DAB	Leyland-DAB ADP67D
2012 C112HDT	1985 Leyland-DAB	Leyland-DAB ADP67D
2013 C113HDT	1985 Leyland-DAB	Leyland-DAB ADP67D

2101 - 2140

1981 Dennis Dominator DDA133   Alexander RH H46/32F

2101 KKU101W	2111 KKU111W	2121 KKU121W	2131 MWB851W
2102 KKU102W	2112 KKU112W	2122 KKU122W	2132 MWB852W
2103 KKU103W	2113 KKU113W	2123 KKU123W	2133 MWB853W
2104 KKU104W	2114 KKU114W	2124 KKU124W	2134 MWB854W
2105 KKU105W	2115 KKU115W	2125 KKU125W	2135 MWB855W
2106 KKU106W	2116 KKU116W	2126 KKU126W	2136 MWB856W
2107 KKU107W	2117 KKU117W	2127 KKU127W	2137 OWE137X
2108 KKU108W	2118 KKU118W	2128 KKU128W	2138 OWE138X
2109 KKU109W	2119 KKU119W	2129 MWB849W	2139 OWE139X
2110 KKU110W	2120 KKU120W	2130 MWB850W	2140 OWE140X

2141 - 2220

1981/2 Dennis Dominator DDA133   Alexander RH H46/32F

2141 NKU141X	2161 NKU161X	2181 NKU181X	2201 NKU201X
2142 NKU142X	2162 NKU162X	2182 NKU182X	2202 NKU202X
2143 NKU143X	2163 NKU163X	2183 NKU183X	2203 NKU203X
2144 NKU144X	2164 NKU164X	2184 NKU184X	2204 NKU204X
2145 NKU145X	2165 NKU165X	2185 NKU185X	2205 NKU205X
2146 NKU146X	2166 NKU166X	2186 NKU186X	2206 NKU206X
2147 NKU147X	2167 NKU167X	2187 NKU187X	2207 NKU207X
2148 NKU148X	2168 NKU168X	2188 NKU188X	2208 NKU208X
2149 NKU149X	2169 NKU169X	2189 NKU189X	2209 NKU209X
2150 NKU150X	2170 NKU170X	2190 NKU190X	2210 NKU210X
2151 NKU151X	2171 NKU171X	2191 NKU191X	2211 NKU211X
2152 NKU152X	2172 NKU172X	2192 NKU192X	2212 NKU212X
2153 NKU153X	2173 NKU173X	2193 NKU193X	2213 NKU213X
2154 NKU154X	2174 NKU174X	2194 NKU194X	2214 NKU214X
2155 NKU155X	2175 NKU175X	2195 NKU195X	2215 NKU215X
2156 NKU156X	2176 NKU176X	2196 NKU196X	2216 NKU216X
2157 NKU157X	2177 NKU177X	2197 NKU197X	2217 NKU217X
2158 NKU158X	2178 NKU178X	2198 NKU198X	2218 NKU218X
2159 NKU159X	2179 NKU179X	2199 NKU199X	2219 NKU219X
2160 NKU160X	2180 NKU180X	2200 NKU200X	2220 NKU220X

2221 - 2274

1982 Dennis Dominator DDA133   Alexander RH H46/32F

2221 SDT221Y	2235 SDT235Y	2248 SDT248Y	2216 SDT261Y
2222 SDT222Y	2236 SDT236Y	2249 SDT249Y	2262 SDT262Y
2223 SDT223Y	2237 SDT237Y	2250 SDT250Y	2263 SDT263Y
2224 SDT224Y	2238 SDT238Y	2251 SDT251Y	2264 SDT264Y
2225 SDT225Y	2239 SDT239Y	2252 SDT252Y	2265 SDT265Y
2226 SDT226Y	2240 SDT240Y	2253 SDT253Y	2266 SDT266Y
2227 SDT227Y	2241 SDT241Y	2254 SDT254Y	2267 SDT267Y
2228 SDT228Y	2242 SDT242Y	2255 SDT255Y	2268 SDT268Y
2229 SDT229Y	2243 SDT243Y	2256 SDT256Y	2270 SDT270Y
2230 SDT230Y	2244 SDT244Y	2257 SDT257Y	2271 SDT271Y
2231 SDT231Y	2245 SDT245Y	2258 SDT258Y	2272 SDT272Y
2232 SDT232Y	2246 SDT246Y	2259 SDT259Y	2273 SDT273Y
2233 SDT233Y	2247 SDT247Y	2260 SDT260Y	2274 SDT274Y
2234 SDT234Y			

2275 - 2304

1983 Dennis Dominator DDA165 Alexander RH H46/32F (*H46/33F)

2275*	UWJ275Y	2283	UWJ283Y	2291	UWJ291Y	2298	A298XAK
2276	UWJ276Y	2284	UWJ284Y	2292	UWJ292Y	2299	A299XAK
2277	UWJ277Y	2285	UWJ285Y	2293	UWJ293Y	2300	A300XAK
2278	UWJ278Y	2286	UWJ286Y	2294	UWJ294Y	2301	A301XAK
2279	UWJ279Y	2287	UWJ287Y	2295	A295XAK	2302	A302XAK
2280	UWJ280Y	2288	UWJ288Y	2296	A296XAK	2303	A303XAK
2281	UWJ281Y	2289	UWJ289Y	2297	A297XAK	2304	A304XAK
2282	UWJ282Y	2290	UWJ290Y				

2311 - 2320

1983 Dennis Dominator DDA165 Northern Counties H7/33F

2311	A311XAK	2314	A314XAK	2317	A317XAK	2319	A319XAK
2312	A312XAK	2315	A315XAK	2318	A318XAK	2320	A320XAK
2313	A313XAK	2316	A316XAK				

2351 - 2365

1984 Dennis Dominator DDA901 East Lancs H46/33F

2351	B351CDT	2355	B355CDT	2359	B359CDT	2363	B363CDT
2352	B352CDT	2356	B356CDT	2360	B360CDT	2364	B364CDT
2355	B355CDT	2357	B357CDT	2361	B361CDT	2365	B365CDT
2354	B354CDT	2358	B358CDT	2362	B362CDT		

2401 - 2449

1984 Dennis Dominator DDA901 Alexander RH H46/32F

2401	A401YAK	2413	A413YAK	2426	A426YAK	2438	A438YAK
2402	A402YAK	2414	A414YAK	2427	A427YAK	2439	B439CKW
2403	A403YAK	2415	A415YAK	2428	A428YAK	2440	B440CKW
2404	A404YAK	2416	A416YAK	2429	A429YAK	2441	B441CKW
2405	A405YAK	2417	A417YAK	2430	A430YAK	2442	B442CKW
2406	A406YAK	2418	A418YAK	2431	A431YAK	2443	B443CKW
2407	A407YAK	2419	A419YAK	2432	A432YAK	2444	B444CKW
2408	A408YAK	2420	A420YAK	2433	A433YAK	2445	B445CKW
2409	A409YAK	2421	A421YAK	2434	A434YAK	2446	B446CKW
2410	A410YAK	2423	A423YAK	2435	A435YAK	2447	B447CKW
2411	A411YAK	2424	A424YAK	2436	A436YAK	2448	B448CKW
2412	A412YAK	2425	A425YAK	2437	A437YAK	2449	B449CKW

2451 - 2470

2985 Dennis Dominator DDA910 Alexander RH H46/32F

2451	C871JWE	2456	C876JWE	2461	C881JWE	2466	C886JWE
2452	C872JWE	2457	C877JWE	2462	C882JWE	2466	C886JWE
2453	C873JWE	2458	C878JWE	2463	C883JWE	2468	C888JWE
2454	C874JWE	2459	C879JWE	2464	C884JWE	2469	C889JWE
2455	C875JWE	2460	C880JWE	2465	C885JWE	2470	C890JWE

2471 - 2485

1986 Dennis Dominator DDA1011 Alexander RH CH45/33F

2471	D471OWE	2475	D475OWE	2479	D479OWE	2483	D483OWE
2472	D472OWE	2476	D476OWE	2480	D480OWE	2484	D484OWE
2473	D473OWE	2477	D477OWE	2481	D481OWE	2485	D485OWE
2474	D474OWE	2478	D478OWE	2482	D482OWE		

2486 - 2490

1986 Dennis Dominator DDA1011 Alexander RH CH45/24F

2486	D486OWE	2488	D488OWE	2489	D489OWE	2490	D490OWE
2487	D487OWE						

Don Valley Buses   Fleet list

29	D129OWG	1987	Dodge S56	Reeve Burgess DP25F	*South Yorkshire Trans .92*
30	D303MHS	1986	Dodge S56	Alexander B21F	*Kelvin Central Buses .92*
31	D314MHS	1986	Dodge S56	Alexander B21F	*Kelvin Central Buses .92*
39	D139OWG	1987	Dodge S56	Reeve Burgess B25F	*South Yorkshire Trans .92*
53	D153RAK	1987	Dodge S56	Reeve Burgess B25F	*South Yorkshire Trans .92*
59	D159RAK	1987	Dodge S56	Reeve Burgess B25F	*South Yorkshire Trans .92*
60	G590PKL	1990	Mercedes Benz 811D	Dormobile B24F	*Skill, Sheffield .91*
66	G566SNN	1990	Mercedes Benz 709D	Carlyle B33F	*Skill, Sheffield .91*
68	F68LNU	1989	Mercedes Benz 709D	Robin Hood B29F	*Skill, Sheffield .91*
69	F69LNU	1989	Mercedes Benz 709D	Robin Hood B29F	*Skill, Sheffield .91*
70	F70LAL	1989	Mercedes Benz 811D	Alexander C33F	*Skill, Sheffield .91*
72	F725USF	1989	Mercedes Benz 811D	Alexander C33F	*Skill, Sheffield .91*
75	G750ONN	1990	Mercedes Benz 609D	NWC C24F	*Skill, Sheffield .91*
	B415NJF	1985	Ford Transit	Rootes B16F	*Midland Fox .91*
	B418NJF	1985	Ford Transit	Rootes B16F	*Midland Fox .91*
	B421NJF	1985	Ford Transit	Rootes B16F	*Midland Fox .91*
	C540TFJ	1986	Ford Transit	Rootes B16F	*Stevenson, Spath .91*

SUT (Sheaf Line)   Fleet list

804	TVP853S	1978	Leyland LN11351A/1R	Leyland DP45F	*Tame Valley 1991*
805	NOE595R	1977	Leyland Greenway	(1992) E.Lancs B48F	*London & Country 1992*
806	CWX669T	1979	Leyland Greenway	(1993) E.Lancs B48F	*West Riding 1990*
808	TUG808R	1976	Leyland LN11351A/1R	Leyland B49F	*Sheffield & District 1989*
809	CWX666T	1979	Leyland LN11351A/1R	Leyland B49F	*West Riding 1990*
810	EUM896T	1979	Leyland LN11351A/1R	Leyland B49F	*West Riding 1990*
811	EUM898T	1979	Leyland LN11351A/1R	Leyland B49F	*West Riding 1990*
812	BUH215V	1979	Leyland LN11351A/1R	Leyland B49F	*Tellings-GM 1992*
813	TUG809R	1976	Leyland LN11351A/1R	Leyland B49F	*Sheffield & District 1989*
814	TUG810R	1976	Leyland LN11351A/1R	Leyland B49F	*Sheffield & District 1989*
815	VNO735S	1977	Leyland N11351A/1R	Leyland B49F	*Eastern National 1992*
818	CWX665T	1979	Leyland LN11351A/1R	Leyland B49F	*West Riding 1990*
819	CWX668T	1979	Leyland LN11351A/1R	Leyland B49F	*West Riding 1990*
820	LMA414T	1979	Leyland LN11351A/1R	Leyland B49F	*SUT 1989*
821	UTU982R	1977	Leyland LN11351A/1R	Leyland B49F	*SUT 1989*
823	EUM888T	1979	Leyland LN11351A/1R	Leyland B49F	*West Riding 1990*
825	GUB178N	1974	Leyland LN11351/1R	Leyland B52F	*West Riding 1989*
827	PWW717R	1976	Leyland LN11351A/1R	Leyland B52F	*Sheffield & District 1989*
828	RWX150R	1976	Leyland LN11351A/1R	Leyland B52F	*West Riding 1989*
831	NHL564M	1973	Leyland LN1151/2R	Leyland B50F	*Sheffield & District 1989*
832	NHL565M	1973	Leyland LN1151/2R	Leyland B50F	*West Riding 1989*
833	NHL568M	1973	Leyland LN1151/2R	Leyland B50F	*West Riding 1989*
835	MUA881P	1976	Leyland LN11351A/1R	Leyland B52F	*West Riding 1989*
836	MUA884P	1976	Leyland LN11351A/1R	Leyland B52F	*Sheffield & District 1989*
839	NHL563M	1973	Leyland LN1151/2R	Leyland B50F	*Sheffield & District 1989*
841	GUB180N	1975	Leyland LN11351/1R	Leyland B52F	*Sheffield & District 1989*
842	GUB183N	1975	Leyalnd LN11351/1R	Leyland B52F	*Sheffield & District 1989*
843	MUA879P	1976	Leyland LN11351A/1R	Leyland B52F	*West Riding 1989*
844	HNL158N	1975	Leyland LN11351/1R	Leyland B52F	*SUT 1989*
845	HNL159N	1975	Leyland LN11351/1R	Leyland B52F	*SUT 1989*
847	HNL164N	1975	Leyland LN11351/1R	Leyland B52F	*SUT 1989*
848	OWF424R	1976	Leyland LN11351A/1R	Leyland B52F	*Yorkshire Traction 1989*
849	VAK447S	1978	Leyland LN11351A/1R	Leyland B52F	*Lincs Road Car 1989*
851	YWG469T	1979	Leyland LN11351A/1R	Leyland B52F	*Lincs Road Car 1990*
855	GMB653T	1978	Leyland LN10351B/1R	Leyland B44F	*SUT 1989*
856	JTU581T	1979	Leyland LN10351B/1R	Leyland B44F	*SUT 1989*

857	AAK111T	1979	Leyland LN10351B/1R	Leyland B44F	*SUT 1989*
859	TUG806R	1976	Leyland LN11351A/1R	Leyland B49F	*Sheffield & District 1989*
860	CWX667T	1979	Leyland LN11351A/1R	Leyland B49F	*West Riding 1990*
861	XVV536S	1978	Leyland LN11351A/1R	Leyland B49F	*Kinch, Barrow 1992*
862	GUB185N	1975	Leyland LN11351A/1R	Leyland B52F	*Sheffield & District 1989*
863	MUA877P	1976	Leyland LN11351A/1R	Leyland B52F	*Sheffield & District 1989*
864	PUM691P	1977	Leyland LN11351A/1R	Leyland B52F	*Sheffield & District 1989*
866	PUM676P	1977	Leyland LN11351A/1R	Leyland B52F	*Sheffield & District 1989*
867	PWW710R	1976	Leyland LN11351A/1R	Leyland B52F	*Sheffield & District 1989*
868	PWW718R	1976	Leyland LN11351A/1R	Leyland B52F	*Sheffield & District 1989*
870	TCY730M	1974	Leyland LN11351/1R	Leyland B52F	*Sheffield & District 1989*
871	GBF74N	1974	Leyland LN11351/1R	Leyland B52F	*Sheffield & District 1989*
873	SWE435S	1978	Leyland LN11351A/1R	Leyland B52F	*Lincs Road Car 1990*
874	SWE447S	1978	Leyland LN11351A/1R	Leyland B52F	*Lincs Road Car 1990*
875	WWA121S	1978	Leyland LN11351A/1R	Leyland B52F	*Lincs Road Car 1990*
876	YWG468T	1979	Leyland LN11351A/1R	Leyland B52F	*Lincs Road Car 1989*
877	RKW605R	1976	Leyland LN11351A/1R	Leyland B52F	*Lincs Road Car 1989*
878	PVT238L	1973	Leyland LN1151/1R	Leyland B52F	*Sheffield & District 1989*
879	DMS17V	1980	Leyland NL116L11/1R	Leyland B52F	*SUT 1989*
880	SNS823W	1980	Leyland NL116L11/1R	Leyland B52F	*SUT 1989*
881	KWA21W	1980	Leyland NL116L11/1R	Leyland B49F	*Mainline*
882	SFA286R	1976	Leyland LN11351A/1R	Leyland B49F	*PMT 1993*
883	PJT270R	1977	Leyland LN11351A/1R	Leyland B49F	*Stagecoach South 1993*
884	SFJ135R	1977	Leyland LN11351A/1R	Leyland B52F	*Stagecoach South 1993*
885	UHG728R	1977	Leyland LN11351A/1R	Leyland B49F	*Ribble 1993*
1001	YPD126Y	1983	Leyland TRCTL11/2R	Duple Dom.IV C53F	*Shearline 1989*
1002	YPD142Y	1983	Leyland TRCTL11/2R	Duple Dom.IV C53F	*Shearline 1989*
1003	3910WE	1983	Leyland TRCTL11/3R	Plaxton 3500 C51F	*Yelloway 1986*
1004	3913WE	1983	Leyland TRCTL11/3R	Plaxton 3500 C49FT	*Yelloway 1986*
1005	475HDT	1984	Dennis Dorchester	Plaxton 3200 C44FT	
1006	476HDT	1984	Dennis Dorchester	Plaxton 3200 C44FT	
1007	477HDT	1984	Dennis Dorchester	Plaxton 3200 C44FT	
1008	F78FWG	1989	Dennis Javelin	Duple 320 C53F	
1009	F79FWG	1989	Dennis Javelin	Duple 320 C53F	
1010	E306UUB	1988	Volvo B10M-61	Plaxton 3500 C48FT	*Wallace Arnold 1991*
1011	E307UUB	1988	Volvo B10M-61	Plaxton 3500 C48FT	*Wallace Arnold 1991*
1012	C452OFL	1986	Leyland TRCTL11/3RH	Plaxton 3500 C51F	*Cambus 1994*
1021	PWK10W	1980	Leyland PSU3F/5R	Duple Dom. C45F	*Smith, Alcester 1984*
1064	AKU164T	1979	Leyland LN10351B/1R	Leyland B44F	

1003/4 were originally registered A578KVU & A67GBN. 1005-7 were originally registered B975-7DWG.

10	AAK110T	1979	Leyland LN10351B/1R	Leyland B44F	*Mainline 1994*
25	KWA25W	1980	Leyland NL116L11/1R	Leyland B52F	*Mainline 1994*
27	KWA27W	1980	Leyland NL116L11/1R	Leyland B52F	*Mainline 1994*
69	KIB6110	1977	Leyland PSU3D/4R	(1987) Plaxton Bust'r B55F	*Compass 1989*

69 was originally registered REL401R

1824 - 1834   1981 Leyland AN68B/1R   Marshall H45/29D
            (ex.Mainline 1994)

1824	JKW324W	1827	JKW327W	1833	JKW333W	1834	JKW334W

Strathclyde Buses Ltd., 197 Victoria Road, Glasgow G42 7AD
Comlaw No.313 Ltd., 197 Victoria Road, Glasgow G42 7AD

Formed in 1986 to acquire the bus fleet of Strathclyde PTE which was created on 1 June 1973 to take over the operations of Glasgow Corporation Transport, Strathclyde Buses was sold to its management and employees in February 1993 who registered a new company SB Holdings for this purpose. In order to compete more effectively in the numerous bus wars in the city since deregulation, Strathclyde Buses on 9 February 1993 created a new low-cost unit under the title of Comlaw No.313 Ltd. which traded as GCT and used buses cascaded from the Strathclyde fleet. Seeking further expansion, SB Holdings in October 1994 purchased former Scottish Bus Group subsidiary Kelvin Central Buses from its employees. During the following month, Stagecoach Holdings plc who had only just begun its new Stagecoach Glasgow operation acquired a 20% share in SB Holdings and thus immediately ceased its own competitive operation in the city.

Livery : STRATHCLYDE'S BUSES - Orange & black. GCT - Yellow, green & black

Depots : STRATHCLYDE'S BUSES - Knightswood (shared with GCT); Larkfield; Parkhead; Possilpark. GCT - Knightswood (shared with Strathclyde's Buses).

Strathclyde's Buses   Fleet list

A2 - A39   1981 Volvo B55-10 Mk.III   Alexander RV H44/35F

2	TGG378W	13	CSU221X	22	CSU230X	31	CSU239X
5	TGG381W	14	CSU222X	23	CSU231X	32	CSU240X
7	TGG383W	15	CSU223X	25	CSU233X	33	CSU241X
8	TGG384W	16	CSU224X	26	CSU234X	34	CSU242X
9	TGG385W	17	CSU225X	27	CSU235X	35	CSU243X
10	TGG386W	18	CSU226X	28	CSU236X	37	CSU245X
11	CSU219X	20	CSU228X	29	CSU237X	38	CSU246X
12	CSU220X	21	CSU229X	30	CSU238X	39	CSU247X

A41 - A81   1982 Volvo B55-10 Mk.III   Alexander RV H44/35F

41	KGG101Y	51	KGG111Y	64	KGG124Y	73	KGG133Y
42	KGG102Y	52	KGG112Y	65	KGG121Y	78	KGG138Y
43	KGG103Y	55	KGG115Y	66	KGG126Y	75	KGG135Y
44	KGG104Y	56	KGG116Y	67	KGG127Y	76	KGG136Y
45	KGG105Y	58	KGG118Y	68	KGG128Y	77	KGG137Y
46	KGG106Y	59	KGG119Y	69	KGG129Y	78	KGG138Y
47	KGG107Y	60	KGG141Y	70	KGG130Y	79	KGG139Y
48	KGG108Y	62	KGG122Y	71	KGG131Y	80	KGG140Y
49	KGG109Y	63	KGG123Y	72	KGG132Y	81	KGG120Y
50	KGG110Y						

LA1251 - LA1333 1979 Leyland AN68A/1R Alexander AL H45/33F

1251	FSU68T	1272	FSU89T	1292	FSU109T	1312	LSU369V
1252	FSU69T	1273	FSU90T	1293	FSU110T	1313	LSU370V
1253	FSU70T	1274	FSU91T	1294	FSU111T	1314	LSU371V
1254	FSU71T	1275	FSU92T	1295	FSU112T	1315	LSU372V
1255	FSU72T	1276	FSU93T	1296	FSU113T	1316	LSU373V
1256	FSU73T	1277	FSU94T	1297	FSU114T	1317	LSU374V
1257	FSU74T	1278	FSU95T	1298	FSU115T	1318	LSU375V
1258	FSU76T	1279	FSU96T	1299	FSU116T	1319	LSU376V
1259	FSU76T	1280	FSU97T	1300	FSU117T	1320	LSU377V
1260	FSU77T	1281	FSU98T	1301	FSU118T	1321	LSU378V
1261	FSU78T	1282	FSU99T	1302	FSU119T	1322	LSU379V
1262	FSU79T	1283	FSU100T	1303	FSU120T	1324	LSU381V
1263	FSU80T	1284	FSU101T	1304	FSU121T	1325	LSU382V
1264	FSU81T	1285	FSU102T	1305	FSU122T	1326	LSU383V
1265	FSU82T	1286	FSU103T	1306	FSU123T	1328	LSU385V
1266	FSU23T	1287	FSU104T	1307	FSU124T	1329	LSU386V
1267	FSU84T	1288	FSU105T	1308	FSU125T	1330	LSU387V
1268	FSU85T	1289	FSU106T	1309	FSU126T	1331	LSU388V
1269	FSU86T	1290	FSU107T	1311	LSU368V	1333	LSU390V
1271	FSU88T						

LA1334 - LA1432 1980 Leyland AN68A/1R Alexander AL H45/33F

1334	LSU391V	1358	RDS572W	1382	RDS561W	1406	RDS595W
1334	LSU392V	1359	RDS573W	1383	RDS562W	1408	RDS597W
1336	LSU393V	1359	RDS753W	1383	RDS562W	1409	RDS598W
1337	LSU394V	1361	RDS540W	1385	RDS564W	1410	RDS599W
1338	LSU395V	1362	RDS541W	1386	RDS575W	1411	RDS600W
1339	LSU396V	1353	RDS542W	1387	RDS576W	1412	RDS601W
1340	LSU397V	1364	RDS543W	1388	RDS577W	1413	RDS602W
1341	LSU398V	1365	RDS544W	1389	RDS578W	1414	RDS603W
1342	LSU399V	1366	RDS545W	1390	RDS579W	1415	RDS604W
1343	LSU400V	1367	RDS546W	1391	RDS580W	1416	RDS605W
1344	LSU401V	1368	RDS547W	1392	RDS581W	1417	RDS606W
1345	LSU402V	1369	RDS548W	1393	RDS582W	1418	RDS607W
1346	LSU403V	1370	RDS549W	1394	RDS583W	1419	RDS607W
1347	LSU404V	1371	RDS550W	1395	RDS584W	1420	RDS609W
1348	LSU405V	1372	RDS551W	1296	RDS585W	1422	RDS611W
1349	LSU406V	1373	RDS552W	1397	RDS586W	1423	RDS612W
1350	LSU407V	1374	RDS553W	1398	RDS587W	1424	RDS613W
1351	RDS565W	1375	RDS554W	1399	RDS588W	1425	RDS614W
1352	RDS566W	1376	RDS555W	1400	RDS589W	1426	RDS615W
1353	RDS567W	1377	RDS556W	1402	RDS591W	1427	RDS616W
1354	RDS568W	1378	RDS557W	1403	RDS592W	1428	RDS617W
1355	RDS569W	1379	RDS558W	1404	RDS593W	1429	RDS618W
1356	RDS570W	1380	RDS559W	1405	RDS594W	1432	SUS600W
1357	RDS571W	1381	RDS560W				

LA1433	SUS601W	1981	Leyland AN68A/1R	Alexander AL H45/33F
LA1434	SUS602W	1980	Leyland AN68A/1R	Alexander AL H44/33F

LA1435 - LA1449 1981 Leyland AN68A/1R Alexander AL H44/33F

1435	SUS603W	1439	SUS607W	1443	UGB196W	1447	CUS301X
1436	SUS604W	1440	UGB193W	1444	CUS298X	1448	CUS302X
1437	SUS605W	1441	CUS296X	1445	CUS299X	1449	UGB202W
1438	SUS606W	1442	CUS297X	1446	CUS300X		

LO1   VGB364W   1980   Leyland B45/TL11/1R   Alexander RH H46/30F

LO2 - LO10   1981 Leyland ONTL11/1R   Roe H46/31F

2	CGG825X	8	CGG831X	9	CGG832X	10	CGG833X
6	CGG829X						

LO12 - LO16   1982 Leyland ONTL11/1R   ECW H46/31F

12	CGG835X	14	CGG837X	15	CGG838X	16	CGG839X
13	CGG836X						

LO17 - LO21   1982 Leyland ONTL11/1R   Alexander RH H47/29F

17	ESU4X	18	ESU5X	19	ESU6X	21	ESU8X

LO22 - LO46   1983 Leyland ONTL11/1R   ECW H47/31F

22	KGG142Y	30	KGG150Y	36	KGG156Y	42	A371TGB
23	KGG143Y	31	KGG151Y	37	KGG157Y	43	A372TGB
25	KGG145Y	32	KGG152Y	38	KGG158Y	44	A373TGB
26	KGG146Y	33	KGG153Y	39	KGG159Y	45	A374TGB
27	KFF147Y	34	KGG154Y	40	KGG160Y	46	A375TGB
29	KGG149Y	35	KGG155Y	41	KGG161Y		

LO48	J137FYS	1991	Leyland ON2R50G13Z4	Leyland H47/31F
LO49	J138FYS	1991	Leyland ON2R50G13Z4	Leyland H47/31F

LO50 - LO101   1993 Leyland ON2R50G13Z4   Alexander RH H47/31F

50	K350SDS	63	L163UNS	76	L176UNS	89	L189UNS
51	L551USU	64	L164UNS	77	L177UNS	90	L190UNS
52	L552USU	65	L165UNS	78	L178UNS	91	L191UNS
53	L553USU	66	L166UNS	79	L179UNS	92	L192UNS
54	L554USU	67	L167UNS	80	L180UNS	93	L193UNS
55	L155UNS	68	L168UNS	81	L181UNS	94	L194UNS
56	L156UNS	69	L169UNS	82	L182UNS	95	L195UNS
57	L157UNS	70	L170UNS	83	L183UNS	96	L196UNS
58	L158UNS	71	L171UNS	84	L184UNS	97	L197UNS
59	L159UNS	72	L172UNS	85	L185UNS	98	L198UNS
60	L160UNS	73	L173UNS	86	L186UNS	99	L199UNS
61	L161UNS	74	L174UNS	87	L187UNS	100	L202UNS
62	L162UNS	75	L175UNS	88	L188UNS	101	L201UNS

M39   E55LBK   1988   MCW Metrorider MF150/70   MCW B25F   *Southampton 1990*

M55 - M66   1987 MCW Metrorider MF150/55   MCW B23F

55	E940XYS	60	E945XYS	63	E948XYS	66	E951XYS

M72	E307YDS	1988	MCW Metrorider MF150/56	MCW	B22F
M73	E308YDS	1988	MCW Metrorider MF150/56	MCW	B13FL
M74	E309YDS	1988	MCW Metrorider MF150/56	MCW	B22F
M75	E310YDS	1988	MCW Metrorider MF150/56	MCW	Bl3FL

M76	E311YDS	1988	MCW Metrorider MF150/56	MCW B22F
M77	E312YDS	1988	MCW Metrorider MF150/56	MCW B13FL
M78	E313YDS	1988	MCW Metrorider MF150/56	MCW B22F
M81	E316YDS	1988	MCW Metrorider MF150/56	MCW B13FL

M82 - M112   1988   MCW Metrorider MF154/12   MCW B33F

82	E179BNS	89	E186BNS	96	E193BNS	105	E202BNS
83	E180BNS	90	E187BNS	97	E194BNS	107	E204BNS
84	E181BNS	91	E188BNS	98	E195BNS	108	E205BNS
85	E182BNS	92	E189BNS	99	E196BNS	109	E206BNS
86	E183BNS	93	E190BNS	100	E197BNS	110	E207BNS
87	E184BNS	94	E191BNS	102	E199BNS	111	E208BNS
88	E185BNS	95	E192BNS	103	E200BNS	112	E209BNS

| M115 | H844UUA | 1991 | Optare Metrorider | Optare B29F | *Optare demonstrator 1991* |
| M116 | F111NPU | 1988 | MCW Metrorider MF158 | MCW DP29F | *Colchester 1991* |

M117 - M120   1988   MCW Metrorider MF158   MCW B31F
                            (ex.Colchester 1991)

| 117 | F112NPU | 118 | F113NPU | 119 | F114NPU | 120 | F115NPU |

M121	H398SYG	1990	Optare Metrorider	Optare B31F	*Optare demonstrator 1991*
M122	F201RVN	1988	MCW Metrorider MF154	MCW DP31F	*Eden, West Aucland 1993*
M123	F203RVN	1988	MCW Metrorider MF154	MCW DP31F	*Eden, West Auckland 1993*

MB1 - MB5   1979   MCW Metrobus DR101/5   MCW H46/31F

| 1 | GGA750T | 3 | GGA752T | 4 | GGA753T | 5 | GGA754T |
| 2 | GGA751T | | | | | | |

MB6 - MB20   1982   MCW Metrobus DR102/66   Alexander RH H45/33F

6	EUS101X	10	EUS105X	14	EUS109X	18	EUS113X
7	EUS102X	11	EUS106X	15	EUS110X	19	EUS114X
8	EUS103X	12	EUS107X	16	EUS111X	20	EUS115X
9	EUS104X	13	EUS108X	17	EUS112X		

MB21 - MB30   1983   MCW Metrobus DR102/31   MCW H46/31F

21	KGG162Y	24	KGG165Y	27	KGG168Y	29	KGG170Y
22	KGG163Y	25	KGG166Y	28	KGG169Y	30	KGG171Y
23	KGG164Y	26	KGG167Y				

MB31 - MB43   1983   MCW Metrobus DR102/36   MCW H46/31F (*H46/23FL)

31	MUS309Y	35	MUS313Y	38	A732RNS	41	A735RNS
32	MUS310Y	36	A730RNS	39	A733RNS	42	A737RNS
33	MUS311Y	37	A731RNS	40	A734RNS	43	A737RNS
34	MUS312Y						

| MB44 | A738RNS | 1983 | MCW Metrobus DR132/4 | MCW H46/31F |
| MB45 | A739RNS | 1983 | MCW Metrobus DR132/4 | MCW H46/31F |

MB46 - MB61   1989   MCW Metrobus DR102/72   MCW H46/31F

46	G384OGD	50	G388OGD	54	G392OGD	58	G396OGD
47	G385OGD	51	G389OGD	55	G393OGD	59	G397OGD
48	G386OGD	52	G390OGD	56	G394OGD	60	G398OGD
49	G387OGD	53	G391OGD	57	G395OGD	61	G399OGD

MBC62 - MBC66   1989   MCW Mterobus DR102/72   MCW DPH43/29F

| 62 | G400OGD | 64 | G402OGD | 65 | G403OGD | 66 | G404OGD |
| 63 | G401OGD |

MB67 - MB70   1989   MCW Metrobus DR102/72   MCW H46/31F

| 67 | G405OGD | 68 | G406OGD | 69 | G407OGD | 70 | G408OGD |

| SS1 | H912HRO | 1991 | Scania N113CRB | Plaxton B47F | *Demonstrator 1993* |
| SS2 | J113XSX | 1992 | Scania N113CRB | Plaxton B51F | *Demonstrator 1993* |

065-100   1994   Volvo B10M-55   Alexander PS DP48F
(ex.Stagecoach Glasgow 11.94)

065	M765PRS	070	M770PRS	075	M775PRS	079	M779PRS
066	M766PRS	071	M771PRS	076	M776PRS	080	M780PRS
067	M767PRS	072	M772PRS	077	M877PRS	081	M781PRS
068	M768PRS	073	M773PRS	078	M778PRS	100	M428RRN
069	M769PRS	074	M774PRS

1982   Leyland AN68C/1R   Roe H43/31F
(ex.Kingston-upon Hull City Transport 10.94)

| WAG370X | WAG374X | WAG377X | WAG379X |
| WAG373X | WAG376X | WAG378X | WAG381X |

VET606S	1978	Leyland AN68A/1R	Roe H45/29D	*South Yorkshire 1994*
CWG720V	1980	Leyland AN68A/1R	Alexander H45/29D	*South Yorkshire 1994*
CWG771V	1980	Leyland AN68A/1R	Roe H45/29D	*South Yorkshire 1994*
CWG772V	1980	Leyland AN68A/1R	Roe H45/29D	*South Yorkshire 1994*
JKW319W	1981	Leyland AN68A/1R	Marshall H45/29D	*South Yorkshire 1994*
JKW329W	1981	Leyland AN68A/1R	Marshall H45/29D	*South Yorkshire 1994*
A102FPL	1984	Leyland ONTL11/2R	ECW CH45/27F	*Northumbria 1994*
C448BKM	1985	Leyland ONTL11/2R	ECW CH45/27F	*Maidstone & District 10.94*

1985   Leyland ONTL11/2R   ECW CH45/27F
(ex.Northumbria 10.94)

| B697BPU | C211UPD | C212UPD | C213UPD |

ANCILLARY VEHICLES

LA680	HGD886L	1973	Leyland AN68/1R	Alexander AL H45/30C	Driver trainer
LA682	HGD888L	1973	Leyland AN68/1R	Alexander AL H45/30C	Driver trainer
LA697	HGD903L	1973	Leyland AN68/1R	Alexander AL H45/30C	Driver trainer
LA698	HGD904L	1973	Leyland AN68/1R	Alexander AL H45/30C	Driver trainer

LA710 HGD916L	1973	Leyland AN68/1R	Alexander AL H45/30C	Driver trainer
LN20 GGE175T	1979	Leyland LN10351A/1R	Leyland B--F	Publicity unit
M18 A348VDS	1983	Ford Transit	Mellor DP16F	Driver trainer
R1		Leyland Hippo		Recovery wagon
R9		Bedford TK (fwd)		Recovery wagon
SVN601K	1972	Dodge 6-wheel		Recovery wagon
RV2 CHE540K	1973	Leyland PSU4B/4R	Marshall	Towing wagon
RV4 CHE535K	1973	Leyland PSU4B/4R	Marshall	Towing wagon

SVN601K was originally registered CGD272K. RV2/4 were ex.Yorkshire Traction.

GCT   Fleet list

GLA1 NGB125M	1974	Leyland AN68/1R	Alexander AL H45/31F	*Strathclyde's Buses 1993*
GLA2 OYS162M	1974	Leyland AN68/1R	Alexander AL H45/31F	*Strathclyde's Buses 1993*
GLA3 OYS178M	1974	Leyland AN68/1R	Alexander AL H45/31F	*Strathclyde's Buses 1993*

GLA4 - GLA8   1974   Leyland AN68/1R   East Lancs H45/33F
(ex.Strathclyde's Buses 1993)

| 4 | OTO554M | 6 | OTO566M | 7 | OTO567M | 8 | OTO581M |
| 5 | OTO561M | | | | | | |

GLA9 JAL877N	1975	Leyland AN68/1R	East Lancs H45/34F	*Strathclyde's Buses 1993*
GLA10 JAL879N	1975	Leyland AN68/1R	East Lancs H45/34F	*Strathclyde's Buses 1993*
GLA11 JVK234P	1976	Leyland AN68A/1R	Alexander AL H45/31F	*Strathclyde's Buses 1993*
GLA12 JVK238P	1976	Leyland AN68A/1R	Alexander AL H45/31F	*Strathclyde's Buses 1993*
GLA13 MVK502R	1976	Leyland AN68A/2R	Alexander AL H48/34F	*Strathclyde's Buses 1993*
GLA14 MVK506R	1976	Leyland AN68A/2R	Alexander AL H48/33F	*Strathclyde's Buses 1993*
GLA15 MVK508R	1976	Leyland AN68A/2R	Alexander AL H48/33F	*Strathclyde's Buses 1993*
GLA16 MVK512R	1976	Leyland AN68A/2R	Alexander AL H48/30F	*Strathclyde's Buses 1993*
GLA17 MVK516R	1976	Leyland AN68A/2R	Alexander AL H48/33F	*Strathclyde's Buses 1993*
GLA18 MVK528R	1976	Leyland AN68A/2R	Alexander AL H48/33F	*Strathclyde's Buses 1993*
GLA19 MVK552R	1976	Leyland AN68A/2R	Alexander AL H48/33F	*Strathclyde's Buses 1993*
GLA20 MVK567R	1976	Leyland AN68A/2R	Alexander AL H48/33F	*Strathclyde's Buses 1993*
GLA21 JVK235P	1976	Leyland AN68A/1R	Alexander AL H45/31F	*Strathclyde's Buses 1993*
GLA22 JVK236R	1976	Leyland AN68A/1R	Alexander AL H45/31F	*Strathclyde's Buses 1993*
GLA23 MVK520R	1976	Leyland AN68A/2R	Alexander AL H48/33F	*Strathclyde's Buses 1993*
GLA24 MVK527R	1976	Leyland AN68A/2R	Alexander AL H48/33F	*Strathclyde's Buses 1993*

GLA26 - GLA30   1978   Leyland AN68A/2R   Alexander AL H49/37F
(ex.Strathclyde's Buses 1993)

| 26 | VCU305T | 28 | VCU308T | 29 | VCU311T | 30 | VCU313T |
| 27 | VCU307T | | | | | | |

GLA31 JVK240P	1976	Leyland AN68A/1R	Alexander AL H45/31F	*Strathclyde's Buses 1993*
GLA32 JVK243P	1976	Leyland AN68A/1R	Alexander AL H45/31F	*Strathclyde's Buses 1993*
GLA33 MVK503R	1976	Leyland AN68A/2R	Alexander AL H48/34F	*Strathclyde's Buses 1993*
GLA34 MVK529R	1976	Leyland AN68A/2R	Alexander AL H48/33F	*Strathclyde's Buses 1993*
GLA35 SCN272S	1978	Leyland AN68A/2R	Alexander AL H49/37F	*Strathclyde's Buses 1993*
GLA36 UVK293T	1978	Leyland AN68A/2R	Alexander AL H49/37F	*Strathclyde's Buses 1993*
GLA37 UVK296T	1978	Leyland AN68A/2R	Alexander AL H49/37F	*Strathclyde's Buses 1993*
GLA38 OYS172M	1974	Leyland AN68/1R	Alexander AL H45/31F	*Strathclyde's Buses 1993*
GLA39 KSU827P	1975	Leyland AN68/1R	Alexander AL H45/31F	*Strathclyde's Buses 1993*
GLA40 KSU828P	1975	Leyland AN68/1R	Alexander AL H45/31F	*Strathclyde's Buses 1993*

GLA41 - GLA49

1977 Leyland AN68/1R   Alexander AL H45/31F
(ex.Strathclyde's Buses 1994)

41	TGE823R	44	RUS350R	46	TGE832R	48	TGE839R
42	TGE828R	45	TGE827R	47	TGE837R	49	TGE736R
43	RUS348R						

GLO1	C807KHS	1986	Leyland ONLXB/1RH	Alexander RL CH47/27F	*Kelvin Central 1993*
GLO2	C808KHS	1986	Leyland ONLXB/1RH	Alexander RL CH47/27F	*Kelvin Central 1993*
GLO3	C810KHS	1986	Leyland ONLXB/1RH	Alexander RL CH47/27F	*Kelvin Central 1993*
GLO4	C113BTS	1986	Leyland ONLXB/1RV	Alexander RL H47/32F	*Kelvin Central 1993*
GLO5	C114BTS	1986	Leyland ONLXB/1RV	Alexander RL H47/32F	*Kelvin Central 1993*
GLO6	C115BTS	1986	Leyland ONLXB/1RV	Alexander RL H47/32F	*Kelvin Central 1993*

GM1 - GM7

1987 MCW Metrorider   MCW B23F
(ex.Strathclyde's Buses 1993)

1	E995WNS	3	E928XYS	5	E932XYS	7	E934XYS
2	E996WNS	4	E930XYS	6	E933XYS		

GM8 F238EDS 1989 MCW Metrorider MF154   MCW C28F   *Strathclyde's Buses 1994*

GM9 - GM15

1987 MCW Met4rorider   MCW B23F
(ex.Strathclyde's Buses 1994)

9	E942XYS	11	949XYS	13	E952XYS	15	E955XYS
10	E943XYS	12	E950XYS	14	E953XYS		

GM16	E201BNS	1988	MCW Metrorider MF154/12	MCW B33F	*Strathclyde's Buses 1994*
GM17	E203BNS	1988	MCW Metrorider MF154/12	MCW B33F	*Strathclyde's Buses 1994*
GM18	E929XYS	1987	MCW Metrorider MF150/55	MCW B23F	*Strathclyde's Buses 1994*
GM19	E931XYS	1987	MCW Metrorider MF150/55	MCW B23F	*Strathclyde's Buses 1994*
GM20	E939XYS	1987	MCW Metrorider MF150/55	MCW B23F	*Strathclyde's Buses 1994*
GM21	E314YDS	1988	MCW Metrorider MF150/56	MCW B13FL	*Strathclyde's Buses 1994*
GM22	E315YDS	1988	MCW Metrorider MF150/56	MCW B22F	*Strathclyde's Buses 1994*
GM23	E937XYS	1987	MCW Metrorider MF150/55	MCW B23F	*trSathclyde's Buses 1994*

LA664 HGD670L 1973 Leyland AN68/1R   Alexander AL H45/29F *Strathclyde's Buses 1994*

SS3	TIB8511	1994	Scania K93	East Lancs DP49F	
SS4	TIB8512	1994	Scania K93	East Lancs DP49F	
SS5	TIB8513	1994	Scania K93	East Lancs DP49F	

100 YEARS OF PUBLIC TRANSPORT IN GLASGOW
1894
1994

KCB NETWORK

Kelvin Central Buses Ltd., Traction House, Hamilton Road, Motherwell ML1 3DS

Formed in 1989 by the merging of Kelvin Scottish Omnibuses, a company born out of the 1985 restructuring of the Scottish Bus Group and Central Scottish Omnibuses which was also part of the SBG, the new enlarged company was purchased by its employees in 1991 since when expansion has been achieved by the purchase of several independent operators including Greens, Kirkintilloch, McKenna of Uddingston, Beaton of Blantyre, Morrow of Clydebank, McDade, Uddingston and McKindless of Wishaw. Despite being sold to SB Holdings in October 1994, the company is to retain its existing livery and KCB Network fleet name.

Livery : Dark red & cream.

Depots : Airdrie; Cumbernauld; Kirkintilloch; Motherwell; Old Kilpatrick; Stepps

KCB Network Fleet list

1001	C546TJF	1986	Ford Transit 190	Rootes B16F	*Stevenson, Spath 1991*
1002	C556TUT	1986	Ford Transit 190	Rootes B16F	*Stenenson, Spath 1991*
1003	C193KBH	1986	Ford Transit 190	Carlyle B16F	*Luton & District 1992*
1004	C194KBH	1986	Ford Transit 190	Carlyle B16F	*Luton & District 1992*

1013 - 1018 1992 Dennis Dart 9.8SDL Alexander AM Dash B41F

(ex.Magicbus 1992)

1013	J513FPS	1015	J515FPS	1017	J517FPS	1018	J518FPS
1014	J514FPS	1016	J516FPS				

1021 - 1026 1994 Volvo B6 Alexander AM Dash B40F

1021	L101WYS	1023	L103WYS	1025	L105XSU	1026	L106XSU
1022	L102WYS	1024	L104WYS				

1067	F349TSX	1988	Mercedes Bena 811D	Alexander AM B31F	*Duncan, K.Rannoch 1991*
1068	H255XDS	1990	Mercedes Benz 811D	Scott B33F	*Whitelaw, Stoneh'se 1992*

1091 - 1099 1987 Iveco 49.10 Robin Hood B19F

(ex.Ribble 1993)

1091	D407FRV	1094	D730YBV	1016	D733YBV	1018	D856FOT
1092	D408FRV	1095	D732YBV	1097	D736YBV	1099	D858FOT
1093	D409FRV						

1100	TWH697T	1979	Leyland FE30AGR	NCME B36F	*Morrow, Clydebank 1992*
1101	NFM842M	1974	Leyland LN1151/1R	Leyland DP48F	*Morrow, Clydebank 1992*
1103	NFM854M	1974	Leyland LN1151/1R	Leyland DP48F	*Morrow, Clydebank 1992*
1104	ORP459M	1974	Leyland LN1151/1R	Leyland B49F	*Morrow, Clydebank 1992*
1105	RFM879M	1974	Leyland LN1151/1R	Leyland B49F	*Morrow, Clydebank 1992*
1106	HCA967N	1975	Leyland LN11351/1R	Leyland DP48F	*Morrow, Clydebank 1992*
1107	HFM175N	1975	Leyland LN11351/1R	Leyland B48F	*Morrow, Clydebank 1992*
1108	HPF304N	1975	Leyland LN10351/1R	Leyland B39F	*Morrow, Clydebank 1992*

1109	HPF320N	1975	Leyland LN10351/1R	Leyland B39F	*Morrow, Clydebank 1992*
1110	MLG962P	1975	Leyland LN11351/1R	Leyland DP48F	*Morrow, Clydebank 1992*
1111	PJI4708	1977	Leyland LN11351A/1R	Leyland B49F	*McKindless, Wishaw 1994*
1112	OVV517R	1976	Leyland LN11351A/1R	Leyland B49F	*Morrow, Clydebank 1992*
1113	PVF358R	1976	Leyland LN11351A/1R	Leyland B49F	*Morrow, Clydebank 1992*
1114	SPC288R	1976	Leyland LN10351A/1R	Leyland B41F	*Morrow, Clydebank 1992*
1115	SGR556R	1976	Leyland LN11351A/1R	Leyland B49F	*Morrow, Clydebank 1992*
1116	TVF615R	1976	Leyland LN11351A/1R	Leyland B49F	*Morrow, Clydebank 1992*
1117	TVF618R	1976	Leyland LN11351A/1R	Leyland B49F	*Morrow, Clydebank 1992*
1118	PJJ347S	1977	Leyland LN10351A/1R	Leyland B41F	*Morrow, Clydebank 1992*
1119	PJJ350S	1977	Leyland LN10351A/1R	Leyland B41F	*Morrow, Clydebank 1992*
1120	UPB295S	1977	Leyland LN10351A/1R	Leyland B41F	*Morrow, Clydebank 1992*
1121	OLS812T	1978	Leyland LN10351B/1R	Leyland B44F	*Midland Bluebird 1992*

1111 was originally registered EPT883S

1122 - 1128
1978 Leyland LN11351A/1R   Leyland B49F
(ex.Green, Kirkintilloch 1991)

1122	CCL779T	1124	DPW783T	1126	WBN463T	1128	WBN476T
1123	CCL780T	1125	DPW784T	1127	WBN467T		

1129	XNG761S	1979	Leyland LN11351A/1R	Leyland B52F	*Green, Kirkintilloch 1991*
1130	KMA408T	1978	Leyland LN11351A/1R	Leyland B49F	*McColl, Bowling 1992*

1131 - 1144
1980 Leyland NL116L11/1R   Leyland B52F
(ex.Kelvin Scottish 1989)

1131	MDS855V	1136	MDS860V	1140	MDS864V	1143	WAS766V
1132	MDS856V	1137	MDS861V	1141	MDS867V	1144	WAS769V
1133	MDS857V	1139	MDS863V	1142	MDS868V		

1145	SWX534X	1982	Leyland NL116L11/1R	Leyland B52F	*Keighley & District 1994*
1146	UWY66X	1982	Leyland NL116L11/1R	Leyland B52F	*Keighley & District 1994*

1147 - 1150
1981 Leyland NL116L11/1R   Leyland B52F
(ex.Kelvin Scottish 1989)

1147	SNS827W	1148	YFS301W	1149	YSF306W	1150	YSF307W

1151 - 1160
1981 Leyland NL116L11/1R   Leyland B49F
(ex.Kelvin Scottish 1989)

1151	AST151W	1155	AST155W	1157	AST157W	1159	AST159W
1153	AST153W	1156	AST156W	1158	AST158W	1160	AST160W
1154	AST154W						

1161	UFG50S	1978	Leyland LN11351A/2R	Leyland B44F	*Morrow, Clydebank 1992*
1162	YYE279T	1979	Leyland LN10351A/2R	Leyland B36F	*Morrow, Clydebank 1992*
1163	YYE286T	1979	Leyland LN10351A/2R	Leyland B36F	*Morrow, Clydebank 1992*
1164	BYW392V	1980	Leyland LN10351A/1R	Leyland B36F	*Morrow, Clydebank 1992*
1165	KSO65P	1976	Leyland LN10351/2R	Leyland B36F	*Grampian 1992*
1166	OLS810T	1978	Leyland LN10351B/1R	Leyland B44F	*Midland Bluebird 1992*
1167	MSO17W	1981	Leyland NL106L11/1R	Leyland B44F	*Bluebird Northern 1993*
1168	PJI4709	1979	Leyland LN11351A/1R	Leyland B49F	*McKindless, Wishaw 1994*
1169	NTC620M	1974	Leyland LN1151/1R	Leyland B47F	*McKindless, Wishaw 1994*
1170	NEL861M	1974	Leyland LN1151/1R	Leyland B52F	*McKindless, Wishaw 1994*
1171	GAO707N	1975	Leyland LN11351A/1R	Leyland B49F	*McKindless, Wishaw 1994*
1172	GAO708N	1975	Leyland LN11351A/1R	Leyland B49F	*McKindless, Wishaw 1994*
1173	FUG323T	1979	Leyland LN10351B/1R	Leyland B44F	*Harrogate & District 1994*

1168 was originally registered LUP898T

1181 - 1185   1983 Dennis Dorchester SDA806   Alexander TS B53F
                    (ex. Central Scottish 1989)

1181 A101RGE	1183 A103RGE	1184 A104RGE	1185 A105RGE
1182 A102RGE			

1218 - 1227   1983 Leyland TRBL11/2R   Alexander TS B53F
                    (ex. Central Scottish 1989)

1218 OUS18Y	1221 OUS11Y	1224 OUS14Y	1226 OUS16Y
1219 OUS19Y	1222 OUS12Y	1225 OUS15Y	1227 OUS17Y
1220 OUS20Y	1223 OUS13Y		

1233 - 1252   1984 Leyland TRBLXB/2RH   Alexander TS B53F
                    (ex. Central Scottish 1989)

1233 A33VDS	1238 A38VDS	1243 A23VDS	1248 A28VDS
1234 A34VDS	1239 A39VDS	1244 A24VDS	1249 A29VDS
1235 A35VDS	1240 A40VDS	1245 A25VDS	1250 A30VDS
1236 A36VDS	1241 A21VDS	1246 A26VDS	1251 A31VDS
1237 A37VDS	1242 A22VDS	1247 A27VDS	1252 A32VDS

1253 - 1275   1985 Leyland TRBLXB/2RH   Alexander TS B53F
                    (ex. Central Scottish 1989)

1253 B253BYS	1259 B259BYS	1265 B245BYS	1271 B251BYS
1254 B254BYS	1260 B260BYS	1266 B246BYS	1272 B252BYS
1255 B255BYS	1261 B261BYS	1267 B247BYS	1273 B241BYS
1256 B256BYS	1262 B262BYS	1268 B248BYS	1274 B242BYS
1257 B257BYS	1263 B264BYS	1269 B249BYS	1275 B243BYS
1258 B258BYS	1264 B244BYS	1270 B250BYS	

1284 - 1298   1987 Leyland TRBLXB/2RH   Alexander TS B53F
                    (ex. Central Scottish 1989)

1284 D369OSU	1288 D373OSU	1292 D377OSU	1296 D381OSU
1285 D370OSU	1289 D374OSU	1293 D378OSU	1297 D382OSU
1286 D371OSU	1290 D375OSU	1294 D379OSU	1298 D383OSU
1287 D372OSU	1291 D376OSU	1295 D380OSU	

1301 - 1310   1993/4 Volvo B10B-58   Alexander PS B51F

1301 L301VSU	1304 L304VSU	1307 L307VSU	1309 L309VSU
1302 L302VSU	1305 L305VSU	1308 L308VSU	1310 L310VSU
1303 L303VSU	1306 L306VSU		

1391 LGE724Y	1982	Volvo B58-56	Duple Dom. B55F	*McKenna, Uddingston 1992*
1410 MHS28P	1976	Leyland PSU3C/3R	Alexander AYS B53F	*Central Scottish 1989*
1421 MHS39P	1976	Leyland PSU3C/3R	Alexander AYS B53F	*Central Scottish 1989*
1427 GMS307S	1978	Leyland PSU3E/4R	Alexander AYS B53F	*Midland Scottish 1992*
1428 FSF728S	1978	Leyland PSU3E/4R	Duple Dom. B53F	*Midland Bluebird 1993*
1429 GMS298S	1978	Leyland PSU3E/4R	Alexander AYS B53F	*Midland Bluebird 1993*
1431 GMS281S	1978	Leyland PSU3E/4R	Alexander AYS B53F	*Midland Scottish 1992*
1432 YSF92S	1977	Leyland PSU3E/4R	Alexander AYS B53F	*Fife Scottish 1990*
1433 GMS304S	1978	Leyland PSU3E/4R	Alexander AYS B53F	*Midland Bluebird 1993*

1437 - 1447   1977 Leyland PSU3C/3R   Alexander AYS B53F
                    (ex. Central Scottish 1989)

1437 WSU437S	1438 WSU438S	1440 WSU440S	1447 WSU447S

1452	YHS282S	1977	Leyland PSU3E/4R	Duple Dom. B55F	*Midland Scottish 1992*
1453	WSU453S	1977	Leyland PSU3C/3R	Alexander AYS B53F	*Central Scottish 1989*
1455	GMS288S	1978	Leyland PSU3E/4R	Alexander AYS B53F	*Kelvin Scottish 1989*
1456	GMS290S	1978	Leyland PSU3E/4R	Alexander AYS B53F	*Kelvin Scottish 1989*
1457	GMS293S	1978	Leyland PSU3E/4R	Alexander AYS B53F	*Kelvin Scottish 1989*

1458 - 1489

1978 Leyland PSU3C/3R   Alexander AYS B53F
(ex.Central Scottish 1989)

1458	EGB58T	1468	EGB68T	1475	EGB75T	1483	EGB53T
1460	EGB60T	1469	EGB69T	1476	EGB76T	1484	EGB54T
1462	EGB62T	1470	EGB70T	1477	EBG47T	1485	EGB55T
1463	EGB63T	1471	EGB71T	1478	EGB48T	1487	EGB57T
1464	EGB64T	1472	EGB72T	1479	EGB49T	1488	EGB45T
1466	EGB66T	1473	EGB73T	1480	EGB50T	1489	EGB46T
1467	EGB67T	1474	EGB74T	1481	EGB51T		

1490	ULS317T	1979	Leyland PSU3E/4R	Alexander AYS B53F	*Kelvin Scottish 1989*

1494 - 1498

1979 Leyland PSU3C/3R   Alexander AYS B53F
(ex.Central Scottish 1989)

1494	GSU834T	1496	GSU836T	1497	GSU837T	1498	GSU838T
1495	GSU835T						

1499	MGR912T	1979	Leyland PSU3E/4R	Duple Dom. B55F	*McKenna, Uddingston 1992*

1500 - 1530

1979 Leyland PSU3C/3R   Alexander AYS B53F
(ex.Central Scottish 1989)

1500	GSU840T	1507	GSU847T	1520	GSU860T	1526	GSU866T
1502	GSU842T	1508	GSU848T	1521	GSU861T	1527	GSU827T
1503	GSU843T	1509	GSU849T	1522	GSU862T	1528	GSU828T
1504	GSU844T	1517	GSU857T	1523	GSU863T	1529	GSU829T
1505	GSU845T	1518	GSU858T	1525	GSU865T	1530	GSU830T
1506	GSU846T	1519	GSU859T				

1540 - 1546

1981 Leyland PSU3F/4R   Alexander AYS B53F
(ex.Central Scottish 1989)

1540	PUS150W	1542	PUS152W	1544	PUS154W	1546	PUS156W
1541	PUS151W	1543	PUS153W	1545	PUS155W		

1547 - 1557

1981 Leyland PSU3G/4R   Alexander AYS B53F
(ex.Central Scottish 1989)

1547	TSU647W	1550	TSU650W	1553	TSU653W	1556	TSU646W
1548	TSU648W	1551	TSU651W	1554	TSU644W	1557	TSU643W
1549	TSU649W	1552	TSU652W	1555	TSU645W		

1563 - 1572

1982 Leyland PSU3G/4R   Alexander AYS B53F
(ex.Central Scottish 1989)

1563	LUS433Y	1566	LUS436Y	1569	LUS439Y	1571	LUS431Y
1564	LUS434Y	1567	LUS437Y	1570	LUS440Y	1572	LUS432Y
1465	LUS435Y	1468	LUS438Y				

1603 BLS672V 1979   MCW Metrobus DR102/3 Alexander AD H43/30F *Kelvin Scottish 1989*

1612 - 1632
1982 MCW Metrobus DR102   Alexander RL H45/33F
(* MCW Metrobus DR104)
(ex.Kelvin Scottish 1989)

1612*	CKS392X	1625	ULS625X	1627	ULS629X	1632*	ULS640X
1619	ULS619X	1626	ULS626X	1629	ULS635X		

1633 - 1650
1983 MCW Metrobus DR102   Alexander RL H45/33F
(ex.Kelvin Scottish 1989)

1633	BLS422Y	1638	BLS429Y	1643	BLS436Y	1647	BLS441Y
1634	BLS425Y	1639	BLS430Y	1644	BLS438Y	1648	BLS442Y
1635	BLS426Y	1640	BLS430Y	1645	BLS439Y	1649	BLS444Y
1636	BLS427Y	1642	BLS435Y	1646	BLS440Y	1650	BLS445Y
1637	BLS428Y						

1638 received a new body in 1985

1651 - 1667
1984 MCW Metrobus DR102   Alexander RL H45/33F
(ex.Kelvin Scottish 1989)

1651	A469GMS	1655	A474GMS	1659	B579MLS	1665	B90PKS
1652	A471GMS	1656	A475GMS	1660	B580MLS	1666	B91PKS
1653	A472GMS	1657	A476GMS	1662	B586MLS	1667	B92PKS
1654	A473GMS	1658	A478GMS	1664	B89PKS		

1691	LMS166W	1981	Leyland FE30AGR	Alexander H44/31F	*Midland Scottish 1992*
1692	LMS152W	1981	Leyland FE30AGR	Alexander H44/31F	*Midland Bluebird 1992*

1693 - 1696
1979 Leyland FE30AGR   ECW H43/32F
(ex.Midland Bluebird 1993)

1693	ULS675T	1694	ULS662T	1695	ULS671T	1696	ULS672T

1698	LMS151W	1981	Leyland FE30AGR	Alexander H44/31F	*Midland Bluebird 1993*
1699	LMS155W	1981	Leyland FE30AGR	Alexander H44/31F	*Midland Bluebird 1993*
1701	EGB77T	1978	Dennis Dominator DD110	Alexander H43/31F	*Central Scottish 1989*

1702 - 1714
1981 Dennis Dominator DD137B Alexander RL H45/34F
(ex.Kelvin Scottish 1989)

1702	TYS260W	1705	TYS265W	1709	TYS269W	1712	TYS272W
1703	TYS262W	1706	TYS266W	1710	TYS270W	1713	TYS273W
1704	TYS263W	1708	TYS268W	1711	TYS271W	1714	TYS274W

1715	FGE435X	1982	Dennis Dominator DD137B	Alexander H45/34F	*Central Scottish 1989*
1716	FGE436X	1982	Dennis Dominator DD137B	Alexander H45/34F	*Central Scottish 1989*
1717	FGE437X	1982	Dennis Dominator DD137B	Alexander H45/34F	*Central Scottish 1989*
1718	FGE438X	1982	Dennis Dominator DD137B	Alexander H45/34F	*Kelvin Scottish 1989*
1719	FGE439X	1982	Dennis Dominator DD137B	Alexander H45/34F	*Kelvin Scottish 1989*
1720	FGE440X	1982	Dennis Dominator DD137B	Alexander H45/34F	*Central Scottish 1989*
1721	FGE441X	1982	Dennis Dominator DD137B	Alexander H45/34F	*Central Scottish 1989*

1722 - 1728

1982 Dennis Dominator DD137B   Alexander RL H45/34F
(ex. Kelvin Scottish 1989)

1722	FGE422X	1724	FGE424X	1726	FGE426X	1728	FGE428X
1723	FGE423X	1725	FGE425X	1727	FGE427X		

1729 - 1734

1982 Dennis Dominator DD137B   Alexander RL H45/34F
(ex. Central Scottish 1989)

1729	FGE429X	1732	WLT367	1733	FGE433X	1734	FGE434X
1730	FGE430X						

1732 was originally registered FGE432X

1735 - 1744

1983 Dennis Dominator DD162   Alexander RL H45/34F
(ex. Central Scottish 1989)

1735	MNS45Y	1738	MNS48Y	1741	MNS51Y	1743	MNS43Y
1736	MNS46Y	1739	MNS49Y	1742	MNS42Y	1744	MNS44Y
1737	MNS47Y						

1745	DEM83X	1981	Dennis Dominator DDA145 Alexander RL H45/33F	*Merseybus 1992*

1746 - 1753

1981 Dennis Dominator DDA157   Alexander RL H45/33F
(ex. Merseybus 1992)

1746	CHF346X	1748	CHF348X	1750	CHF350X	1752	CHF352X
1747	CHF347X	1749	CHF349X	1751	CHF351X	1753	CHF353X

1754	DEM84X	1981	Dennis Dominator DDA145 Alexander RL H45/33F	*Merseybus 1992*

1801 - 1804

1982 Leyland ONLXB/1R   ECW H45/32F
(ex. Kelvin Scottish 1989)

1801	ULS96X	1802	ULS97X	1803	ULS98X	1804	ULS99X

1805 - 1808

1983 Leyland ONLXB/1R   Alexander RL H45/32F
(ex. Kelvin Scottish 1989)

1805	ALS120Y	1806	ALS121Y	1807	ALS130Y	1808	ALS131Y

1819	C112BTS	1986	Leyland ONLXB/1RV Alexander RL H47/32F	*Strathtay Scottish 1989*

1823 - 1826

1983 Leyland ONLXB/1R   Alexander RL H45/32F
(ex. Fife Scottish 1989)

1823	A981FLS	1824	A982FLS	1825	A983FLS	1826	A984FLS

1827 - 1843

1994 Volvo Olympian   Alexander Royale H43/31F

1827	L827YGA	1832	L832YGA	1836	M836DUS	1840	M840DUS
1828	L828YGA	1833	L833YGA	1837	M837DUS	1841	M841DUS
1829	L829YGA	1834	M834DUS	1838	M838DUS	1842	M842DUS
1830	L830YGA	1835	M835DUS	1839	M839DUS	1843	M843DUS
1831	L831YGA						

1951 - 1969 1979 Ailsa B55-10 MkII Alexander AV H44/35F
(ex. Central Scottish 1989)

1951	LHS751V		1959	LHS739V	1963	LHS743V	1967	LHS747V
1957	LHS737V		1961	LHS741V	1964	LHS744V	1968	LHS748V
1958	LHS738V		1962	LHS742V	1965	LHS745V	1969	LHS749V

| 1970 | YMS704R | 1977 | Ailsa B55-10 | Alexander AV H44/35F | *Strathtay Scottish 1991* |

1971 - 1977 1977 Ailsa B55-10 Alexander AV H44/35F
(ex. Midland Scottish 1990)

| 1971 | YMS705R | | 1973 | YMS708R | 1976 | YMS711R | 1977 | YMS712R |
| 1972 | YMS707R | | 1975 | YMS710R | | | | |

1980	YMS701R	1977	Ailsa B55-10	Alexander AV H44/35F	*Strathtay Scottish 1991*
1981	YMS703R	1977	Ailsa B55-10	Alexander AV H44/35F	*Strathtay Scottish 1991*
2065	E39OMS	1987	Mercedes Benz 709D	Alexander DP24F	*Munro, Uddingston 1994*
2066	F94JGE	1988	Mercedes Benz 609D	NW Conversions C24F	*Munro, Uddingston 1994*
2069	E511YSU	1987	Mercedes Benz 709D	Alexander C25F	*McKenna, Uddingston 1992*
2070	F94KDS	1988	Mercedes Benz 811D	Alexander C33F	*McKenna, Uddingston 1992*
2071	F126HGD	1988	Mercedes Benz 609D	Reeve Burgess C23F	*Coakley, New Steton 1992*
2072	F852LHS	1988	Mercedes Benz 811D	Alexander C33F	*McKenna, Uddingston 1992*
2073	H125YGG	1990	Mercedes Benz 609D	Rapier C24F	*Coakley, New Steton 1992*
2074	H907YGA	1990	Mercedes Benz 811D	Reeve Burgess C33F	*Coakley, New Steton 1992*

2202 - 2206 1982 Leyland TRBTL11/2R Alexander AT C49F
(ex. Kelvin Scottish 1989)

| 2202 | FGG602X | 2204 | FGE604X | 2205 | FGE605X | 2206 | FGE601X |
| 2203 | FGE603X | | | | | | |

2207	ALS104Y	1983	Leyland TRBTL11/2R	Alexander AT C49F	*Kelvin Scottish 1989*
2454	GLS274S	1978	Leyland PSU3E/4R	Alexander AT C49F	*Kelvin Scottish 1989*
2531	EMS359V	1980	Leyland PSU3E/4R	Alexander AT C49F	*Kelvin Scottish 1989*

2533 - 2537 1980 Leyland PSU3F/4R Alexander AT C49F
(ex. Central Scottish 1989)

| 2533 | PGA833V | 2535 | PGA825V | 2536 | PGA826V | 2537 | PGA827V |
| 2534 | PGA834V | | | | | | |

| 2538 | PGA830V | 1980 | Leyland PSU3F/4R | Alexander AT C49F | *Kelvin Scottish 1989* |
| 2539 | PGA832V | 1980 | Leyland PSU3F/4R | Alexander AT C49F | *Central Scottish 1989* |

2809 - 2816 1986 Leyland ONLXB/1RH Alexander RL H47/27F
(ex. Central Scottish 1989)

| 2809 | C809KHS | 2812 | C802KHS | 2814 | C804KHS | 2816 | C806KHS |
| 2811 | C801KHS | 2813 | C803KHS | 2815 | C805KHS | | |

2573	VNH158W	1981	Leyland PSU3F/4RT	Duple Dom.IV C49F	*Green, Kirkintilloch 1991*
2576	VNH164W	1981	Leyland PSU3F/4RT	Duple Dom.IV C49F	*Green, Kirkintilloch 1991*
2577	VNH165W	1981	Leyland PSU3F/4RT	Duple Dom.IV C49F	*Green, Kirkintilloch 1991*
2578	NNH190Y	1983	Leyland PSU5C/4R	Duple Dom.IV C57F	*Green, Kirkintilloch 1991*
2579	NNH189Y	1983	Leyland PSU5C/4R	Duple Dom.IV C57F	*Green, Kirkintilloch 1991*
2580	VNH168W	1981	Leyland PSU3F/4RT	Duple Dom.IV C49F	*Green, Kirkintilloch 1991*

Kelvin Central **171**

2581	HVG801V	1979	Leyland PSU3E/4R	Duple Dom.II C49F	*Green, Kirkintilloch 1991*
2582	HVG803V	1979	Leyland PSU3E/4R	Duple Dom.II C49F	*Green, Kirkintilloch 1991*
2583	LCL805V	1980	Leyland PSU3E/4R	Duple Dom.II C49F	*Green, Kirkintilloch 1991*
2584	LCL806V	1980	Leyland PSU3E/4R	Duple Dom.II C49F	*Green, Kirkintilloch 1991*
2585	MRP242V	1980	Leyland PSU3E/4RT	Plaxton Sup.IV C49F	*United Counties 1991*
2586	MRP243V	1980	Leyland PSU3E/4RT	Plaxton Sup.IV C49F	*United Counties 1991*
2587	VNH163W	1981	Leyland PSU3F/4RT	Duple Dom.IV C49F	*United Counties 1991*
2588	VNH166W	1981	Leyland PSU3F/4RT	Duple Dom.IV C49F	*United Counties 1991*
2598	VNH167W	1981	Leyland PSU3F/4RT	Duple Dom.IV C49F	*United Counties 1991*
2590	WGA644V	1979	Leyland PSU3E/4R	Plaxton Sup.IV C53F	*Marbill, Beith 1992*
2591	VUD28X	1982	Leyland PSU3G/4R	ECW C49F	*Whitelaw, Stonehse 1992*
2592	VUD32X	1982	Leyland PSU3G/4R	ECW C51F	*Whitelaw, Stonehse 1992*
2593	MPL127W	1981	Leyland PSU3E/4R	Duple Dom. C53F	*Hynes, Bearsden 1992*
2594	MPL130W	1981	Leyland PSU3E/4R	Duple Dom. C53F	*Hynes, Bearsden 1992*

2844 - 2849   1994 Volvo Olympian   Alexander Royale DPH47/27F

2844	M844DUS	2846	M846DUS	2848	M848DUS	2849 M849DUS
2845	M845DUS	2847	M847DUS			

3201	WLT760	1981	Leyland TRCTL11/3R	Duple Dom.III C46FT	*Kelvin Scottish 1989*

3201 was originally registered BSG548W

3208	WLT910	1983	Leyland TRCTL11.3R	Duple Dom.II C47F	*Kelvin Scottish 1989*
3209	WLT357	1983	Leyland TRCTL11/2R	Plaxton 3200 C49F	*Kelvin Scottish 1989*
3210	WLT741	1983	Leyland TRCTL11/2R	Plaxton 3200 C49F	*Kelvin Scottish 1989*
3212	WLT408	1983	Leyland TRCTL11/2R	Plaxton 3200 C49F	*Kelvin Scottish 1989*
3213	WLT770	1983	Leyland TRCTL11/3R	Plaxton 3200 C52F	*Luton & District 1991*
3214	WLT976	1983	Leyland TRCTL11/3R	Plaxton 3200 C52F	*Luton & District 1991*
3215	KCB758	1983	Leyland TRCTL11/2R	Plaxton 3200 C52F	*Luton & District 1991*
3216	BXI521	1985	Leyland TRCTL11/3RH	Plaxton 3200 C50FT	*Luton & District 1991*

3208/9 were originally registered BLS106Y & TFS318Y. 3210 was previously registered PGE442Y and WLT371 and was originally TFS319Y. 3213-6 were originally registered NBD106/7Y, A104EPA & B287KPF.

3228	WLT388	1983	Leyland TRCTL11/3R	Plaxton 3200 C49FT	*Central Scottish 1989*
3229	A9KCB	1983	Leyland TRCTL11/2RP	Alexander TE C47F	*Kelvin Scottish 1989*
3231	WLT677	1984	Leyland TRCTL11/3RH	Duple Laser C47FT	*Kelvin Scottish 1989*
3232	WLT678	1984	Leyland TRCTL11/3RH	Duple Laser C55F	*Kelvin Scottish 1989*

3228 was originally registered VTY131Y. 3229 was previously registered WLT770 and was originally A119GLS. 3231/2 were originally registered A125/8ESG.

3299	CSU932	1986	Leyland TRCTL11/3RH	Duple C50F	*Luton & District 1992*
3300	C257SPC	1986	Leyland TRCTL11/3RH	Duple C53F	*Munro, Uddingston 1994*

3299 was originally registered C259SPC

4138	MDS862V	1994	Leyland LN Greenway	East Lancs B49F	

4138 was rebuilt from 1138, 1980 Leyland NL116L11/1R.

ANCILLARY VEHICLES

S54	HGM427E	1967	Leyland PSU3/1R	Towing wagon	
S56	HGM430E	1967	Leyland PSU3/1R	Towing wagon	
S58	HGM428E	1967	Leyland PSU3/1R	Towing wagon	
S61	HGM426E	1967	Leyland PSU3/1R	Towing wagon	
S82	AGM672L	1974	Leyland PSU3/3R	Towing wagon	
S970	AMS295B	1964	Leyland PSU3/3R	Towing wagon	
S972	DMS359C	1965	Leyland PSU3/3R	Towing wagon	
S973	DMS367C	1965	Leyland PSU3/3R	Towing wagon	
S974	AMS513K	1972	Leyland PSU3/3R	Towing wagon	
0991	OSG546M	1975	Leyland PSU3/3R	Alexander AY C49F	Driver trainer
0992	MHS1P	1976	Leyland PSU3C/3R	Alexander AYS B53F	Driver trainer
0993	WSU433S	1977	Leyland PSU3C/3R	Alexander AYS B53F	Driver trainer

LATE FLEET AMENDMENTS

BLUEBIRD BUSES

Delete :

242/3 (C902HWF, B803XUS)

Loans :

432/6 (PSO177W, RRS225X) to Ribble

STAGECOACH RED & WHITE

Addition :

C902HWF 1985 Mercedes Benz L608D   Reeve Burgess DPl9F Bluebird Buses 11.94

STAGECOACH RIBBLE

Hired :

PSO177W	1981	Leyland TRCTL11/3R	Duple C53F	Bluebird Buses 12.94
RRS225X	1982	Leyland TCTL11/3R	Duple DP53F	Bluebird Buses 12.94

STAGECOACH SELKENT

Additions :

RH58 F58AVV	1989	Iveco 49.10	Robin Hood B23F	United Counties 11.94
RH59 F59AVV	1989	Iveco 49.10	Robin Hood B23F	United Counties 11.94
RH60 F60AVV	1989	Iveco 49.10	Robin Hood B23F	United Counties 11.94
RH61 G61JVV	1989	Iveco 49.10	Robin Hood B23F	United Counties 11.94

Delete :

T1126/7/30 ((WDA1/2/5T)

STAGECOACH SOUTH - COASTLINE

Additions :

WDA1T	1978	Leyland TNLXB/1RF	Park Royal CH43/29F	Selkent 11.94
WDA2T	1978	Leyland TNLXB/1RF	Park Royal CH43/29F	Selkent 11.94
WDA5T	1978	Leyland TNLXB/1RF	Park Royal CH43/29F	Selkent 11.94

STAGECOACH UNITED COUNTIES

Delete :

58-61 (F58-60AVV, G61JVV)

STAGECOACH WESTERN SCOTTISH

Addition :

S100 PSG842P 1976 Seddon Pennine 7   Alexander C24FL

CITYLINE AUCKLAND

Addition :

7611 - 7615   1986 Mercedes Benz L608D   B20F

7611 SZ8591	7613 TA7462	7614 TA7468	7615 SZ8598
7612 SZ8592			

The UK identity of these ex.Stagecoach South & Stagecoach Red & White buses is not known at the time of writing.

CITYLINE HUTT VALLEY

Additions :

7601 - 7608   1986   Mercedes Benz L608D   B20F

7601 SN7472	7603 ST9430	7605 SX6698	7607 SZ205
7602 ST9425	7604 SW6560	7606 SX6699	7608 TA7124

The UK identity of these ex.Stagecoach South & Stagecoach Red & White buses is not known at the time of writing.

STAGECOACH WELLINGTON

501 - 514   1994   MAN 11.190   Designline B39D

501 SS5537	506 SW4400	509 SY1641	512 SZ5918
502 SS5538	507 SW4435	510 SY1631	513 TA2267
503 ST7109	508 SW4436	511 SY5917	514 TA2691
504 SX7724			

These are the only examples of the 80 buses on order of this type to have entered service by 10 December 1994.

TO BE ALLOCATED

       1994   Volvo B6   Alexander AM Dash DP40F

M741PRS	M847PRS	M753PRS	M759PRS
M742PRS	M748PRS	M754PRS	M760PRS
M743PRS	M749PRS	M755PRS	M761PRS
M744PRS	M750PRS	M756PRS	M762PRS
M745PRS	M751PRS	M757PRS	M763PRS
M746PRS	M752PRS	M758PRS	M764PRS

STAGECOACH HOLDINGS PORTFOLIO

Companies purchased by Stagecoach Holdings plc or its subsidiaries.

11.11.83	Adamson & Low, Edinburgh *(Stagecoach)* (sold 5.85)
7.11.85	A & C McLennan, Spittalfield *(Stagecoach)*
2.4.87	Hampshire Bus, Southampton
2.4.87	Pilgrim Coaches, Southampton (closed 4.87) .
23.7.87	Cumberland Motor Services, Whitehaven
12.10.87	Cotters, Glasgow (Express services) *(Stagecoach)*
19.11.87	United Counties Omnibus Co., Northampton
5.88	Yeowart, Whitehaven *(Cumberland)*
5.88	Kirkpatrick, Brigham *(Cumberland)*
21.9.88	Brownrigg, Egremont *(Cumberland)*
15.11.88	Speedybus Enterprises, Hong Kong (50% share)
2.89	Highwayman Coaches, Errol *(Stagecoach)*
31.1.89	United Transport International, Blantyre, Malawi

7.4.89	East Midland Motor Services, Chesterfield
21.4.89	Ribble Motor Services, Preston
21.4.89	Bee Line Buzz Co., Preston
2.5.89	Stephenson, Maryport *(Cumberland)*
26.5.89	Barrow Borough Transport *(Ribble)*
16.8.89	Southdown Motor Services, Brighton
17.8.89	Top Line Buses, Hastings (49%)
25.9.89	Cedar Travel, Worthing *(Southdown)*
20.10.89	Inverness Traction, Inverness
26.11.89	Portsmouth Citybus *(Southdown)* (sold 1.91)
11.89	Mercers, Longridge *(Ribble)*
1.12.89	W.A.Palmer, Carlisle *(Cumberland)*
8.12.89	Hastings & District, Hastings
2.2.90	Maun, Mansfield (50%) *(East Midland)*
7.4.90	Maun, Mansfield (50%) *(East Midland)*
6.90	Gray Coach Lines, Toronto, Canada (sold 12.92)
19.11.90	Vine, Cleator Moor *(Cumberland)*
27.3.91	Bluebird Northern, Aberdeen
4.91	Clark, Banchory *(Bluebird Northern)*
23.7.91	Fife Scottish Omnibuses, Kirkcaldy
15.11.91	Kenya Bus Services, Nairobi, Kenya
3.3.92	National Transport Tokens, Manchester (50%)
23.10.92	Alder Valley, Aldershot
28.10.92	Wellington City Transport, New Zealand
23.8.93	Lancaster City Transport, Morecambe *(Ribble)*
7.9.93	East Kent Road Car Co., Canterbury
18.11.93	Grimsby Cleethorpes Transport, Grimsby
25.11.93	Cheltenham & Gloucester Omnibus Co., Cheltenham
25.11.93	Cheltenham District Traction Co., Cheltenham
25.11.93	Swindon & District Bus Co., Cheltenham
25.11.93	Midland Red South, Rugby
25.11.93	G & G Travel, Leamington Spa
25.11.93	Vanguard Coaches, Bedworth
25.11.93	Red & White Services, Cwmbran
25.11.93	The Valleys Bus Co., Cwmbran
25.11.93	Eastern Valleys Bus Co., Cwmbran
25.11.93	Western Valleys Bus Co., Cwmbran
25.11.93	Aberdare Bus Co., Cwmbran
1.94	Norrie, New Deer *(Bluebird Buses)*
2.94	Pegasus Express Parcels, Aberdeen
6.94	Eastbourne Bus Co. Wellington, New Zealand
4.7.94	Mainline, Sheffield (20%)
26.7.94	Busways Travel Servives, Newcastle-upon-Tyne
1.8.94	Western Scottish Omnibuses, Kilmarnock
6.9.94	East London Bus & Coach Co. Ilford
6.9.94	South East London & Kent Bus CO., Catford
1.10.94	Arran Transport & Trading Co., Brodick *(Western Scottish)*
26.10.94	Cleveland Transit, Stockton-on-Tees
26.10.94	Kingston-upon-Hull City Transport, Hull
15.11.94	SB Holdings, Glasgow (20%)
11.12.94	Hartlepool Transport, Hartlepool

Mainline, Sheffield in December 1994 submitted a bid for Chesterfield Transport.

STAGECOACH HOLDINGS FLEET STATISTICS

	Single deck/ coaches	Mini/ midibuses	Double deck	+Trolleybus * Cable car	Fleet total
Armstrong Galley	20		3		23
Blue Bus Services	34	35	20		89
Bluebird Buses	105	56	59		220
Cheltenham District	26	33	7		66
Cleveland Transit	42	18	55		115
Cleveland Coaches	18	3	1		22
Coastline	54	39	43		136
Cumberland	140	83	80		303
Darlington	21	23	10		54
East Kent	58	69	97		224
East London	20	159	405		584
East Midland	53	50	88		191
Economic Service	5	2	15		22
Favourite Services	8	12	7		27
Fife Scottish	116	142	72		330
G & G	12	8	11		31
Gloucester Citybus	13	31	10		54
Grimsby Cleethorpes	35	10	44		89
Hampshire Bus	61	28	56		145
Hants & Surrey	17	26	53		96
Hartlepool	68				68
Inverness	9	28	18		55
KHCT	18	11	82		111
Manchester	23	3			26
Midland Red South	84	123	34		241
Newcastle Busways	43	68	133		244
Red & White	147	86	26		259
Ribble Buses	152	132	136		420
Selkent	28	107	267		402
South Coast Buses	60	36	29		125
South Shields Busways	12	33	23		68
Stagecoach Buses	35	8	40		83
Stroud Valleys	16	18	11		45
Sunderland Busways	18	43	69		130
Swindon & District	5	9	22		36
Tees Valley	2	1	2		5
United Counties	46	113	186		345
Vanguard	24	2	2		28
Western Scottish	208	133	60		401
Cityline Auckland	34	5			39
Cityline Hutt Valley	53	8			61
Eastbourne Bus Co.	20				20
Hong Kong	5				5
Kelburn Cable Car				2*	2
Kenya Bus	280				280
Kenya Bus (Mombassa)	71				71
Malawi	302	4	33		339
Wellington	123	8		73+	204
Total U.K.	1856	1781	2276		5914
Total overseas	888	25	33	75	1021
International total	2744	1806	2309	75	6935

Pegasus Express Parcels 31 commercial vehicles   National Transport Tokens 1 van